CW00603057

25

Seasons at Goodison

The Complete Record

1977-78 to 2001-02

David Powter

British Library Cataloguing in Publication Data
A catalogue record for this book is available from the British Library

ISBN 1-86223-069-2

 (01472 696226)
72 St. Peter's Avenue, Cleethorpes, N.E. Lincolnshire, DN35 8HU, England

Web site http://www.soccer-books.co.uk
e-mail info@soccer-books.co.uk

The Publishers, and the Football Clubs itemised are unable to accept liability for any loss, damage or injury caused by error or inaccuracy in the information published in this guide.

Printed by Bookcraft

CONTENTS

EVERTON 25 SEASONS 1977-78 TO 2001-2002

EVERTON FC CLUB RECORD

Year Formed: 1878

Turned Professional: 1885

Ground: Goodison Park, Liverpool, L4 4EL

Telephone: 0151 330-2200

Capacity: 40,170

Record Attendance: 78,299 vs Liverpool in 1948-49

Pitch Measurements: 110 x 70 yards

Colours: Royal blue shirts with white panels, white shorts with blue trim, black stockings with white trim.

Nickname: The Toffeemen/The Toffees

Previous Name: 1878 – St Domingo (became Everton in 1879)

Previous Grounds: Stanley Park (1878), Priory Road (1882), Anfield Road (1884). Moved to Goodison Park in 1892.

League History: 1888 – Football League Founder Members • 1930-31 – Division 2 • 1931-51 – Division 1 • 1951-54 – Division 2 • 1954-92 – Division 1 • 1992 – F.A. Premier League Founder Members

Record League Victory: 9-1 vs Manchester City (1906-07)

Record League Defeat: 4-10 vs Tottenham Hotspur (1958-59)

Most League Points (2 for a win): 66 in the First Division (1969-70)

Most League Points (3 for a win): 90 in the First Division (1984-85)

Most League Goals: 121 in the Second Division (1930-31)

Highest League Scorer (in aggregate): 349 goals – Dixie Dean (1925-37)

Highest League Scorer (in a season): 60 goals – Dixie Dean (1927-28) – a Football League Record

Most Goals in a game: 6 goals – Jack Southworth vs West Bromwich Albion (1893-94)

Most League appearances: 578 – Neville Southall (1981-82 to 1997-98)

Longest Sequence of League Wins: 12 (from 24/3/1894 to 13/10/1894)

Longest Sequence of League Defeats: 6 (from 26/12/1996 to 29/1/1997)

Longest Sequence of Unbeaten League Games: 20 (from 29/4/1978 to 16/12/1978)

Longest Sequence of League Games without a Win: 14 (from 6/3/1937 to 4/9/1937)

Most Capped Player: 92 – Neville Southall (for Wales)

Record Transfer Fee Received: £10 million for Francis Jeffers (from Arsenal, June 2001)

Record Transfer Fee Paid: £5.75 million for Nick Barmby (to Middlesbrough, October 1996)

MAJOR HONOURS (15 TROPHIES)

Football League Champions on 9 occasions: 1890-91, 1914-15, 1927-28, 1931-32, 1938-39, 1962-63, 1969-70, 1984-85 and 1986-87
F.A. Cup Winners on 5 occasions: 1905-06, 1932-33, 1965-66, 1983-84 and 1994-95
European Cup Winners' Cup Winners: 1984-85

OTHER HONOURS

Football League Second Division Champions: 1930-31

EVERTON FC CLUB RECORD DURING THE 25 SEASONS 1977-78 TO 2001-02

Highest League Victory: 7-1 vs Southampton (1996-97)
Highest League Defeat: 2-6 vs Manchester United (1977-78) & Aston Villa (1989-90)
Most League Points (2 for a win): 55 in the First Division (1977-78)
Most League Points (3 for a win): 90 in the First Division (1984-85)
Most League Goals Scored: 88 in the First Division (1984-85)
Most League Goals Conceded: 63 in the First Division (1993-94)
Highest League Scorer (in aggregate): 111 goals – Graeme Sharp
Highest League Scorer (in a season): 30 goals – Bob Latchford (1977-78) and Gary Lineker (1985-86)
Most Goals in a game: 4 goals – Bob Latchford vs QPR (1977-78) and Graeme Sharp vs Southampton (1987-88)
Number of League Hat-tricks: 17 (includes 4 goals in a game twice)
Leading Scorer over most Seasons: Tony Cottee – 5 occasions
Most League appearances: 578 – Neville Southall
Number of Ever-Present Players throughout a Season: 15
Most Seasons Ever-Present: 7 – Neville Southall
Highest Average Home League Attendance: 39,513 (1977-78)
Highest Home League Crowd: 53,131 vs Liverpool (1978-79)
Lowest Home League Crowd: 12,972 vs Coventry City (1982-83)
Longest Sequence of League Wins: 7 (from 14/3/1987 to 20/4/1987)
Longest Sequence of League Defeats: 6 (from 26/12/1996 to 29/1/1997)

Longest Sequence of Unbeaten League Games: 20 (from 29/4/1978 to 16/12/1978)
Longest Sequence of League Games without a Win: 12 (20/8/1994 to 29/10/1994)
Most Capped Player: 92 – Neville Southall (Wales)
Record Transfer Fee Received: £10 million for Francis Jeffers (from Arsenal, June 2001)
Record Transfer Fee Paid: £5.75 million for Nick Barmby (to Middlesbrough, October 1996)

MAJOR HONOURS (5 TROPHIES)

Football League Champions on 2 occasions: 1984-85 and 1986-87
F.A. Cup Winners on 2 occasions: 1983-84 and 1994-95
European Cup Winners' Cup: 1984-85

EVERTON 25 FIVE SEASONS 1977-78 TO 2001-02

INTRODUCTION

With a relatively new manager in David Moyes, Everton fans looked forward to the 2002-03 season with great anticipation. There were parallels with 25 years before, during the summer of 1977, when Gordon Lee was about to embark on his first full campaign at Goodison Park. Lee had taken the reins midway through 1976-77 after Billy Bingham was axed.

Gordon Lee was not the 'big name' that the fans expected, but there were still high hopes that he would turnaround the club's fortunes. Everton had not collected a trophy since Harry Catterick's team had lifted the League Championship in 1969-70. They had finished in mid-table in both 1975-76 and 1976-77. However, Everton had gone close in both cup competitions in that latter campaign. They reached the League Cup Final, but were defeated in a second replay by Aston Villa at Old Trafford. And they battled through to an F.A. Cup semi-final meeting with Liverpool, but lost a Maine Road replay, after the first game had ended 2-2.

Lee inherited some very good players. These included skipper Mick Lyons, Bob Latchford, Duncan McKenzie, Martin Dobson, Bruce Rioch and Andy King. Also on the books were two promising young defenders – Mark Higgins and Billy Wright.

Former Stoke City left-back Mike Pejic had been recruited before the transfer deadline and, during the summer, Lee signed speedy winger Dave Thomas from QPR and goalie George Wood from Blackpool. Lee's jigsaw had begun to take shape and the spirit at Goodison Park was rising.

EVERTON 25 SEASONS 1977-78 TO 2001-02

1977-78

Despite losing the opening two games of 1977-78, Gordon Lee's side picked up momentum with an unbeaten run of 18 games. However, any realistic hopes of making a serious tilt at the title were crushed when Manchester United romped to a 6-2 victory at Goodison Park on Boxing Day, followed by another reverse at Leeds a day later. The Toffees never got back on terms with Nottingham Forest (who finished as comprehensive champions) and another sticky patch in April – when they slid to three more defeats – cost them the runners-up spot (to Liverpool). The third place finish was Everton's highest since the title was won in 1969-70.

Bob Latchford netted 30 times to be the First Division's leading scorer in 1977-78. It was the fourth successive campaign that the big striker had headed the club's list of scorers. That 30 goal haul enabled Latchford to collect a £10,000 prize. This was an incentive offered by the Daily Express, as no player had reached the 30-goal mark in the top-flight in six years. Bob, who only netted the last two of his tally in the final quarter of the ultimate game of the season, shared the prize with his team-mates.

Lee's rebuilding of the the squad continued during 1977-78 with midfielder Trevor Ross joining from Arsenal. The unhappy Bruce Rioch returned to Derby County and another big name to leave during the summer of 1978 was the skilful Duncan McKenzie. The fans' favourite was sold to Chelsea. There was a trio of new men, though, in Mickey Walsh, Geoff Nulty and Colin Todd.

FACTFILE 1977-78

Manager: Gordon Lee

LEAGUE STATISTICS

Final position: 3rd place in Division One
Games played: 42 **Points:** 55

Biggest Victory: 6-0 vs Coventry City (H) and also vs Chelsea (H)
Biggest Defeat: 2-6 vs Manchester United (H)
Leading Goalscorer: Bob Latchford (30 goals)
Ever-Present: Andy King, Mick Lyons and George Wood
Four-Goal Hero: Latchford
Other Hat-Trick Heroes: Latchford
Average Home Attendance: 39,513
Highest Home Crowd: 52,798 vs Liverpool
Lowest Home Crowd: 33,402 vs Ipswich Town

CUPS

F.A.Cup: Round 4
League Cup: Quarter-final

1978-79

The two Merseyside giants dominated the early stages of 1978-79. Liverpool led the way with ten wins out of eleven; but Everton kept pace with an unbeaten record until losing narrowly at snowy Coventry just before Christmas. Lee's side faded out of contention afterwards and had to be content with fourth place at the season's end. The springtime signing of strikers Brian Kidd and Peter Eastoe failed to propel the Toffees to the title.

Earlier in 1978-79 Everton enjoyed themselves by twice hammering Finn Harps 5-0 in the UEFA Cup first round. However, they perished in the next round on away goals to Dukla Prague. Gordon Lee's side also had one glorious evening in the League Cup, with an 8-0 annihilation of Wimbledon. Bob Latchford netted five against the Dons, who were then a Fourth Division side.

Lee brought in two new men during the summer of 1979. Keeper Martin Hodge (from Plymouth Argyle) and left-back John Bailey (from Blackburn Rovers). Martin Dobson and four of Lee's own signings played their last matches for Everton in 1978-79. They were Mickey Walsh (who left as part of the Eastoe deal), Mike Pejic, Colin Todd and Dave Thomas.

FACTFILE 1978-79

Manager: Gordon Lee

LEAGUE STATISTICS

Final position: 4th place in Division One
Games played: 42 **Points:** 51
Biggest Victory: 4-1 vs Bristol City (H)
Biggest Defeat: 0-3 vs Southampton (A)
Leading Goalscorer: Andy King (12 goals)
Ever-Present: George Wood
Hat-Trick Hero: King
Average Home Attendance: 35,456
Highest Home Crowd: 53,141 vs Liverpool
Lowest Home Crowd: 22,958 vs Birmingham City

CUPS

F.A. Cup: Round 3
League Cup: Round 5
UEFA Cup: Round 2

1979-80

Gordon Lee got out the cheque-book again in the early part of 1979-80. He recruited full-back John Gidman and midfielders Asa Hartford and Gary Stanley. However, Everton's fortunes took a further dip during this campaign. They exited the UEFA Cup to Feyenoord in the first round, and performed even worse in the League, winning only five times in the first half of the season and just four more times in the second half. Two of those victories were crucial ones in April, though, ensuring relegation was avoided by four points. Even so, a final finish of 19th was Everton's worst since they regained their top-flight status in 1955. Gordon Lee would probably have paid the price with his job but for his side's fine run in the F.A. Cup.

Aldershot, Wigan Athletic, Wrexham and Ipswich Town were side-stepped as Lee's side glided through to a semi-final clash with Second Division West Ham United. The first match at Villa Park ended 1-1, with Brian Kidd opening the scoring from the spot before getting sent-off. It was the Hammers who were celebrating at the end of extra-time of the Elland Road replay. Bob Latchford scored Everton's goal in a 2-1 defeat and West Ham went on to win the F.A. Cup.

Kidd and Andy King were sold during the summer of 1980. Geoff Nulty also played his last game in 1979-80, having been forced to retire with a knee injury.

FACTFILE 1979-1980

Manager: Gordon Lee

LEAGUE STATISTICS

Final position: 19th place in Division One
Games played: 42 **Points:** 35
Biggest Victory: 5-1 vs Leeds United (H)
Biggest Defeat: 0-4 vs Ipswich Town (H)
Leading Goalscorer: Brian Kidd (10 goals)
Ever-Presents: None
Hat-Trick Hero: Bob Latchford
Average Home Attendance: 28,711
Highest Home Crowd: 53,018 vs Liverpool
Lowest Home Crowd: 20,356 vs West Bromwich Albion

CUPS

F.A. Cup: Semi-final
League Cup: Round 4
UEFA Cup: Round 1

1980-81

The main highlights of 1980-81 came in the F.A. Cup competition. The Toffeemen accounted for Arsenal in the third round and then defeated Liverpool 2-1 in a memorable tie at Goodison Park. Southampton were side-stepped in the fifth round but Gordon Lee's outfit ran out of steam at the quarter-final stage. Manchester City defeated them 3-1 in a replay at Maine Road.

Everton's League form was very uneven in 1980-81: they won six games on the trot in the autumn; but then won only six of their last 32 games to finish 15th. The Goodison faithful started to vote with their feet. Only 15,352 spectators watched the final home game of the season and, for Lee, the writing was on the wall.

Lee was dismissed two days after the end of the 1980-81 campaign. He had been in charge for nearly four and a half campaigns. He had brought some improvements to Goodison, especially in the defensive department; but not for the first time in his career it was felt he was unable to get the best out of the star performers.

The new manager was quickly announced as former Everton midfielder Howard Kendall, who was then manager of Blackburn Rovers. Kendall soon set about a recruitment drive, with strikers Alan Biley and Mick Ferguson, and midfielder Mickey Thomas among the new faces. One man who made his last appearance in an Everton shirt in 1980-81 was Bob Latchford. The big striker joined Swansea City after netting 106 League goals for the Toffees – at a rate of around one goal every two games.

FACTFILE 1980-81

Manager: Gordon Lee

LEAGUE STATISTICS

Final position: 15th place in Division One
Games played: 42 **Points**: 36
Biggest Victory: 5-0 vs Crystal Palace (H) and also vs Coventry City (A)
Biggest Defeat: 0-4 vs Ipswich Town (A)
Leading Goalscorer: Peter Eastoe (15 goals)
Ever-Present: Eastoe (including one appearance as a sub)
Hat-Trick Hero: Bob Latchford
Average Home Attendance: 26,105
Highest Home Crowd: 52,565 vs Liverpool
Lowest Home Crowd: 15,352 vs Stoke City

CUPS

F.A.Cup: Quarter-final
League Cup: Round 3

1981-82

Howard Kendall laid the groundwork for future successes in his first season at the helm. Gary Stevens, Neville Southall (signed from Bury), Kevin Richardson and Adrian Heath (signed from Stoke City) all made their Everton debuts. Graeme

Sharp (signed by Lee from Dumbarton) also gained a regular first-team berth. Five victories and a draw in the last six games underlined the improvement and Everton finished 1981-82 in eighth place.

Alan Biley and Mickey Thomas both failed to settle and only played in their debut campaigns at Goodison. Meanwhile Mick Ferguson received a bad injury and only made eight League appearances for the club. Other departures during 1981-82 included Asa Hartford (to Manchester City) and Peter Eastoe (to WBA in exchange for the returning Andy King). Former skipper Mick Lyons made his 389th and last League appearance for the Toffees in 1981-82, before joining Sheffield Wednesday.

FACTFILE 1981-82

Manager: Howard Kendall

LEAGUE STATISTICS

Final position: 8th place in Division One
Games played: 42 **Points:** 64
Biggest Victory: 3-0 vs Wolverhampton Wanderers (A)
Biggest Defeat: 0-3 vs Tottenham Hotspur (A) and also vs Ipswich Town (A)
Leading Goalscorer: Graeme Sharp (15 goals)
Ever-Presents: None
Hat-Trick Heroes: None
Average Home Attendance: 24,673
Highest Home Crowd: 51,847 vs Liverpool
Lowest Home Crowd: 15,460 vs Nottingham Forest

CUPS

F.A. Cup: Round 3
League Cup: Round 4

1982-83

Some more improvement was noticeable at Goodison Park during 1982-83. Another late flourish, when they won six of their last eight games, lifted the Toffeemen one place to seventh. Any chance of F.A. Cup glory evaporated with an injury-time defeat at Old Trafford at the quarter-final stage.

Among the new faces at Goodison Park in 1982-83 were centre-half Derek Mountfield (from Tranmere Rovers) and Kevin Sheedy. The Liverpool reserve midfielder Sheedy became the first man in 20 years to make the trip across Stanley Park. Former Evertonian David Johnson also arrived from Anfield and midfielder Peter Reid joined from Bolton Wanderers. A huge disappointment at the end of the season was the departure of promising England Under-23 midfielder Steve McMahon to Aston Villa. Another player who made his last Everton appearance in 1982-83 was Billy Wright. The centre-back was dropped before a match at Ipswich in December, for being overweight, and later transferred to Birmingham City.

FACTFILE 1982-83

Manager: Howard Kendall

LEAGUE STATISTICS

Final position: 7th place in Division One

Games played: 42 **Points**: 64

Biggest Victory: 5-0 vs Aston Villa (H)

Biggest Defeat: 0-5 vs Liverpool (A)

Leading Goalscorer: Graeme Sharp (15 goals)

Ever-Presents: None

Hat-Trick Heroes: None

Average Home Attendance: 20,277

Highest Home Crowd: 52,741 vs Liverpool

Lowest Home Crowd: 12,972 vs Coventry City

CUPS

F.A. Cup: Quarter-final

League Cup: Round 3

1983-84

Howard Kendall's job appeared to be very much on the line during the course of 1983-84. By mid-January his side had sunk to 18th place and looked destined to exit the League Cup at Oxford. Yet Everton rallied, won a replay and completely turned around their season. They gradually climbed the table and finished seventh. And reached Wembley twice!

The Toffees visited Wembley for the first time in six years when they reached the League Cup Final. It was the very first all-Merseyside Cup Final at the famous stadium. The game ended goalless but, sadly for Evertonians, the replay was won 1-0 by Liverpool. However, glory and their first trophy in 14 years, was just around the corner. The Toffeemen stuck to their task in the F.A. Cup and knocked out Stoke City, Gillingham, Shrewsbury Town, Notts County and Southampton (after extra-time in the semi-final). Everton got the better of Watford in the Final, with Trevor Steven (signed from Burnley) causing havoc on the right-wing. Goals by Graeme Sharp and Andy Gray (bought from Wolves in November), either side of half-time, eventually punctured Elton John's dreams. Kevin Ratcliffe became only the fourth Everton skipper to hold the F.A. Cup aloft. Everton won another trophy during 1983-84 when their youngsters lifted the F.A. Youth Cup.

On a less happy note, skipper Mark Higgins played his last game in 1983-84 due to a serious pelvic injury.

FACTFILE 1983-84

Manager: Howard Kendall

LEAGUE STATISTICS

Final position: 7th place in Division One
Games played: 42 **Points**: 62
Biggest Victory: 4-1 vs Notts County (H)
Biggest Defeat: 0-3 vs Ipswich Town (A), vs Liverpool (A), vs Wolverhampton Wands (A)
Leading Goalscorer: Adrian Heath (12 goals)
Ever-Presents: None
Hat-Trick Hero: Heath
Average Home Attendance: 19,343
Highest Home Crowd: 51,245 vs Liverpool
Lowest Home Crowd: 13,016 vs Notts County

CUPS

F.A. Cup: Winners
League Cup: Finalists

1984-85

Without a shadow of doubt, 1984-85 was the finest season in the history of Everton FC. The Toffeemen romped to the League Championship, 13 points ahead of runners-up Liverpool. Their record haul of 90 points would have been even higher but for three defeats in their final four fixtures, when the title was already secured. Everton also enjoyed a marvellous European campaign, culminating in a memorable May evening in Rotterdam when Andy Gray, Trevor Steven and Kevin Sheedy scored in a 3-1 victory over Rapid Vienna in the European Cup Winners' Cup Final. Only a magnificent curling strike by Manchester United's Norman Whiteside crushed their hopes of a unique treble in extra-time of the F.A. Cup Final. It was one game too many for Howard Kendall's side, who looked fatigued after their European exploits.

Awards and plaudits flowed in to Goodison from all directions. Kendall was the 'Manager of the Year', goalkeeper Neville Southall was the Football Writers' 'Footballer of the Year' and Peter Reid took the PFA 'Player of the Season' award. Southall, Reid, Gary Stevens, Steven, Graeme Sharp, Gray, Sheedy, Pat Van den Hauwe (signed from Birmingham City), Paul Bracewell (signed from Sunderland) and Kevin Ratcliffe all received international recognition from their respective countries; while consistent centre-half Derek Mountfield (who contributed ten League goals) was very unlucky to miss out on full international honours.

FACTFILE 1984-85

Manager: Howard Kendall

LEAGUE STATISTICS

Final position: Champions of Division One

Games played: 42 **Points:** 90

Biggest Victory: 5-0 vs Manchester United (H) and also vs Nottingham Forest (H)

Biggest Defeat: 1-4 vs Tottenham Hotspur (H) and also vs Coventry City (A)

Leading Goalscorer: Graeme Sharp (21 goals)

Ever-Present: Neville Southall

Hat-Trick Heroes: None

Average Home Attendance: 32,725

Highest Home Crowd: 51,045 vs Liverpool

Lowest Home Crowd: 20,013 vs Coventry City

CUPS

F.A. Cup: Finalists
League Cup: Round 4
European Cup Winners' Cup: Winners

1985-86

Events involving Liverpool fans at the Heysel Stadium, in May 1985, prevented Everton returning to Europe for a crack at the senior competition in 1985-86. Andy Gray moved to Aston Villa and was replaced up front by a youthful Gary Lineker, a £800,000 signing from Leicester City. Lineker's only season at Goodison proved extremely fruitful. He netted 38 times, including 30 in the League to top the list of First Division scorers. However, those goals were not quite enough for Everton to retain the Championship as Liverpool won a tight three cornered fight that also featured West Ham United. Everton defeated the Hammers in the final match to collect second place, two points behind Kenny Dalglish's team.

Liverpool also broke Everton hearts in the F.A. Cup Final. Lineker put the Toffees in front in the first half, but Liverpool deservedly won the game, with three goals in the second period.

In addition to Lineker (who moved to Barcelona the following summer for £2.6 million), John Bailey made his last Everton appearance in 1985-86. He moved on to Newcastle United, while another full-back, Neil Pointon, joined from Scunthorpe United. One significant arrival in the summer of 1986 was centre-half Dave Watson from Norwich City for a club record £900,000 fee.

FACTFILE 1985-86

Manager: Howard Kendall

LEAGUE STATISTICS

Final position: 2nd place in Division One
Games played: 42 **Points:** 86
Biggest Victory: 6-1 vs Arsenal (H) and also vs Southampton (H)
Biggest Defeat: 0-3 vs Queen's Park Rangers (A)
Leading Goalscorer: Gary Lineker (30 goals)

Ever-Presents: None
Hat-Trick Hero: Lineker (on three occasions)
Average Home Attendance: 32,226
Highest Home Crowd: 51,509 vs Liverpool
Lowest Home Crowd: 23,347 vs Leicester City

CUPS

F.A. Cup: Finalists
League Cup: Round 4

1986-87

It was the blue half of Merseyside that enjoyed League Championship success in 1986-87, even though Howard Kendall was forced to call upon 23 different players (with only Kevin Ratcliffe being ever-present) due to a string of injuries. In a fine all-round performance, Everton finished nine points clear of second placed Liverpool. The goals were spread around with 16 different scorers. Trevor Steven top scored with 14 – all but four of which were from the penalty spot.

Along with Dave Watson, the new faces in 1986-87 were midfielder Ian Snodin (from Leeds United), Paul Power (from Manchester City) and Wayne Clarke (from Birmingham City). Clarke netted five times during the run-in (including the only goal at Highbury and a hat-trick against Newcastle United).

After bringing four major trophies to Goodison Park, Kendall surprised the football world by leaving for Athletic Bilbao during the summer of 1987. His assistant Colin Harvey was the natural choice to follow him into the Goodison manager's chair.

FACTFILE 1986-87

Manager: Howard Kendall

LEAGUE STATISTICS

Final position: Champions of Division One
Games played: 42 **Points:** 86
Biggest Victory: 5-1 vs Leicester City (H)
Biggest Defeat: 1-3 vs Liverpool (A)
Leading Goalscorer: Trevor Steven (14 goals)

Ever-Present: Kevin Ratcliffe
Hat-Trick Hero: Wayne Clarke
Average Home Attendance: 32,935
Highest Home Crowd: 48,247 vs Liverpool
Lowest Home Crowd: 25,553 vs Wimbledon

CUPS

F.A.Cup: Round 5
League Cup: Quarter-final

1987-88

Injuries to Paul Bracewell, Adrian Heath, Paul Power and Kevin Sheedy hampered Everton's chances of retaining their crown. Colin Harvey's side made a stuttering start; but five straight wins early in 1988 improved their position. Nevertheless the Toffees finished in fourth place, 20 points behind Liverpool.

Everton made a bold bid to win the League Cup in 1987-88. Rotherham United, Liverpool (who got their revenge by beating Everton in the F.A. Cup), Oldham Athletic and Manchester City were defeated en route to the last four. However, hopes of another trip to Wembley were ended by a 4-1 aggregate defeat to Arsenal in the two-legged semi-final.

The only major arrival during the 1987-88 campaign was Scottish midfielder Ian Wilson, from Leicester City. However, in a bid to improve his side's scoring rate, Harvey paid West Ham a club record £2.3 million for England international Tony Cottee in the summer of 1988. Cottee was just one part of a £4.6 million spending spree. Others to join were Stuart McCall, Pat Nevin and Neil McDonald. Those leaving Goodison Park included Derek Mountfield (to Aston Villa), Gary Stevens (to Glasgow Rangers) and Alan Harper (to Sheffield Wednesday).

FACTFILE 1987-88

Manager: Colin Harvey

LEAGUE STATISTICS

Final position: 4th place in Division One
Games played: 40 **Points:** 70

Biggest Victory: 4-0 vs Sheffield Wednesday (H) and also vs Southampton (A)
Biggest Defeat: 0-2 vs Liverpool (A)
Leading Goalscorer: Graeme Sharp (13 goals)
Ever-Presents: None
Four-Goal Hero: Sharp
Other Hat-Trick Heroes: None
Average Home Attendance: 27,770
Highest Home Crowd: 44,162 vs Liverpool
Lowest Home Crowd: 20,351 vs Wimbledon

CUPS

F.A. Cup: Round 5
League Cup: Semi-final

1988-89

The new season started brightly when record signing Tony Cottee scored within a minute of his debut. He completed a hat-trick in that 4-0 victory over Newcastle United and finished the season with 13 goals to be the club's top scorer. However, a string of mediocre performances by the team meant that Everton slipped down the table to finish eighth. There was the consolation of two Wembley Cup Finals. Both were thrilling affairs but both ended in Everton defeats. Nottingham Forest won the Simod Cup Final 4-3, while – much more heartbreakingly – it was Liverpool who yet again got the better of them in the F.A. Cup Final.

WBA, Plymouth Argyle, Barnsley, Wimbledon and Norwich City were all defeated as Colin Harvey's side battled through to meet the Reds in the F.A. Cup Final. Liverpool had the edge throughout and, although substitute Stuart McCall twice equalised, the Reds finished as 3-2 winners at the end of extra-time.

Among the men who played their last games for Everton during 1988-89 were Peter Reid and Adrian Heath, who moved to QPR and Espanyol, respectively. A disillusioned Trevor Steven moved to Glasgow Rangers in the summer of 1989, while Wayne Clarke (to Leicester City), Paul Bracewell (back to Sunderland) and Pat Van den Hauwe (to Tottenham Hotspur) also moved on. As part of the Clarke deal, Everton gained striker Mike Newell. In addition, Martin Keown (from

Aston Villa) and Norman Whiteside (from Manchester United) also became Evertonians.

FACTFILE 1988-89

Manager: Colin Harvey

LEAGUE STATISTICS

Final position: 8th place in Division One
Games played: 38 **Points:** 54
Biggest Victory: 4-0 vs Newcastle United (H)
Biggest Defeat: 1-3 vs Arsenal (H)
Leading Goalscorer: Tony Cottee (13 goals)
Ever-Present: Neville Southall
Hat-Trick Hero: Cottee
Average Home Attendance: 27,765
Highest Home Crowd: 45,994 vs Liverpool
Lowest Home Crowd: 16,316 vs Charlton Athletic

CUPS

F.A. Cup: Finalists
League Cup: Round 4

1989-90

Everton improved two places to finish sixth in 1989-90 and, but for an end of season blip, when they failed to win any of their last three fixtures, they might have finished third. They failed to pull up any trees in the cups, though. They were tumbled out of the League Cup by Nottingham Forest (in the fourth round) and exited the F.A. Cup to Oldham Athletic, in a fifth round replay.

Winger Peter Beagrie arrived from Stoke City during 1989-90. Colin Harvey also signed Swede Stefan Rehn and Dutchman Ray Atteveld. Rehn went on to start only one Football League match, but goes down in history as Everton's very first overseas signing. During the summer of 1990 defender Andy Hinchcliffe was recruited from Manchester City.

FACTFILE 1989-90

Manager: Colin Harvey

LEAGUE STATISTICS

Final position: 6th place in Division One

Games played: 38 **Points:** 59

Biggest Victory: 4-0 vs Crystal Palace (H) and also vs Nottingham Forest (H)

Biggest Defeat: 2-6 vs Aston Villa (A)

Leading Goalscorer: Tony Cottee (13 goals)

Ever-Present: Neville Southall

Hat-Trick Hero: Cottee

Average Home Attendance: 26,280

Highest Home Crowd: 42,453 vs Liverpool

Lowest Home Crowd: 17,591 vs Nottingham Forest

CUPS

F.A. Cup: Round 5

League Cup: Round 4

1990-91

The Toffees made a dismal start to the 1990-91 campaign, losing their first three League games. Neville Southall made an incredible protest during the half-time interval of the first game of the season. With Everton losing 3-0 to Leeds United, the big keeper left before the end of Colin Harvey's team-talk and returned to his goalmouth. Only one of the first ten League games ended in an Everton victory and the team's morale was low. They did defeat Wrexham 5-0 and 6-0 in the League Cup; but in the next round exited 2-1 at Bramall Lane. The following day the board relieved Colin Harvey of his duties.

Coach Jimmy Gabriel acted as caretaker and Everton beat QPR 3-0 at home. However, a permanent manager soon arrived in the form of old boss Howard Kendall. Having returned to England to manage Manchester City, Kendall just could not resist the lure of Goodison Park. Interestingly, the man he selected as his number two was the axed former manager Harvey.

Everton's League form improved gradually and an unbeaten six game run at the end of the season enabled them to claw their way up to ninth place. Everton also enjoyed some cup success, but failed to gain a trophy. Crystal Palace beat them in the Zenith Data Systems Cup Final at Wembley and West Ham United defeated them in the quarter-final of the F.A. Cup. In the previous round Everton had to battle bravely to see off Liverpool, equalising four times in a Goodison Park replay. Substitute Tony Cottee made it 3-3 in the last minute of normal time and then squared matters at 4-4 in the second half of extra-time. With Kenny Dalglish sensationally giving up his job, caretaker Ronnie Moran was in charge of Liverpool in the second replay which the Toffees won 1-0.

Kendall had only recruited Polish winger Robert Warzycha during 1990-91, but was busy with the cheque-book in the summer of 1991. He signed two former Evertonians, Mark Ward and Alan Harper, from his previous club Manchester City. But his biggest coup was to persuade Peter Beardsley to join from Liverpool for £1 million. One man who made his final Everton appearance in 1990-91 was Graeme Sharp, who moved to Oldham Athletic. Sharp netted 111 League goals, more than any other Everton player apart from the legendary Dixie Dean.

FACTFILE 1990-91

Managers: Colin Harvey and Howard Kendall

LEAGUE STATISTICS

Final position: 9th place in Division One
Games played: 38 **Points:** 51
Biggest Victory: 3-0 vs Southampton (H) and also Queen's Park Rangers (H)
Biggest Defeat: 1-3 vs Coventry City (A), vs Nottingham Forest (A) and vs Liverpool (A)
Leading Goalscorer: Tony Cottee (10 goals)
Ever-Present: Neville Southall
Hat-Trick Hero: Cottee
Average Home Attendance: 25,028
Highest Home Crowd: 39,847 vs Liverpool
Lowest Home Crowd: 14,590 vs Wimbledon

CUPS

F.A. Cup: Quarter-final
League Cup: Round 6

1991-92

The arrival of Peter Beardsley raised Goodison Park spirits in 1991-92; however Howard Kendall's side failed to overcome a sluggish start. They only won just one of their first eight games and eventually finished 12th. Beardsley finished top scorer, with 20 goals (all but five in the League) but, with little cup joy either, it was a mediocre campaign for Evertonians.

Among the other new faces in 1991-92 were Matt Jackson (from Luton Town), Gary Ablett (from Liverpool) and striker Mo Johnston (from Glasgow Rangers). Kendall's recruitment drive continued in the summer of 1992, with Barry Horne (from Southampton), Paul Rideout (from Glasgow Rangers) and, Yugoslav winger, Preki all joining the fold.

One man who left Goodison Park in 1991-92 was former captain Kevin Ratcliffe. He joined Cardiff City, after making 359 League appearances in an Everton jersey.

FACTFILE 1991-92

Manager: Howard Kendall

LEAGUE STATISTICS

Final position: 12th place in Division One
Games played: 42 **Points:** 53
Biggest Victory: 4-0 vs West Ham United (H)
Biggest Defeat: 2-4 vs Arsenal (A)
Leading Goalscorer: Peter Beardsley (15 goals)
Ever-Presents: Peter Beardsley and Neville Southall
Hat-Trick Heroes: Peter Beardsley and Tony Cottee
Average Home Attendance: 23,148
Highest Home Crowd: 37,681 vs Liverpool
Lowest Home Crowd: 15,201 vs Southampton

CUPS

F.A.Cup: Round 4
League Cup: Round 4

1992-93

In terms of their League position, Everton only slipped one place to 13th in 1992-93; however, that is far from the full story. In the first season of the Premier League, they only finished four points ahead of the third relegated club (Crystal Palace). Everton would have been even more uncomfortably placed, but for an important 5-2 victory at Maine Road on the final day of the campaign.

At the end of the season the club was put up for sale, with Peter Johnson and Bill Kenwright battling for control. Howard Kendall had some money to spend and recruited Graham Stuart from Chelsea.

FACTFILE 1992-93

Manager: Howard Kendall

LEAGUE STATISTICS

Final position: 13th in the F.A. Premier League
Games played: 38 **Points:** 53
Biggest Victory: 5-2 vs Manchester City (A)
Biggest Defeat: 3-5 vs Queen's Park Rangers (H)
Leading Goalscorer: Tony Cottee (12 goals)
Ever-Presents: None
Hat-Trick Heroes: None
Average Home Attendance: 20,445
Highest Home Crowd: 35,826 vs Liverpool
Lowest Home Crowd: 14,051 vs Southampton

CUPS

F.A. Cup: Round 3
League Cup: Round 4

1993-94

Everton began 1993-94 in bright form, with three successive victories. However, they lost the next three games and before the end of September had suffered an embarrassing 5-1 home defeat at the hands of Norwich City.

The Toffees won their seventh League game, against Southampton, on 4th

December. However, later that evening Howard Kendall (and Colin Harvey) resigned after the board refused to meet Manchester United's evaluation of Dion Dublin, Kendall's number one target in the transfer market. Jimmy Gabriel again took over as caretaker manager and Everton's plight worsened with a six match run that yielded just one point.

Mike Walker, manager of Norwich City, became Everton's new boss in early 1994. His new side responded with a 6-2 hammering of Swindon Town. Walker quickly brought in striker Brett Angell (from Southend United) and Swedish winger Anders Limpar (from Arsenal). However, the side still struggled and it looked quite likely that Walker would be the first manager since Cliff Britton (in 1951) to take Everton into the second-flight.

Everton went into the final game of 1993-94 at home to Wimbledon, on 7th May 1994, with their fate out of their own hands. The Dons took a 2-0 lead to leave the Blues looking doomed. However, Graham Stuart kept his cool to convert a penalty (the first he had ever scored) after Anders Limpar was adjudged to have been fouled. In the second half Barry Horne equalised with a long-shot and, with Everton pulses racing, Stuart mis-hit the winning goal. A see-saw turn of events elsewhere ensured that Everton avoided the drop. The Toffees finished in 17th place, safe by just two points.

Off the pitch, Peter Johnson won control of the club and was appointed chairman. He provided Walker with some extra funding to bring in Nigerian striker Daniel Amokachi and midfielder Vinnie Samways (from Spurs). However, a significant departure at the end of 1993-94 was Peter Beardsley, who re-joined Newcastle United.

FACTFILE 1993-94

Managers: Howard Kendall and Mike Walker

LEAGUE STATISTICS

Final position: 17th in the F.A. Premiership
Games played: 42 **Points:** 44
Biggest Victory: 6-2 vs Swindon Town (H)
Biggest Defeat: 1-5 vs Norwich City (H) and also vs Sheffield Wednesday (A)
Leading Goalscorer: Tony Cottee (16 goals)

Ever-Present: Neville Southall

Hat-Trick Hero: Cottee (on two occasions)

Average Home Attendance: 22,876

Highest Home Crowd: 38,157 vs Liverpool

Lowest Home Crowd: 13,265 vs Southampton

CUPS

F.A.Cup: Round 3

League Cup: Round 4

1994-95

Everton made an appalling start to 1994-95. They mustered just eight points during the first third of the campaign and their first victory did not come until 1st November 1995. However, seven days later, Mike Walker lost his job after less than nine months at the helm. Former Everton striker Joe Royle quickly moved into the Goodison hot-seat. He got off to a dream start when goals by on-loan Duncan Ferguson and Paul Rideout enabled the Toffees to defeat Liverpool 2-0 at Goodison Park.

Royle's side gradually climbed up the table; however, it was not until the penultimate fixture of 1994-95 that safety was secured. Meanwhile a string of victories were recorded in the F.A. Cup. Derby County, Bristol City, Norwich City and Newcastle United were all side-stepped as Everton reached the last four.

Ferguson (now a permanent signing from Glasgow Rangers for a club record fee of £4.3 million) was a major influence up front, but he was unavailable for the semi-final clash with Tottenham Hotspur at Elland Road. The Londoners were considered to be the favourites, but Royle's men out-played them on the day to win 4-1. Daniel Amokachi came off the bench to bag a brace.

Everton also started as underdogs in the Final against Manchester United; but Royle's tactics were spot-on and Paul Rideout's first half header proved enough to give Everton the F.A. Cup for the fifth time in their history. The triumph was also the passport for the club's first European adventure in eleven years.

Among the men joining Everton in 1994-95 was full-back David Burrows, who arrived from West Ham United. One man making the trip in the other direction was Tony Cottee. The diminutive striker returned to his first club having scored 72 League goals for the Toffees – more than any other Evertonian, since the Second World War, apart from Graeme Sharp. Royle's most important signing during the summer of 1995 was winger Andrei Kanchelskis (from Manchester United) for a club record £5.5 million.

FACTFILE 1994-95

Managers: Mike Walker and Joe Royle

LEAGUE STATISTICS

Final position: 15th in the F.A. Premiership
Games played: 42 **Points:** 50
Biggest Victory: 4-1 vs Ipswich Town (H)
Biggest Defeat: 0-4 vs Manchester City (A)
Leading Goalscorer: Paul Rideout (14 goals)
Ever-Presents: None
Hat-Trick Heroes: None
Average Home Attendance: 31,291
Highest Home Crowd: 40,011 vs Manchester United
Lowest Home Crowd: 23,295 vs Norwich City

CUPS

F.A. Cup: Winners
League Cup: Round 2

1995-96

The European Cup Winners' Cup run of 1995-96 only embraced four games. After knocking out KR Reykjavik, the Toffeemen slipped out 1-0, on aggregate, to Feyenoord.

After winning only two of their first eleven fixtures, Everton showed greatly improved League form and finished sixth. Andrei Kanchelskis's arrival from Manchester United proved to be the catalyst and the winger finished top scorer in 1995-96, with 16 goals.

Royle's rebuilding continued during the summer of 1996 with the arrival of Leeds United midfielder Gary Speed.

FACTFILE 1995-96

Manager: Joe Royle

LEAGUE STATISTICS

Final position: 6th in the F.A. Premiership

Games played: 38 **Points:** 61

Biggest Victory: 4-0 vs Middlesbrough (H)

Biggest Defeat: 2-4 vs Wimbledon (A)

Leading Goalscorer: Andrei Kanchelskis (16 goals)

Ever-Presents: None

Hat-Trick Heroes: None

Average Home Attendance: 35,435

Highest Home Crowd: 40,127 vs Aston Villa

Lowest Home Crowd: 30,009 vs Queen's Park Rangers

CUPS

F.A. Cup: Round 4

League Cup: Round 2

1996-97

Gary Speed netted a goal on his debut as Everton began 1996-97 brightly by beating Newcastle United and then holding the champions Manchester United at Old Trafford. Joe Royle added Nicky Barmby to his squad, paying Middlesbrough a club record £5.75 million. A 7-1 hammering of Southampton came during a run of eight games without defeat and the omens looked good, with Everton lying in sixth place.

Far less satisfactory were the defeats in the League Cup and F.A. Cup, to lower division outfits, York City and Bradford City, respectively. Even less impressive was the run of six successive League defeats, around the turn of the year, which sent the Toffees spiralling into relegation trouble.

Royle resigned towards the end of March, after the board refused to give him the funds to purchase Norwegians Tore Andre Flo and Claus Eftevaag. Veteran skipper Dave Watson was given the job of caretaker manager. Safety was achieved, but not by a very big margin. With only one of the last eight games won, Everton slid to 15th place – only two points above relegated Sunderland.

It was fully expected that former Evertonian Andy Gray would take over as the club's manager during the summer of 1997. However, at the last moment, the BSkyB football pundit changed his mind and turned down the board's offer. Instead the man given the job of rebuilding Everton was Howard Kendall, who returned for an unprecedented third spell. His assistant was former Everton player Adrian Heath.

Among the men who played their last games for Everton in 1996-97 were Andrei Kanchelskis (sold to Fiorentina for £8 million), Anders Limpar (to Birmingham City) and Paul Rideout (who went to China). In addition defender David Unsworth joined West Ham United; however he was to return twelve months later via a very brief stay at Villa Park.

Several new faces arrived at Goodison Park during the summer of 1997, including Slaven Bilic (from West Ham United), Gareth Farrelly (from Aston Villa) and Tony Thomas (from Tranmere Rovers).

FACTFILE 1996-97

Managers: Joe Royle and Howard Kendall

LEAGUE STATISTICS

Final position: 15th in the F.A. Premiership
Games played: 38 **Points:** 42
Biggest Victory: 7-1 v Southampton (H)
Biggest Defeat: 0-4 v Wimbledon (A)
Leading Goalscorer: Duncan Ferguson (10 goals)
Ever-Presents: None
Hat-Trick Hero: Gary Speed
Average Home Attendance: 36,189
Highest Home Crowd: 40,177 vs Liverpool
Lowest Home Crowd: 30,368 vs Leicester City

CUPS

F.A.Cup: Round 4
League Cup: Round 2

1997-98

Kendall's side made a poor start to 1997-98, winning only three of their first 18 fixtures. Three successive victories around the turn of the year moved them into mid-table but another slump took them to the edge of the cliff again. By the final round of games Everton were precariously placed in the relegation zone and once again their fate was not in their own hands.

On the last day of the season Everton welcomed Coventry City to Goodison Park, while Bolton Wanderers (who had one more point) visited Chelsea. The Toffeemen (with their superior goal difference) needed to achieve a better outcome than the Trotters. Things seemed to be swinging Everton's way when Gareth Farrelly gave them a first half lead. And their survival prospects got even brighter when Bolton went behind at Stamford Bridge. However, there were some more twists and turns to come. Nicky Barmby had a penalty saved and soon afterwards Coventry equalised. A City winner or a Bolton equaliser in London would have spelt relegation for Everton; however, the only other scoring came from Chelsea and it was the Trotters who dropped out of the Premiership. Kendall's side finished in 17th place – surviving only because they conceded five goals less than Bolton.

Everton did lift one trophy in 1997-98 when their youngsters lifted the F.A. Youth Cup. Among the many jewels in the youth squad was Danny Cadamarteri, who had made a big impact during his run in the first team earlier in the term.

The were two key departures from Goodison Park during 1997-98. Veteran keeper Neville Southall joined Stoke City, after making a club record 578 League appearances over a period of 17 seasons. Much more of a surprise was the departure of skipper Gary Speed, who eventually joined Newcastle United after handing in a shock transfer request.

Another significant departure took place during the summer of 1998 when Kendall's third spell at the Goodison helm ended "by mutual consent". His successor was the former Glasgow Rangers boss Walter Smith.

FACTFILE 1997-98

Manager: Howard Kendall

LEAGUE STATISTICS

Final position: 17th in the F.A. Premiership

Games played: 38 **Points:** 40
Biggest Victory: 4-2 vs Barnsley (H)
Biggest Defeat: 0-4 vs Arsenal (A)
Leading Goalscorer: Duncan Ferguson (11 goals)
Ever-Presents: None
Hat-Trick Hero: Ferguson
Average Home Attendance: 35,376
Highest Home Crowd: 40,479 vs Manchester United
Lowest Home Crowd: 28,533 vs Wimbledon

CUPS

F.A. Cup: Round 3
League Cup: Round 3

1998-99

Walter Smith's side struggled in front of goal for much of 1998-99. Their first home goal did not come until the end of October and they only found the net three times in their first 12 Goodison fixtures. The mid-February 5-0 home victory over Middlesbrough relieved the drought, but it was the on-loan signing of striker Kevin Campbell which effectively ensured the Toffees' safety. Campbell (who later became a permanent signing), ended up as the top scorer with eight goals. He netted in each of four crucial victories in the spring which enabled Smith's side to finish in 14th place – seven points above the relegation line.

Everton enjoyed some success in the F.A. Cup, defeating Bristol City, Ipswich Town and Coventry City before exiting 4-1 at Newcastle at the quarter-final stage. Injuries seriously blighted the club in 1998-99, with midfielder John Collins (signed from Monaco) one of several senior players forced to sit out a chunk of the campaign.

There was huge outrage when skipper Duncan Ferguson was sold to Newcastle United for £8 million in late November. The transfer was agreed behind the manager's back and Smith threatened to resign unless the full truth was made public. As a result it was chairman Peter Johnson who was to hand in his resignation.

Among the new faces appearing on the pitch at Goodison Park in 1998-99 were former Strasbourg midfielder Olivier Dacourt (who stayed just one season) and defender David Weir (signed from Hearts). There were more arrivals during the summer of 1999. Veteran defender Richard Gough, midfielder Mark Pembridge and defender Abel Xavier being the most notable signings from Nottingham Forest, Benfica and PSV Eindhoven, respectively.

FACTFILE 1998-99

Manager: Howard Kendall

LEAGUE STATISTICS

Final position: 14th in the F.A. Premiership
Games played: 38 **Points:** 43
Biggest Victory: 6-0 vs West Ham United (H)
Biggest Defeat: 0-3 vs Coventry City (A) and also vs Aston Villa (A)
Leading Goalscorer: Kevin Campbell (9 goals)
Ever-Presents: None
Hat-Trick Heroes: Kevin Campbell and Duncan Ferguson
Average Home Attendance: 36,202
Highest Home Crowd: 40,185 vs Liverpool
Lowest Home Crowd: 30,357 vs Newcastle United

CUPS

F.A. Cup: Quarter-final
League Cup: Round 4

1999-2000

Walter Smith's side improved by one place in 1999-2000 to finish 13th. For much of the campaign, an even better position seemed possible and, for a while, it looked as if they might finish inside the top half of the table. The prospect of collecting silverware appeared bright, too, with Exeter City, Birmingham City and Preston North all being side-stepped in the F.A. Cup. However, Aston Villa destroyed Everton dreams by defeating them 2-1 at Goodison.

Among the new men Smith brought in during 1999-2000 were Joe-Max Moore (from New England Revolution), Stephen Hughes (from Arsenal) and veteran striker Mark Hughes (from Southampton).

Most Everton fans were pleased to hear the announcement during 1999-2000 that Bill Kenwright's 'True Blue Holdings' consortium had acquired Peter Johnson's shares. The Goodison faithful were even more delighted when their former favourite Duncan Ferguson was bought back from Newcastle United for £3.75 million during the summer of 2000. Another important summer signing was that of former England midfielder Paul Gascoigne (who Smith had previously managed at Ibrox).

Niclas Alexandersson (from Sheffield Wednesday) and Thomas Gravesen (from SV Hamburg) also arrived during the summer of 2000. However, among the departures was Nicky Barmby. He sensationally joined Liverpool for £6 million and became the first Evertonian to make the direct move to Anfield since Dave Hickson in 1959.

FACTFILE 1999-2000

Manager: Walter Smith

LEAGUE STATISTICS

Final position: 14th in the F.A. Premiership
Games played: 38 **Points:** 50
Biggest Victory: 5-0 vs Sunderland (H)
Biggest Defeat: 1-5 vs Manchester United (A)
Leading Goalscorer: Kevin Campbell (12 goals)
Ever-Presents: None
Hat-Trick Hero: Nick Barmby
Average Home Attendance: 34,880
Highest Home Crowd: 40,052 vs Liverpool
Lowest Home Crowd: 30,490 vs Leicester City

CUPS

F.A. Cup: Quarter-final
League Cup: Round 2

2000-01

Everton spent virtually the whole of 2000-01 stuck in mid-table. They lost three of their last five fixtures and finished in 16th place, eight points above the relegation zone. A long injury list which included Duncan Ferguson, Paul Gascoigne and promising striker Francis Jeffers hampered Walter Smith's hopes of pushing the club forward. For the third consecutive campaign skipper Kevin Campbell finished as the top scorer.

There was little cup joy in 2000-01, with Everton slipping out of both competitions to lower division opposition. Among Walter Smith's signings during 2000-01 were Gary Naysmith (from Hearts) and Alessandro Pistone (from Newcastle United). It was a season in which Richard Gough played his last game for the club. So, too, did Francis Jeffers who moved to Arsenal in the summer of 2001 for a club record fee of £10 million.

FACTFILE 2000-01

Manager: Walter Smith

LEAGUE STATISTICS

Final position: 16th in the F.A. Premiership
Games played: 38 **Points:** 42
Biggest Victory: 3-0 vs Charlton Athletic (H)
Biggest Defeat: 0-5 vs Manchester City (A)
Leading Goalscorer: Kevin Campbell (9 goals)
Ever-Presents: None
Hat-Trick Heroes: None
Average Home Attendance: 34,130
Highest Home Crowd: 40,260 vs Liverpool
Lowest Home Crowd: 27,670 vs Aston

CUPS

F.A. Cup: Round 4
League Cup: Round 2

2001-02

Goals were again in short supply during 2000-01 with new signing Tomasz Radzinski and the injury-hit Duncan Ferguson being the joint top scorers in spite of only netting six times each. Among the men who played their last games for Everton in 2001-02 were Danny Cadamarteri (who joined Bradford City),

Abel Xavier (who joined Liverpool) and Paul Gascoigne (who joined Burnley).

The departure of Gazza came shortly after Everton and Water Smith parted company in March. The Toffees were 15th in the table at the time of Smith's departure following a string of mediocre performances. There had been strong hopes that his side would lift the F.A. Cup. Stoke City, Leyton Orient and Crewe Alexandra were all side-stepped, but Middlesbrough proved too strong for Everton at the quarter-final stage. That 3-0 defeat at the Riverside Stadium proved to be the last straw and two days later Smith was gone.

The man chosen to be Everton's new manager was the Preston North End boss David Moyes. His new side celebrated his arrival by winning matches back-to-back for the first time in the campaign. All-told Everton collected 13 points from nine matches, under Moyes, to finish in 15th place. Having again cemented their Premiership place, Everton had ensured that they would enter 2002-03 as the very first club to celebrate 100 seasons of top-flight football.

FACTFILE 2001-02

Managers: Walter Smith and David Moyes

LEAGUE STATISTICS

Final position: 15th in the F.A. Premiership

Games played: 38 **Points:** 43

Biggest Victory: 5-0 vs West Ham United (H)

Biggest Defeat: 2-6 vs Newcastle United (A)

Leading Goalscorers: Duncan Ferguson and Tomasz Radzinski (6 goals each)

Ever-Presents: None

Hat-Trick Heroes: None

Highest Home Attendance: 34,004

Highest Home Crowd: 39,948 vs Manchester United

Lowest Home Crowd: 29,503 vs Tottenham Hotspur

CUPS

F.A. Cup: Quarter-final

League Cup: Round 2

THE FUTURE

2001-02 had been another mediocre campaign for Everton, but there was a great deal of optimism around Goodison Park during the summer of 2002. In fact there had been a strong injection of optimism around the club ever since the arrival of manager David Moyes in March. The fans eagerly awaited the new season with the strong belief that their side could finish inside the top half of the table for the first time in seven seasons.

Moyes was busy in the transfer market during the close season. His biggest outlay was £5 million on Nigerian defender Joseph Yobo (from Marseille). Two Chinese players were recruited in the form of Li Tie (for £1.25 million) and Li Weifeng (on loan). In addition, Juliano Rodrigo was signed from Botafogo (for £1.25 million) and Richard Wright was purchased from Arsenal (for £3.5 million). The 24 year-old goalkeeper won a League Championship medal with the Gunners the previous May, but saw the move to Goodison Park as a big opportunity for him to cement a regular first-team spot and regain his place in the England squad.

Another man expected to make his mark at Goodison Park during 2002-03 was 16 year-old striker Wayne Rooney. Having scored 17 goals in only 15 Academy matches, he was being touted as the "blue Michael Owen". Moyes promised not to over play his teenage prodigy in 2002-03, nevertheless Rooney looked set to become the second youngest player (after Joe Royle) to represent the Toffees in League action.

Among the men who were released in the summer of 2002 were the experienced trio of David Ginola, Jesper Blomqvist and Alec Cleland.

With a brand new 55,000 seater stadium at the prestigious King's Dock planned to open in 2005-06, Everton supporters had a lot to look forward to in the medium term. More immediately, though, the fans saw the 2002-03 season as a chance for Everton to rebuild and consolidate under Moyes. There was certainly a strong belief that it would be a campaign free of relegation worries, spiced by a long run in at least one of the cups.

EVERTON 25 SEASONS 1977-78 TO 2001-02

A-Z OF THE 25 MOST INFLUENTIAL PLAYERS

PETER BEARDSLEY

Peter Beardsley was already 30 years old when he made the surprise move across Stanley Park in 1991. Nevertheless he was worth every penny of the £1 million fee. Peter was the club's top scorer in his first season, with a tally of 15 League goals. He struck ten more times in 1992-93 before moving back to his native Newcastle for a £1.4 million fee.

Beardsley delighted Goodison Park even though his stay fell during an undistinguished period for the team. He displayed the full range of skills which earned him 59 England caps. He began his career with Carlisle United and had spells with Vancouver Whitecaps and Manchester United (making just one League Cup appearance), before making his name with Newcastle United. Four other League clubs utilised his enthusiasm and experience after he left St James' Park for the second time. All-told he made 658 League appearances, but many at Goodison Park would have loved him to have made a lot more than 81 in an Everton shirt.

FACTFILE

Born: Newcastle-Upon-Tyne, 18th January 1961
Position: Striker
Everton 25 Seasons League Record: 81 appearances – 25 goals
Everton Career League Record: As above
Other League apps (Pre-Everton): Carlisle United (104 apps. – 22 goals), Newcastle United (147 apps. – 61 goals), Liverpool (131 apps. – 46 goals)
Other League apps (Post-Everton): Newcastle United (129 apps. – 46 goals), Bolton Wanderers (17 apps. – 2 goals), Manchester City (on loan 6 apps. – 0 goals), Fulham (on loan 21 apps. – 4 goals), Hartlepool United (22 apps. – 2 goals)

25 SEASONS EVERTON LEAGUE RECORD

Season	Apps	Goals
1991-1992	42	15

1992-1993	39	10
25 Season Total	81	25

KEVIN CAMPBELL

Kevin Campbell exploded on the scene at Goodison Park with nine goals in eight appearances, when on loan from Trabzonspur, at the end of the 1998-99 campaign. A hat-trick against West Ham United numbered amongst his quick-fire tally, which proved enough to make him Everton's leading scorer that season. Having signed permanently for the Toffees for £3 million, Kevin followed up by again being the club's leading scorer in both 1999-2000 and 2000-01 and thus emulating another Londoner, Tony Cottee, who was also top-scorer during each of his first three seasons at Goodison.

Looking more lethal than at any time in his career, his move to Merseyside has given Kevin Campbell a new lease of life. Scoring at a rate of a goal every other game, Kevin was a popular choice to skipper the side. The strong striker again made a significant contribution in 2001-02, even though he was blighted by injury. Kevin initially made his name with Arsenal in the early 1990s before moving to Nottingham Forest in the summer of 1995. His spell in Turkey, in 1998-99, was a nightmare; however, despite a string of injuries, life at Goodison Park has been going like a dream.

FACTFILE

Born: Lambeth, 4th February 1970
Position: Striker
Everton 25 Seasons League Record: 86 appearances – 34 goals
Everton Career League Record: As above
Other League apps (Pre-Everton): Arsenal (166 apps. – 46 goals), Leyton Orient (on loan 16 apps. – 9 goals), Leicester City (on loan 11 apps. – 5 goals), Nottingham Forest (80 apps. – 32 goals)

25 SEASONS EVERTON LEAGUE RECORD

Season	Apps	Goals
1998-1999	8	9
1999-2000	26	12

2000-2001	29	9
2001-2002	23	4
25 Seasons Total	86	34

TONY COTTEE

Tony Cottee joined Everton in the summer of 1988 for a record £2.3 million from his beloved West Ham United. An excellent goal-poacher, he headed the club's list of scorers in five of his six full campaigns at Goodison. His Everton career got off to a memorable start, with a goal inside the first minute of a match (against Newcastle United) in which he went on to complete a hat-trick. Tony went on to register three more hat-tricks for the club. He was a member of the side which played in the 1989 F.A. Cup Final and also scored twice in the Simod Cup Final earlier in 1988-89.

Only Cottee's former strike-partner, Graeme Sharp, netted more goals for Everton in the quarter of a century up to the summer of 2002. Tony's goals' tally for the Toffees fell just one short of the century mark (72 of which were in the League) when he returned to East London in September 1994. He subsequently experienced a nightmare spell in Malaysia (with Selangor) before returning to the Premiership with Leicester City. He scored some valuable goals for the Foxes and appeared in two League Cup Finals, the second of which brought Tony his first winners' medal in senior football. He played in all four levels of English senior football during 2000-01. He played for Leicester, Norwich City, Barnet and, finally, Millwall. His first spell in management was unfortunate, as Barnet dropped out of the Football League two months after he was dismissed. Four of Tony Cottee's seven England caps were awarded while was an Everton player and the diminutive hit-man has several scrapbooks full of happy memories from his spell at Goodison Park.

FACTFILE

Born: West Ham, 11th July 1965
Position: Striker
Everton 25 Seasons League Record: 184 appearances – 72 goals
Everton League Career: As above
Other League apps (Pre-Everton): West Ham United (212 apps. – 92 goals)

Other League apps (Post-Everton): West Ham United (67 apps. – 23 goals), Leicester City (85 apps. – 27 goals), Birmingham City (on loan 5 apps. – 1 goals), Norwich City (7 apps. – 1 goal), Barnet (16 apps. – 9 goals), Millwall (2 apps. – 0 goals)

25 SEASONS EVERTON LEAGUE RECORD

Season	Apps	Goals
1988-1989	36	13
1989-1990	27	13
1991-1992	29	10
1992-1993	24	8
1993-1994	26	12
1994-1995	39	16
1995-1996	3	0
25 Seasons Total	184	72

PETER EASTOE

Peter Eastoe arrived at Goodison Park in March 1979 from QPR, in exchange for Mickey Walsh. He began his career with Wolves, but made his name by scoring a bucket full of goals for Swindon Town. Eastoe's best season at Goodison Park was 1980-81. He featured in every League game (coming on as substitute in the first) and was top scorer (with 15 goals).

Eastoe netted 26 League goals for the Toffees before he left in 1981-82, in exchange for the returning Andy King. This was a reasonable record considering the team struggled for much of his time at the club. Peter later made appearances for four other sides on loan (including his first club Wolves).

FACTFILE

Born: Tamworth, 2nd August 1953
Position: Striker
Everton 25 Seasons League Record: 95 appearances – 26 goals
Everton Career League Record: As above
Other League apps (Pre-Everton): Wolverhampton Wanderers (6 apps. – 0 goals), Swindon Town (91 apps. – 43 goals), Queen's Park Rangers (72 apps. – 15 goals)

Other League apps (Post-Everton): West Bromwich Albion (31 apps. – 8 goals), Leicester City (on loan 11 apps. – 2 goals), Huddersfield T. (on loan 10 apps. – 0 goals), Walsall (on loan 6 apps. – 1 goals), Wolverhampton Wands. (on loan 8 apps. – 0 goals)

25 SEASONS EVERTON LEAGUE RECORD

Season	Apps	Goals
1978-1979	8	0
1979-1980	26	6
1980-1981	42	15
1981-1982	19	5
25 Seasons Total	95	26

JOHN EBBRELL

John Ebbrell joined Everton as an associated schoolboy and became a trainee in 1986. This committed midfielder made his League debut in 1988-89 and for six seasons in the early 1990's was a regular member of the first-team squad.

Handicapped by injury, Ebbrell's Everton career fizzled out and he rejoined his former manager Howard Kendall at Sheffield United for a £1 million fee in March 1997. His career with the Blades was tragically cut short by further injuries. The hard-working John Ebbrell won an England B cap and 14 Under-21 caps, but with a little more luck might have achieved so much more in the game.

FACTFILE

Born: Bromborough, 1st October 1969
Position: Midfield
Everton 25 Seasons League Record: 217 appearances – 13 goals
Everton Career League Record: As above
Other League apps (Post-Everton): Sheffield United (1 appearance – 0 goals)

25 SEASONS EVERTON LEAGUE RECORD

Season	Apps	Goals
1988-1989	4	0
1989-1990	17	0

1990-1991	36	3
1991-1992	39	1
1992-1993	24	1
1993-1994	39	4
1994-1995	26	0
1995-1996	25	4
1996-1997	7	0
25 Seasons Total	217	13

DUNCAN FERGUSON

The tough, tall, Scot first joined Everton in October 1995 when Joe Royle paid Glasgow Rangers a fee of £4.4 million. His intimidating physical presence helped the Toffees capture the F.A. Cup in his first term with Everton. With his important goals against Liverpool, Duncan quickly gained 'hero' status at Goodison Park. There was enormous heart-break and indignation when Duncan was transferred to Newcastle United for a fee of over £7 million in November 1998.

To the great delight of the blue half of Merseyside, Duncan returned to Goodison Park for a cut-price fee of £3.75 million in August 2000. Injuries prevented him from making more than a dozen appearances in 2000-01, but his tally of six goals helped Everton steer clear of relegation. Another injury disrupted season followed in 2001-02 but Ferguson was again the club's joint top scorer (with six goals). When fully fit, and too sadly this is not often enough, Duncan is one of the most potent strikers in the Premiership. He is renowned for his ability in the air, but he's also surprisingly skilful on the ground. Duncan Ferguson began his career with Dundee United. He won seven Scotland caps, three while on the books of Everton.

FACTFILE

Born: Stirling, 27th December 1971
Position: Striker
Everton 25 Seasons League Record: 150 appearances – 49 goals
Everton Career League Record: As above

Other League apps (Between spells at Everton): Newcastle U (30 apps. – 8 goals)

25 SEASONS EVERTON LEAGUE RECORD

Season	Apps	Goals
1994-1995	23	7
1995-1996	18	5
1996-1997	33	10
1997-1998	29	11
1998-1999	13	4
2000-2001	12	6
2001-2002	22	6
25 Seasons Total	150	49

ADRIAN HEATH

Adrian Heath was a very useful member of Howard Kendall's successful 1980's squad. Adrian scored on a consistent basis, 71 in total in the League, with only Graeme Sharp and Tony Cottee netting more times for the club during the quarter of a century up to the summer of 2002. Heath was the club's top scorer during the 1983-84 season, with 12 League goals. The following campaign saw him net 11 times in only 17 appearances before being side-lined by injury.

Adrian began his career with Stoke City. He signed for Everton in January 1982 for a club record fee of £700,000. He won two League Championship medals and played in the F.A. Cup winning side of 1984. He also came on as substitute in the 1986 F.A. Cup Final and played in the League Cup Final in 1983-84. An England B international, Heath left the club in November 1988 to join Espanyol. He later saw service with five other League clubs (including Stoke again). His playing days ended at Burnley, whom he went on to manage. Adrian Heath was Howard Kendall's assistant-manager during his third spell as manager at Goodison Park. He also managed Sheffield United and later became Peter Reid's assistant at Sunderland.

FACTFILE

Born: Stoke-On-Trent, 11th January 1961

Position: Midfield/Striker

Everton 25 Seasons League Record: 226 appearances – 71 goals

Everton Career League Record: As above

Other League apps (Pre-Everton): Stoke City (95 apps. – 16 goals)

Other League apps (Post-Everton): Aston Villa (9 apps. – 0 goals), Manchester City (75 apps. – 4 goals), Stoke City (6 apps. – 0 goals), Burnley (120 apps. – 29 goals), Sheffield United (on loan 4 apps. – 0 goals)

25 SEASONS EVERTON LEAGUE RECORD

Season	Apps	Goals
1981-1982	22	6
1982-1983	38	10
1983-1984	36	12
1984-1985	17	11
1985-1986	36	10
1986-1987	41	11
1987-1988	29	9
1988-1989	7	2
25 Seasons Total	226	71

ANDY HINCHCLIFFE

Andy Hinchcliffe joined Everton from Manchester City (for £800,000) in July 1990. He was a thoughtful attacking defender with a cultivated left-foot. He stayed at Goodison for eight campaigns and, if it was not for a series of injuries, would have made even more impact. He was a member of the 1995 F.A. Cup team, but played some of his best football during 1996-97. Andy was then on the crest of a wave, having won three England caps as Glenn Hoddle's left wing-back, but tragically his season was truncated in December when he damaged his cruciate ligament.

After seven months on the side-lines, Hinchcliffe returned to first-team action in 1997-98 and did well enough to win back his England place. However, a well-publicised spat with Howard Kendall meant his Everton days were soon numbered. He joined Sheffield Wednesday for £2.85 million in January 1998, a month after a proposed move to Spurs collapsed due to injury. He suffered further injury frustration at Hillsborough. Andy Hinchcliffe collected four of his seven caps while he was an Evertonian and will be best remembered for his ability to send across deadly corners and free-kicks.

FACTFILE

Born: Manchester, 5th February 1969
Position: Defender
Everton 25 Seasons League Record: 182 appearances – 7 goals
Everton Career League Record: As above
Other League Apps (Pre-Everton): Manchester City (112 apps. – 8 goals)
Other League Apps (Post-Everton): Sheffield Wednesday (86 apps. – 7 goals)

25 SEASONS EVERTON LEAGUE RECORD

Season	Apps	Goals
1990-1991	21	1
1991-1992	18	0
1992-1993	25	1
1993-1994	26	0
1994-1995	29	2
1995-1996	28	2
1996-1997	18	1
1997-1998	17	0
25 Seasons Total	182	7

ANDREI KANCHELSKIS

Andrei Kanchelskis joined Everton (for a record £5.5 million) in the summer of 1995 after falling out with Alex Ferguson at Manchester United. The Ukrainian winger's first two goals for the Toffees were in a memorable 2-1 win at Anfield. Andrei produced many of the best performances of his career in 1995-96, when he netted 16 times to become the club's leading scorer in the League.

Kanchelskis failed to replicate that fine form during the first half of the following season and was sold to Fiorentina (for £8 million) in January 1997. He later returned to Britain when he joined Glasgow Rangers, but was a pale shadow of the man who electrified Goodison Park during 1995-96. In addition to scoring 20 times in only 52 League appearances, Andrei Kanchelskis created countless other chances with a stream of pin-point crosses. It is a shame that he was unable to sustain his best form for more than one full season on Merseyside.

FACTFILE

Born: Kirovograd (Ukraine), 23rd January 1969
Position: Midfield
Everton 25 Seasons League Record: 52 appearances – 20 goals
Everton Career League Record: As above
Other League apps (Pre-Everton): Manchester United (123 apps. – 28 goals)

25 SEASONS EVERTON LEAGUE RECORD

Season	Apps	Goals
1995-1996	32	16
1997-1997	20	4
25 Seasons Total	52	20

ANDY KING

The whole-hearted Andy King had two spells playing at Goodison Park, making 195 League appearances in total. He initially joined the club at the end of the 1975-76 campaign from his home-town side Luton Town (for £35,000). His enthusiasm and goals quickly made him a big favourite of the fans. He was the club's leading scorer in 1978-79, with 12 goals.

King was part of the Everton team which reached the League Cup Final in 1976-77. His most memorable goal for the Toffees was the dipping long-shot in October 1978, which gave his side their first victory over Liverpool since November 1971. Andy moved on to QPR in 1980 and then played for WBA. The midfielder returned to Goodison in 1982, in a deal which saw Peter Eastoe go to the Hawthorns. Andy King made 44 League appearances during his second spell at Everton, in which he netted ten more goals.

FACTFILE

Born: Luton, 14th August 1956
Position: Midfield
Everton 25 Seasons League Record: 155 appearances – 40 goals
Everton Career League Record: 195 appearances – 49 goals
Other League apps (Pre-Everton): Luton Town (33 apps. – 9 goals)
Other League apps (Between spells with Everton): QPR (30 apps. – 9 goals), West Bromwich Albion (25 apps. – 4 goals)

25 SEASONS EVERTON LEAGUE RECORD

Season	Apps	Goals
1977-1978	42	8
1978-1979	40	12
1979-1980	29	9
1982-1983	24	9
1983-1984	20	2
25 Seasons Total	155	40

BOB LATCHFORD

Bob Latchford enjoyed seven excellent years at Goodison Park after joining from Birmingham City (for £350,000) in February 1974. He was the club's leading scorer in four successive seasons between 1974-75 and 1977-78. The latter campaign was his most prolific, when he netted 32 times – all but two of these goals coming in the League. He was the first Everton player since Joe Royle (in 1969-70) to net 30 League goals. This feat was repeated eight years later by Gary Lineker.

Latchford scored 106 League goals in total for the club. He netted four goals in one League game (at QPR) in 1977-78 and hit hat-tricks on three other occasions. Bob netted in both the replay and the second replay (which was lost) of the 1976-77 League Cup Final. All twelve of Bob Latchford's England caps were awarded while he was Evertonian. He moved to Swansea City in 1980-81 and helped the Welsh side reach the First Division for the first time. He left

Swansea in 1984 to join NAC Breda in Holland.

FACTFILE

Born: Birmingham, 18th January 1951
Position: Striker
Everton 25 Seasons League Record: 120 appearances – 53 goals
Everton Career League Record: 236 appearances – 106 goals
Other League apps (Pre-Everton): Birmingham City (160/159 apps. – 68 goals)
Other League apps (Post-Everton): Swansea City (87 apps. – 35 goals)

25 SEASONS EVERTON LEAGUE RECORD

Season	Apps	Goals
1977-1978	39	30
1978-1979	36	11
1979-1980	26	6
1980-1981	19	6
25 Seasons Total	120	53

GARY LINEKER

Gary Lineker's Everton career lasted only one season but that 1985-86 campaign was a very memorable one. Lineker became the first Evertonian since Bob Latchford, eight years before, to register 30 League goals in a season. His electric pace and his predatory instinct in front of goal unsettled a succession of defences. The Toffees just failed to win both the League and the F.A. Cup in 1985-86, finishing runners-up to Liverpool in both competitions. It was Gary who opened the scoring in the F.A. Cup Final, but Everton lost 3-1.

Lineker was signed as a replacement for Andy Gray for £800,000 from Leicester City. He took a little time to win over some of the fans; but by the end of the campaign he was the First Division's leading scorer. His scoring exploits on Merseyside, in 1985-86, were fully acknowledged when he was voted the Football Writers' Association's 'Footballer of the Year' and the PFA 'Player of the Year'. Everton received a £2.75 fee when Lineker left for Barcelona (where he won a Spanish Championship medal). He won his only major honour in England when he helped Spurs win the 1991 FA Cup. He later played for Grampus Eight, in Japan, before hanging up his boots and becoming a very successful radio and TV presenter with the BBC. Gary Lineker won 11 of his 80 England caps while he was on Everton's books. His tally of 48 goals makes him second only to Sir Bobby Charlton in the England scoring list.

FACTFILE

Born: Leicester, 30th November 1960
Position: Forward
Everton 25 Seasons League Record: 41 appearances – 30 goals
Everton Career League Record: As above
Other League apps (Pre-Everton): Leicester City (194 apps. – 95 goals)
Other League apps (Post-Everton): Tottenham Hotspur (105 apps. – 67 goals)

25 SEASONS EVERTON LEAGUE RECORD

Season	Apps	Goals
1985-1986	41	30
25 Seasons Total	41	30

MICK LYONS

Mick Lyons was an integral part of the Everton side for eleven seasons and perhaps one of the club's most accomplished uncapped defenders. He actually started out as a centre-forward but it was in the centre of the defence that he found a regular first-team place. He was solid and consistent and, for the bulk of his career, was injury-free. He was a regular scorer, netting 48 in the League altogether. His best haul was in 1973-74, when his tally of nine goals made him the club's leading scorer. The goal Mick most wants to forget is the 40 yarder into his own net in the October 1979 Anfield derby encounter!

Lyons was made Everton captain in 1975-76 and skippered the side that reached the League Cup Final in 1976-77. He scored in the second replay, but his side lost 3-2 to Aston Villa. Although Mick was called into the England squad in 1978, he never won a full cap, but was recognised at Under-23 and B international levels. He was ever-present in Everton's team in 1975-76 and 1977-78. Lyons moved to Sheffield Wednesday in 1982 and helped the Owls win promotion to the First Division. Afterwards he became Grimsby Town's player-manager. Mick Lyons returned to Everton to coach the reserve-team in 1987, but later coached in Brunei.

FACTFILE

Born: Liverpool, 8th December 1951
Position: Defender
Everton 25 Seasons League Record: 177 appearances – 16 goals
Everton Career League Record: 389 appearances – 48 goals
Other League apps (Post-Everton): Sheffield Wednesday (129 apps. – 12 goals), Grimsby Town (50 apps. – 4 goals)

25 SEASONS EVERTON LEAGUE RECORD

Season	Apps	Goals
1977-1978	42	5
1978-1979	37	6
1979-1980	38	0
1980-1981	33	2
1981-1982	27	3
25 Seasons Total	177	16

DEREK MOUNTFIELD

Derek Mountfield was a reliable component of Howard Kendall's triumphant sides of the mid-1980's. He formed a solid centre-back pairing with Kevin Ratcliffe, most notably in 1983-84 and 1984-85. Derek joined Everton for a bargain fee of £30,000 in 1982 after gaining his League baptism with Tranmere Rovers. He was a member of the sides which won the F.A. Cup in 1984 and the European Cup Winners' Cup 12 months later. He also played in the 1983-84 Milk Cup Final and collected F.A. Cup runners-up medals in 1985 and 1987.

Strong in the air, Mountfield was effective in both penalty areas. He netted 19 League goals in total – ten of them coming in the title winning campaign of 1984-85. Injuries and the arrival of Dave Watson curtailed Mountfield's appearances thereafter, but he was still a useful member of the squad. Everton received £450,000 when he moved to Aston Villa in the summer of 1988. Derek later joined Wolves before dropping down the divisions. He won a Third Division Championship medal with Carlisle United in 1994-95. He won one England 'B' cap and one England Under-21 cap. Many less talented centre-backs than Derek Mountfield have won full honours for England.

FACTFILE

Born: Liverpool, 2nd November 1962
Position: Defender
Everton 25 Seasons League Record: 106 appearances – 19 goals
Everton Career League Record: As above
Other League apps (Pre-Everton): Tranmere Rovers (26 apps. – 1 goal)
Other League apps (Post-Everton): Aston Villa (90 apps. – 9 goals), Wolverhampton Wanderers (83 apps. – 4 goals), Carlisle United (31 apps. – 0 goals), Northampton Town (4 apps. – 0 goals), Walsall (97 apps. – 2 goals), Scarborough (6 apps. – 0 goals)

25 SEASONS EVERTON LEAGUE RECORD

Season	Apps	Goals
1982-1983	1	0
1983-1984	31	3
1984-1985	37	10
1985-1986	15	3
1996-1987	13	3
1987-1988	9	0
25 Seasons Total	106	19

KEVIN RATCLIFFE

Kevin Ratcliffe was the most successful captain in Everton's history, leading his side to two League Championships and two cup triumphs. At his peak he possessed electric pace and was strong in the air. He forged excellent partnerships in the middle of the Everton defence with Derek Mountfield and, later, Dave

Watson.

Ratcliffe made his League debut in 1980 and succeeded Mark Higgins as captain in 1983. He skippered Everton in all four of their 1980's F.A. Cup Finals and the 1983-84 League Cup Final. And it was Kevin who held the European Cup Winners' Cup aloft in Rotterdam in May 1985.

Kevin lost his first-team place to Martin Keown during Howard Kendall's second spell at Goodison. He had a brief spell at Dundee and afterwards played for Cardiff City, Nottingham Forest, Derby County and Chester City. He managed the latter club and in November 1999 took the reins of Shrewsbury Town. All but one of his 59 Welsh caps were collected while he was with Everton. Kevin Ratcliffe did so much for Everton FC that it seems a little crass to mention that he only scored twice for the club.

FACTFILE

Born: Mancot, 12th November 1960
Position: Defender
Everton 25 Seasons Record: 359 appearances – 2 goals
Everton Career Record: As above
Other League apps (Post-Everton): Cardiff City (25 apps. – 1 goal), Derby County (6 apps. – 0 goals), Chester City (23 apps. – 0 goals)

25 SEASONS EVERTON LEAGUE RECORD

Season	Apps	Goals
1979-1980	2	0
1980-1981	21	0
1981-1982	25	0
1982-1983	29	1
1983-1984	38	0
1984-1985	40	0
1985-1986	39	1
1986-1987	42	0
1987-1988	24	0
1988-1989	30	0
1989-1990	24	0

1990-1991	36	0
1991-1992	9	0
25 Seasons Total	359	2

PETER REID

Peter Reid was a key cog of the trophy winning teams of the 1980's. He was signed from Bolton Wanderers for a bargain fee of £60,000 and proved to be one of Howard Kendall's best signings. The hard-working midfielder was voted PFA 'Player of the Year' in 1985 and all of his 13 England caps were awarded while he was an Evertonian.

Reid's early days at the club were blighted by injury. However, he went on to collect two League Championship medals and played in the club's first five Cup Finals of the 1980's. Peter's fighting spirit was an inspiration to his team-mates and, even though he was injury-prone, he gave great service to the club. He left Merseyside for QPR in 1988-89 and later played for four other League clubs (most notably Manchester City). Peter Reid was manager at Maine Road between 1990 and 1993. He became manager of Sunderland in March 1995.

FACTFILE

Born: Liverpool, 20th June 1956
Position: Midfield
Everton 25 Seasons League Record: 159 appearances – 8 goals
Everton Career League Record: As above
Other League apps (Pre-Everton): Bolton Wanderers (225 apps. – 23 goals)
Other League apps (Post-Everton): Queen's Park Rangers (29 apps. – 1 goal), Manchester City (103 apps. – 1 goal), Southampton (7 apps. – 0 goals), Notts County (5 apps. – 0 goals), Bury (1 appearance – 0 goals)

25 SEASONS EVERTON LEAGUE RECORD

Season	Apps	Goals
1982-1983	7	0
1983-1984	35	2
1984-1985	36	2
1985-1986	15	1

1986-1987	16	1
1987-1988	32	1
1988-1989	18	1
25 Seasons Total	159	8

PAUL RIDEOUT

Only ten Evertonians scored more League goals than Paul Rideout in the quarter of a century up until the summer of 2002, but it is for one particular F.A. Cup goal that he's remembered most fondly at Goodison. It was Rideout who scored the only goal of the 1995 F.A. Cup Final, heading in a rebound after half an hour. That 1994-95 campaign was easily his most fruitful in an Everton shirt, with his tally of 14 League goals making him the club's leading scorer. The England Under-21 international joined the Toffees from Glasgow Rangers in January 1992 for £500,000. Half of this fee was recouped when he left Goodison in April 1997 for Chinese outfit Huang Dong Vanguards.

Good in the air, Rideout could also be quite nimble on the ground. Much travelled, having played for Italian side Bari while in his early twenties, Paul joined Tranmere Rovers from Chinese side Shengzhen in July 2000. Paul Rideout again made F.A. Cup headlines during 2000-01, when he netted a stunning hat-trick in Rovers' scalping of Premiership Southampton.

FACTFILE

Born: Bournemouth, 14th August 1964
Position: Striker
Everton 25 Seasons League Record: 112 appearances – 29 goals
Everton Career League Record: As above
Other League apps (Pre-Everton): Swindon Town (104 apps. – 39 goals), Aston Villa (54 apps. – 19 goals), Southampton (75 apps. – 19 goals), Notts County (11 apps. – 3 goals)
Other League apps (Post-Everton): Tranmere Rovers (46 apps. – 6 goals)

25 SEASONS EVERTON LEAGUE RECORD

Season	Apps	Goals
1992-1993	24	3
1993-1994	24	6
1994-1995	29	14
1995-1996	25	6
1996-1997	10	0
25 Seasons Total	112	29

GRAEME SHARP

During his 12-year stay at Goodison Park Graeme Sharp scored 159 goals in all competitions to become Everton's leading scorer this side of the Second World War. Only the legendary Dixie Dean netted more goals for the club. Graeme hit 111 League goals, which was 39 more than another other Evertonian managed in the quarter of a century up to the summer of 2002. Graeme possessed a powerful shot and was very strong in the air. He dove-tailed well with several different strike-partners, including Andy Gray, Gary Lineker and Tony Cottee.

Gordon Lee signed Sharp for £120,000 in 1980 from Dumbarton. He claimed a regular first-team place in 1981-82, when he netted 15 League goals to be the club's top-scorer. He also headed the Everton scoring lists at the end of three other campaigns. Graeme was a member of both title winning sides of the 1980s, and played in all six major Cup Finals that Everton played during that same decade. He scored the crucial goal in the 1984 F.A. Cup Final.

Sharp left Goodison Park for Oldham Athletic in 1991 and he then became manager of the Latics between 1994 and 1997. All of Graeme Sharp's 12 Scotland caps were won while he was an Everton player.

FACTFILE

Born: Glasgow, 16th October 1960
Position: Striker
Everton 25 Seasons League Record: 322 appearances – 111 goals
Everton Career League Record: As above
Other League apps (Post-Everton): Oldham Athletic (109 apps. – 30 goals)

25 SEASONS EVERTON LEAGUE RECORD

Season	Apps	Goals
1979-1980	2	0
1980-1981	4	0
1981-1982	29	15
1982-1983	41	15
1983-1984	28	7
1984-1985	36	21
1985-1986	37	19
1986-1987	27	5
1987-1988	32	13
1988-1989	26	7
1989-1990	33	6
1990-1991	27	3
25 Seasons Total	322	111

KEVIN SHEEDY

Kevin Sheedy began his League career with Hereford United, before transferring to Liverpool (where he made only three League appearances). In the first move of its type in 20 years (since John Morrissey), Sheedy moved across Stanley Park to join Everton in 1982. He went on to win two League Championship medals and was a member of the side which triumphed in the 1984-85 European Cup Winners' Cup Final. He also played in all four defeated Cup Final sides of the 1980s. An injury collected in the League Cup Final earlier in the campaign side-lined him from participating in the 1984 F.A. Cup Final.

The skilful midfielder was an accurate passer and dead-ball expert. Kevin's left-foot not only made a string of goals but scored them too. He contributed regularly to the score-sheet, passing double figures in the League on three occasions. He was most prolific in the title winning campaign of 1986-87 when he scored 13 times from 38 appearances. Sheedy left Everton in 1992 for Newcastle United and later played for Blackpool. Although Welsh-born, Kevin played for the Republic of Ireland and all but four of his 45 caps were won while he was on Everton's books. Only four men made more League appearances for Everton than Kevin Sheedy during the quarter of a century up to the summer of 2002, and only his three former colleagues Graeme Sharp, Tony Cottee and Adrian Heath found the net more times.

FACTFILE

Born: Builth Wells, 21st October 1959
Position: Midfield
Everton 25 Seasons League Record: 274 appearances – 67 goals
Everton Career League Record: As above
Other League apps (Pre-Everton): Hereford United (51 apps. – 4 goals), Liverpool (3 apps. – 0 goals)
Other League apps (Post-Everton): Newcastle United (37 apps. – 4 goals), Blackpool (26 apps. – 1 goal)

25 SEASONS EVERTON LEAGUE RECORD

Season	Apps	Goals
1982-1983	40	11
1983-1984	28	4
1984-1985	29	11
1985-1986	31	5
1986-1987	28	13
1987-1988	17	1
1988-1989	26	8
1989-1990	37	9
1990-1991	22	4
1991-1992	16	1
25 Season Total	274	67

NEVILLE SOUTHALL

Neville Southall was probably the finest goalkeeper to play for Everton and, at his peak, was considered to possess the safest pair of hands in British football. Neville stayed at Goodison Park for 17 seasons, during which time he created a club record of 578 League appearances and became Everton's most capped player.

He pulled on the Welsh jersey on 92 occasions – a record for his country.

Southall was a key component of Howard Kendall's two championship winning sides. He missed only 11 League games in 1986-87 and was ever-present in 1984-85. The big custodian also appeared in every League match in the four seasons between 1988-89 and 1991-92 and was again ever-present in 1993-94 and finally, for a seventh time, in 1995-96.

A former Llandudno hod-carrier, Neville made his Football League debut for Bury in 1980-81 after joining from Non-League outfit Winsford United. Neville's stay at Gigg Lane lasted just one season as Howard Kendall paid £150,000 for him in July 1981. He made his First Division debut against Ipswich Town at Goodison Park, on 17th October 1981. A run of 38 consecutive League appearances was halted after his side were on the wrong end of a 5-0 score-line in Goodison derby encounter of 1982-83. He was loaned out to Port Vale later in the campaign; but returned to Merseyside with renewed vigour and, during the early part of 1983-84, established himself as the Toffees' first-choice keeper.

Neville won five major trophies with Everton. In addition to winning two League Championship medals, he was between the sticks at Wembley when the F.A. Cup was won in 1984 and 1995. He was also a key member of the side that collected the European Cup Winners' Cup in 1985. He had all the attributes required to become a goalkeeping great – technique, temperament and great powers of concentration. Neville Southall was voted 'Footballer of the Year' by the Football Writers' Association in 1985 and was awarded a MBE in 1997.

Time eventually caught up with the legendary shot-stopper in 1996-97, the campaign that he made a record 700th first-team appearance. He was axed by manager Joe Royle after Bradford City had inflicted a shock home defeat in the F.A. Cup. It was the first time in 15 years that he had been dropped. Neville quickly regained his first-team place, but the writing was on the wall and, after loan spells at Southend United and Stoke City, he joined the Potters on a free transfer in February 1998. He had continued to set records during his final Goodison campaign. He became the first man to play in 200 Premiership matches and made his 750th and last first-team appearance when Tottenham Hotspur visited Goodison Park on 29th November 1997.

Neville subsequently joined Doncaster Rovers (in the Conference), before quickly returning to League action with Torquay United. Although he was initially signed on a match-by-match basis, Southall was the Gulls' 'Player of the Year' in

1998-99. The following campaign he played a single game for Bradford City, becoming, at 41 years and 178 days, the oldest man to feature for the Bantams in League football. He also responded to a call from his old team-mate Kevin Ratcliffe during 2001-02 and warmed the bench for Shrewsbury Town. Later that campaign he briefly managed Conference side Dover Athletic.

FACTFILE

Born: Llandudno, 16th September 1958
Position: Goalkeeper
Everton 25 Seasons League Record: 578 appearances – 0 goals
Everton Career League Record: As above
Other League apps (Pre-Everton): Bury (39 apps. – 0 goals)
Other League apps (on loan from Everton): Port Vale (9 apps. – 0 goals), Southend United (9 apps. – 0 goals)
Other League apps (Post-Everton): Stoke City (12 apps. – 0 goals), Torquay United (53 apps. – 0 goals), Bradford City (1 appearance – 0 goals)

25 SEASONS EVERTON LEAGUE RECORD

Season	Apps	Goals
1981-1982	26	0
1982-1983	17	0
1983-1984	35	0
1984-1985	42	0
1985-1986	32	0
1986-1987	31	0
1987-1988	32	0
1988-1989	38	0
1989-1990	38	0
1990-1991	38	0
1991-1992	42	0
1992-1993	40	0
1993-1994	42	0
1994-1995	41	0
1995-1996	38	0

1996-1997	34	0
1997-1998	12	0
25 Seasons Total	578	0

TREVOR STEVEN

Trevor Steven was a stylish member of Everton's midfield for six seasons during the glorious 1980's. He played in the three successive F.A. Cup Finals in the mid-1980's, scored in the European Cup Winners' Cup Final triumph and collected two League Championship medals. He was signed from Burnley (for £300,000) in the summer of 1983. He stayed at Goodison six years before joining Glasgow Rangers for a fee of £1.5 million. He later also played for Marseille.

An excellent crosser and passer, Steven was an integral component of Howard Kendall's best teams. He had an excellent game in the 1984 F.A. Cup Final, effectively creating both goals. Steven could score goals as well and one of his most memorable was the fierce drive that put the Toffees 2-0 ahead in Rotterdam in the European Cup Winners' Cup Final. He also netted 48 times for Everton in League football. The wide man's best tally was the 14 he netted in 1986-87, ten of which came from the penalty spot. His composure helped make him the club's leading League scorer in that Championship winning campaign. The first 25 of Trevor Steven's 36 England caps were won while he was on Everton's books.

FACTFILE

Born: Berwick-Upon-Tweed, 21st September 1963
Position: Midfield
Everton 25 Seasons League Record: 214 appearances – 48 goals
Everton Career League Record: As above
Other League apps (Pre-Everton): Burnley (76 apps. – 11 goals)

25 SEASONS EVERTON LEAGUE RECORD

Season	Apps	Goals
1983-1984	27	1
1984-1985	40	12
1985-1986	41	9

1986-1987	41	14
1987-1988	36	6
1988-1989	29	6
25 Seasons Total	214	48

GARY STEVENS

Gary Stevens came through the junior ranks to sign professional forms with Everton in April 1981. This polished and reliable right-back collected two Championship medals and played in Everton's first five Cup Final sides of the 1980's.

Stevens played for England 46 times, the first 26 of his caps were won while he was at Goodison Park. He joined Glasgow Rangers in the summer of 1988 for a fee of £1 million. He won six Scottish Championship medals and appeared in four cup winning sides while at Ibrox. He returned to England in 1994 when he joined Tranmere Rovers for £350,000.

FACTFILE

Born: Barrow, 27th March 1963
Position: Defender
Everton 25 Seasons League Record: 208 appearances – 8 goals
Everton League Career Record: As above
Other League apps (Post-Everton): Tranmere Rovers (125 apps. – 2 goals)

25 SEASONS EVERTON LEAGUE RECORD

Season	Apps	Goals
1981-1982	19	1
1982-1983	28	0
1983-1984	27	1
1984-1985	37	3
1985-1986	41	1
1986-1987	25	2
1987-1988	31	0
25 Seasons Total	208	8

GRAHAM STUART

The versatile Graham Stuart was one of Everton's better performers of the mid-1990's. He began his career with Chelsea and joined Everton for £850,000 in August 1993. He was a member of the Toffees' F.A. Cup winning side in 1995 but is best remembered for his exploits in the last match of the previous campaign. Graham scored the first and third goals in the thrilling 3-2 victory over Wimbledon which allowed Everton to avoid relegation. He had netted only once for the club before the fateful afternoon of 7th May 1994. With his side looking doomed at 2-0 down, he stepped up to convert from the spot after Anders Limpar was adjudged to have been fouled. Few in the crowd realised that Graham had only taken one penalty before and had missed it! After Barry Horne equalised, it was Graham who claimed the winning goal with a mis-hit shot that the Wimbledon keeper somehow failed to stop. Events elsewhere ensured that Everton avoided the drop.

Graham played in several positions for Everton, mostly in midfield or up front but in an emergency he also filled in at right wing-back. His most prolific campaign was 1995-96 when he found the net nine times in League games. He left Everton in November 1997, joining Sheffield United for £850,000. He moved on again in March 1999 to Charlton Athletic. Graham Stuart helped the Addicks win the 1999-2000 First Division title and then performed very consistently in the top-flight in the subsequent two seasons.

FACTFILE

Born: Tooting, 24th October 1970

Position: Midfield/Striker

Everton 25 Seasons League Record: 136 appearances – 22 goals

Everton Career League Record: As above

Other League apps (Pre-Everton): Chelsea (87 apps. – 14 goals)

Other League apps (Post-Everton): Sheffield United (53 apps. – 11 goals), Charlton Athletic (112 apps. – 19 goals)

25 SEASONS EVERTON LEAGUE RECORD

Season	Apps	Goals
1993-1994	30	3

1994-1995	28	3
1995-1996	29	9
1996-1997	35	5
1997-1998	14	2
25 Seasons Total	136	22

DAVID UNSWORTH

David Unsworth scored on his first-team debut in 1991-92 after coming on as a substitute in the 3-3 draw at Tottenham. However, it was not until 1994-95 that this quick player secured a regular place in the side. The left-footed defender formed a solid partnership with Dave Watson and won his solitary England cap in 1995. David was a member of the team that beat Manchester United in the 1995 F.A. Cup Final.

Unsworth moved on to West Ham United in the summer of 1997 for a fee of over £1 million. His powerful tackling and terrific enthusiasm made him extremely popular at the Boleyn Ground. However, David's wife failed to settle in the south and, after only one campaign as a Hammer, he moved to Aston Villa for £3 million. Within a month, and without kicking a ball in anger, Unsworth became an Evertonian again when Walter Smith paid the same £3 million fee in August 1998. This versatile performer has appeared in central defence, at left-back and in midfield. He is usually deadly from the spot and only 11 Everton players scored more League goals than the 26 David Unsworth netted for the club in the quarter of a century up to the summer of 2002.

FACTFILE

Born: Chorley, 16th October 1973

Position: Defender

Everton 25 Seasons League Record: 246 appearances – 26 goals

Everton Career League Record: As above

Other League apps (Between spells at Everton): West Ham U (32 apps. – 2 goals)

Andy King amassed 195 appearances for the Blues during two spells at the club. His enthusiasm and goals made him a big favourite of the fans.

Duncan Ferguson, another great favourite of the fans, has scored a goal every three games for Everton despite many problems with injuries.

Peter Reid was the midfield dynamo of Everton's team in the mid-1980's and was voted PFA 'Player of the Year' in 1985.

Trevor Steven – this stylish midfielder played in almost every one of Everton's games between 1984 and 1988.

Gary Stevens came through the junior ranks to sign professional forms with Everton in April 1981. During his time at the club he made 208 League appearances and earned 26 caps for England.

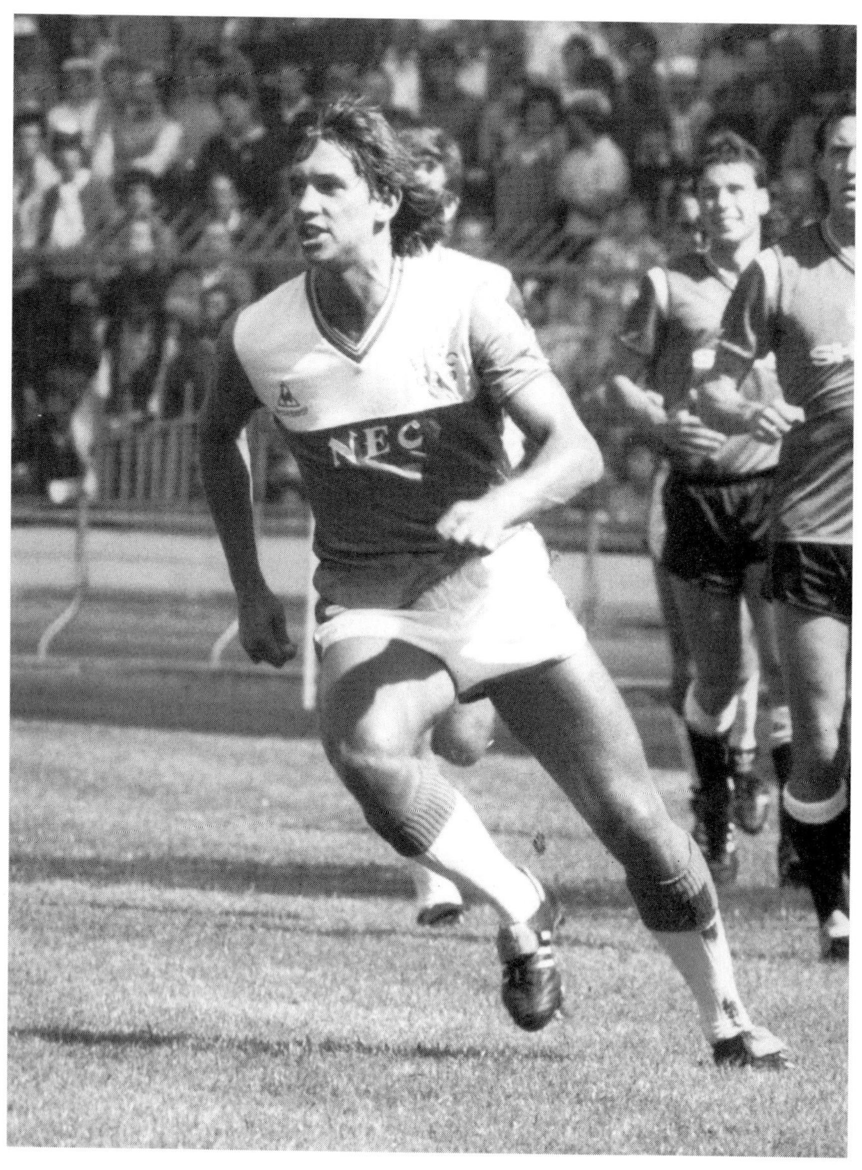

Gary Lineker played for just one season at Goodison, but what a season! In addition to scoring 30 League goals, Gary also won the Football Writers' Association's 'Footballer of the Year' and the PFA 'Player of the Year'.

Derek Mountfield was another key member of Howard Kendall's successes during the 1980's. He was a strong centre-half who won medals in the F.A. Cup in 1984 and the European Cup Winners' Cup 12 months later.

Adrian Heath scored goals consistently during his eight seasons at the club. He later became Howard Kendall's assistant during his third spell as manager at Goodison Park.

25 SEASONS EVERTON LEAGUE RECORD

Season	Apps	Goals
1991-1992	2	1
1992-1993	3	0
1993-1994	8	0
1994-1995	38	3
1995-1996	31	2
1996-1997	34	5
1998-1999	34	1
1999-2000	33	6
2000-2001	29	5
2001-2002	33	3
25 Seasons Total	245	26

DAVE WATSON

Dave Watson is one of the all-time Everton legends. He was a first-team regular for 13 seasons, becoming the club captain and, for a spell, the caretaker manager. He won a League Championship medal in his first campaign at the club and appeared in two F.A. Cup Finals, skippering the side to its triumph of 1995.

A former Liverpool reserve, Dave made his Football League debut for Norwich City in 1980-81 after moving to Carrow Road for £100,000. He won his first six England caps whilst playing for Norwich. He helped the Canaries lift the old Second Division title in 1985-86, immediately before returning to Merseyside for a club record £900,000 fee.

Watson was an inspirational defender, who was good in the air and determined with his tackling. He was the model professional for over a decade and far less accomplished defenders have collected more caps than the 12 he won for England. He acted as caretaker player-manager at the end of the 1996-97 campaign following Joe Royle's resignation. His form was still good enough to demand a first-team place during the twilight of career, even though he was a member of the coaching staff. Dave Watson made his 423rd and final Everton League appearance in 1999-2000. He took over as the manager of Tranmere Rovers in April 2001, but left Prenton Park on the eve of the 2002-03 campaign.

FACTFILE

Born: Liverpool, 20th November 1961

Position: Defender

Everton 25 Seasons League Record: 423 appearances – 23 goals

Everton Career League Record: As above

Other League apps (Pre-Everton): Norwich City (212 apps. – 11 goals)

25 SEASONS EVERTON LEAGUE RECORD

Season	Apps	Goals
1986-1987	35	4
1987-1988	37	4
1988-1989	32	3
1989-1990	29	1
1990-1991	32	2
1991-1992	35	3
1992-1993	40	1
1993-1994	28	1
1994-1995	38	2
1995-1996	34	1
1996-1997	29	1
1997-1998	26	0
1998-1999	22	0
1999-2000	6	0
25 Seasons Total	423	23

EVERTON 25 SEASONS 1977-78 TO 2001-02

JUST ABOUT MANAGING!

Seven different men held the post of manager of Everton FC during the quarter of a century up to the summer of 2002. Howard Kendall was at the helm the longest – just over ten years, comprising three distinct spells spanning six years, three and one, respectively. Mike Walker's reign as manager was the shortest in the club's history – just 305 days. The reigns of the Everton managers embraced the following periods.

JANUARY 1977 TO MAY 1981	GORDON LEE
MAY 1981 TO JUNE 1987	HOWARD KENDALL
JUNE 1987 TO NOVEMBER 1990	COLIN HARVEY
NOVEMBER 1990 TO DECEMBER 1993	HOWARD KENDALL
JANUARY 1994 TO NOVEMBER 1994	MIKE WALKER
NOVEMBER 1994 TO MARCH 1997	JOE ROYLE
JUNE 1997 TO JUNE 1998	HOWARD KENDALL
JULY 1998 TO MARCH 2002	WALTER SMITH
FROM MARCH 2002	DAVID MOYES

GORDON LEE
JANUARY 1977 TO MAY 1981

Gordon Lee replaced Billy Bingham as manager at the end of January 1977. His side initially played some good football but, not for the first time in his career, Lee failed to get the best out of his star names.

His side also played some fantastic free-flowing football in 1977-78, scoring 76 goals (more than other club in the Division) to finish third. Lee's side started the following season in flying form and set a club record unbeaten League run of 18 games. Everton gradually lost their way, under Lee, and it was only a good F.A. Cup run that kept his critics at bay in 1979-80 (when his side finished fourth from bottom of the table). It proved to be no more than a stay of execution, though, and he was sacked in May 1981.

In his playing days, Lee was a full-back with Aston Villa and Shrewsbury Town. He managed Port Vale (1968-74), Blackburn Rovers (1974-75) and Newcastle United (1975-77) before taking the reins at Goodison Park. He later managed Preston North End (1981-83) before taking a coaching role with KR Reykjavik. After leaving Iceland, he coached in the Middle East and at Leicester City.

FACTFILE

Born: Hednesford, 13th July 1934

EVERTON MANAGERIAL RECORD

	Played	Won	Drew	Lost
League	188	69	63	56
F.A. Cup	20	11	4	5
League Cup	21	9	6	6
Europe	6	3	0	3
Total	235	92	73	70

Honours: None

Highest League finish: 3rd in 1978-79

Lowest League finish: 19th in 1979-80

Best F.A. Cup Run: Semi-Final in 1976-77 and 1979-80

Best League Cup Run: Final in 1976-77

Best European Run (UEFA Cup): Round 2 in 1978-79

First Match in charge: 30th January 1977 vs Swindon Town F.A. Cup (won 2-1)

Last Match: 4th May 1981 vs Wolverhampton Wanderers First Division (drew 0-0)

HOWARD KENDALL
MAY 1981 TO JUNE 1987

Howard Kendall was the most successful manager in Everton's history. He had an unprecedented three spells in the Goodison Park hot-seat. He steered the Toffees to four trophies, all in his first spell in the 1980's.

In 1983-84 Kendall's side lifted the F.A. Cup, a competition he never won as a player (having twice played in Finals). A year later Everton just missed out on an historic treble – losing in the F.A. Cup Final, but winning the League Championship and the European Cup Winners' Cup. Everton also won the League Championship again in 1986-87 (having finished second the previous season) under Kendall's stewardship. They also reached the 1985-86 F.A. Cup Final and the 1983-84 League Cup Final. His first spell at the Everton helm ended in June 1987 when he accepted the challenge to manage Athletic Bilbao.

As a player, Howard was one of the best midfielders not to gain England recognition. He started his career at Preston North End and, in 1964, became the youngest man to play in a Wembley F.A. Cup Final (when aged 17 years and 345 days). He later played for Everton, Birmingham City, Stoke City and Blackburn Rovers. He helped the Toffees win the 1969-70 title, forming a great midfield partnership with Alan Ball and Colin Harvey. He also appeared in the 1968 F.A. Cup Final.

Howard's first managerial position was in a player-manager capacity at Blackburn Rovers. His stock rose when he lifted Rovers out of the Third Division in 1979-80. He replaced Gordon Lee as Everton's manager in May 1981. His job was on the line during the first half of 1983-84, but his side went on to reach two Cup Finals that season and the rest is history!

FACTFILE

Born: Ryton-on-Tyne, 22nd May 1946

EVERTON MANAGERIAL RECORD (FIRST SPELL)

	Played	Won	Drew	Lost
League	352	132	59	61
F.A. Cup	31	21	5	5
League Cup	34	17	9	7
Europe	9	7	2	0
Total	326	177	75	73

Honours: Two League Championships, one F.A. Cup & one European Cup Winners' Cup

Highest League finish: Champions in 1984-85 and 1986-87

Lowest League finish: 8th in 1981-82

Best F.A. Cup Run: Winners in 1983-84

Best League Cup Run: Final in 1983-84

Best European Run (European Cup Winners' Cup): Winners in 1984-85

First Match in charge: 29th August 1981 vs Birmingham City Division One (won 3-1)

Last Match in charge: 11th May 1987 vs Tottenham Hotspur Division One (won 1-0)

COLIN HARVEY
JUNE 1987 TO NOVEMBER 1990

Colin Harvey stepped up from his position as assistant-manager to become Everton's Manager when his close friend Howard Kendall departed to Spain in the summer of 1987. Everton finished in the top six in each of his three campaigns at the helm. They also reached the 1989 F.A. Cup Final. Harvey was sacked in 1990, but reverted to being assistant manager under Kendall again.

As a player, Harvey was an unsung midfielder who won one England cap. He signed professional forms at Goodison in 1962. He moved to Sheffield Wednesday in 1974 before retiring through injury. He won the League Championship with the Toffees in 1969-70 and played in the 1966 and 1968 F.A. Cup Finals. The first ending in victory. After leaving Goodison Park, Colin Harvey assisted Graeme Sharp when he was manager of Oldham Athletic.

FACTFILE

Born: Liverpool, 16th November 1944

EVERTON MANAGERIAL RECORD

	Played	Won	Drew	Lost
League	144	51	56	37
F.A. Cup	23	9	11	3
League Cup	19	10	4	5
Europe	0	0	0	0
Total	186	70	71	45

Honours: None

Highest League finish: 4th in 1987-88

Lowest League finish: 6th in 1989-90

Best F.A. Cup Run: Final in 1988-89

Best League Cup Run: Semi-final in 1987-88

First Match in charge: 15th August 1987 v Norwich City First Division (won 1-0)

Last Match in charge: 30th October 1990 v Sheffield United League Cup (lost 1-2)

HOWARD KENDALL
NOVEMBER 1990 TO DECEMBER 1993

Howard Kendall returned to Goodison Park for his second spell as manager in November 1990. He lost his job with Athletic Bilbao in November 1989, but quickly took over at Manchester City. However, the lure of Goodison Park proved too strong and, to the chagrin of the Citizens, he accepted the opportunity to re-take the Everton job in November 1990.

Kendall's second spell lasted just over three years. He quit in December 1993 after the board refused to back his purchase of striker Dion Dublin.

EVERTON MANAGERIAL RECORD (SECOND SPELL)

	Played	Won	Drew	Lost
League	129	46	33	50
F.A. Cup	10	4	3	3
League Cup	15	8	3	4
Europe	0	0	0	0
Total	154	58	39	57

Honours: None

Highest League finish: 9th in 1990-91

Lowest League finish: 12th in 1991-92

Best F.A. Cup Run: Quarter-final in 1990-91

Best League Cup Run: Round 4 in 1992-93

First Match: 10th November 1990 vs Sheffield United First Division (drew 0-0)

Last Match: 4th December 1993 vs Southampton Premier League (won 1-0)

MIKE WALKER
JANUARY 1994 TO NOVEMBER 1994

Mike Walker's reign as Everton manager lasted just 305 days, the shortest in the club's history. When he joined Everton he was one of the most highly sought after young managers in the game. Ten months later his career was on the slide after he failed to come to grips with the task at Goodison.

Walker tried to get his side playing good football but the results were generally poor. Everton only escaped relegation by a narrow margin on the last day of 1993-94. He was sacked in November 1994, after his side made the worst start in the club's history.

As a player, Mike was a Welsh Under-23 goalkeeper. He played for York City, Watford and Colchester United. He cut his managerial teeth with Colchester (1986-87), but really made his name at Norwich City. He took a coaching job at Carrow Road in 1988 before stepping up to be manager in 1992. He took the Canaries to third place in the Premier League in 1992-93. He returned to manage Norwich again in 1996, after his spell on Merseyside, leaving the Norfolk club again in 1998. He later managed in Cyprus. Mike is the father of Leicester City and England keeper Ian.

FACTFILE

Born: Colwyn Bay, 28th September 1945

EVERTON MANAGERIAL RECORD

	Played	Won	Drew	Lost
League	31	6	6	15
F.A. Cup	2	0	1	1
League Cup	2	0	1	1
Europe	0	0	0	0
Total	35	6	8	17

Honours: None
Highest League finish: 17th in 1993-94
Lowest League finish: 17th in 1993-94

Best F.A. Cup Run: Round 3 in 1993-94)

Best League Cup Run: Round 2 in 1994-95)

First Match in charge: 8th January 1984 vs Bolton Wanderers F.A. Cup (drew 1-1)

Last Match in charge: 5th November 1994 vs Norwich City Premiership (drew 0-0)

JOE ROYLE
NOVEMBER 1994 TO MARCH 1997

Joe Royle was a very popular appointment as manager of Everton in November 1994. Not only was he a much liked former player, but at the time of his appointment was one of the most highly rated managers in England. He responded to his task by steering the Toffees to success in the F.A. Cup in May 1995. Further progress followed over the subsequent twelve months (with a sixth place finish) and Joe looked set to be the Everton boss for some considerable time. Sadly, that 1995-96 campaign was his only full season at the helm. He resigned in March 1997 after a dispute with the board over some new players he wanted to recruit.

As player, Joe was the youngest man to pull on an Everton shirt when he took the field against Blackpool, in 1966, aged 16 years and 282 days. He was part of Everton's F.A. Cup side in 1968 and was top scorer (with 23 goals) when the League Championship was won in 1969-70. He later joined Manchester City in 1974-75 and collected a League Cup winners' medal the following campaign. He also played for Bristol City and Norwich City. Joe won six England caps.

He made his name as a manager with Oldham Athletic. He stayed at Boundary Park over twelve years before taking the reins at Goodison Park. Joe became Manchester City's boss in 1998 and took them from the Second Division to the Premiership. He left Maine Road in May 2001 after the Citizens slipped back to the Nationwide League.

FACTFILE

Born: Liverpool, 8th April 1949

EVERTON MANAGERIAL RECORD

	Played	Won	Drew	Lost
League	97	35	32	30

F.A. Cup	12	8	2	2
League Cup	4	0	2	2
Europe	4	2	1	1
Total	117	45	37	35

Honours: F.A. Cup
Highest League finish: 6th in 1995-96
Lowest League finish: 15th in 1994-95
Best F.A. Cup Run: Winners in 1994-95
Best League Cup Run: Second Round in 1995-96 and 1996-97
Best European Run (European Cup Winners' Cup): Second Round in 1995-96
First Match in charge: 21st November 1994 vs Liverpool Premiership (won 2-0)
Last Match in charge: 22nd March 1997 vs Manchester United Premiership (lost 0-2)

HOWARD KENDALL
AUGUST 1997 TO MAY 1998

Howard managed Notts County and Sheffield United in between his second and third spells as Everton manager. He was the shock choice to replace Joe Royle in the summer of 1997. However, his side struggled throughout 1997-98 and relegation was only avoided by the skin of the teeth on the last day of the season. Kendall left Goodison Park soon afterwards.

EVERTON MANAGERIAL RECORD (THIRD SPELL)

	Played	Won	Drew	Lost
League	38	9	13	16
F.A. Cup	1	0	0	1
League Cup	3	2	0	1
Europe	0	0	0	0
Total	42	11	13	18

Honours: None

Highest League finish: 17th in 1997-98

Lowest League finish: 17th in 1997-98

Best F.A. Cup Run: Third Round in 1997-98

Best League Cup Run: Third Round in 1997-98

First Match in charge: 9th August 1997 vs Crystal Palace Premiership (lost 1-2)

Last Match in charge: 10th May 1998 vs Coventry City Premiership (drew 1-1)

WALTER SMITH
JULY 1998 TO MARCH 2002

Walter Smith OBE joined Everton in July 1998 after achieving glory with Glasgow Rangers. He was Graeme Souness's assistant who went on to lead the Ibrox club to even greater success. Smith's reign at Everton was nearly an incredibly short one as he soon threatened to quit over the sale of Duncan Ferguson. Smith stayed on, but his side rarely threatened to climb above mid-table. His teams were usually quite solid at the back; but going forward they generally lacked imagination and found goals difficult to come by. Even the arrival of Paul Gascoigne (who Walter had previously signed for Rangers) failed to spark Everton. Walter Smith left Goodison Park in March 2002 after his lost an F.A. Cup quarter-final 3-0 at Middlesbrough.

Smith trained as an electrician but as a player he was a tough-tackling defender with Dundee United and Dumbarton. After his playing days ended he became assistant-coach of the Scottish youth side. He returned to Dundee United to become assistant-manager to Jim McLean in 1984. United won the title the following season. Souness immediately appointed Smith as his assistant when he was appointed manager of Rangers in 1986. As first assistant-manager and then manager (when Souness left to manage Liverpool in 1991), Smith helped Rangers to win nine titles on the trot. The Gers also won the Scottish F.A. Cup three times and the Scottish League Cup four times while he was at Ibrox. Walter Smith was assistant to Scotland's caretaker manager Alex Ferguson during the 1986 World Cup Finals.

FACTFILE

Born: Glasgow, 24th February 1948

EVERTON MANAGERIAL RECORD

	Played	Won	Drew	Lost
League	143	41	42	60
F.A. Cup	16	10	2	4
League Cup	11	2	6	3
Europe	0	0	0	0
Total	170	53	50	67

Honours: None

Highest League finish: 13th in 1999-2000

Lowest League finish: 16th in 2000-01

Best F.A. Cup Run: Quarter-final in 1999-2000 and 2001-02

Best League Cup Run: Fourth Round in 1998-99

First Match in charge: 15th August 1998 vs Aston Villa Premiership (drew 0-0)

Last Match in charge: 10th March 2002 vs Middlesbrough F.A. Cup (lost 0-3)

DAVID MOYES FROM MARCH 2002

David Moyes became Everton's manager on 14th March 2002. He started brightly by leading his side to victory in his first two games at the helm. His honest style of management quickly won over the players and the fans. The season finished before he had the chance to make many changes, but a fresh wind could be felt throughout the club.

Moyes cut his managerial teeth at Preston North End. He joined the Lilywhites as a player in September 1993 and was subsequently appointed assistant to Gary Peters. He stepped up to become manager in 1998 and steered North End to the Second Division championship in 1999-2000. His side came within one victory of reaching the Premiership 12 months later. Preston finished fourth in Division One to qualify for the play-offs, but lost to Bolton Wanderers in the Final in Cardiff.

As a player, Moyes was a very useful centre-half in the lower divisions. He actually won a League Championship medal with his first club, Glasgow Celtic, in 1981-82. He then played in England for Cambridge United, Bristol City and

Shrewsbury Town. He moved back to Scotland in 1990 and signed for Dunfermline. He briefly played for Hamilton Academical before moving south again to Deepdale. He was a key member of the Preston side which lifted the 1995-96 Third Division title.

FACTFILE

Born: Glasgow, 25th April 1963

EVERTON MANAGERIAL RECORD (UP TO JULY 2002)

	Played	Won	Drew	Lost
League	9	4	1	4
F.A. Cup	0	0	0	0
League Cup	0	0	0	0
Europe	0	0	0	0
Total	9	4	1	4

Honours: None
Highest League finish: 15th in 2001-02
Lowest League finish: 15th in 2001-02
First Match in charge: 16th March 2002 vs Fulham Premiership (won 2-1)

EVERTON 25 SEASONS 1977-78 TO 2001-02

THE CUP FINALS

Everton reached seven major cup finals during the quarter of a century up to the summer of 2002. The Toffees appeared in five F.A. Cup Finals (winning in 1984 and 1995), one League Cup Final (which went to a replay) and were triumphant in the 1984-85 European Cup Winners' Cup Final.

1983-84	LEAGUE CUP	vs LIVERPOOL	DREW
1983-84	LEAGUE CUP REPLAY	vs LIVERPOOL	LOST
1983-84	F.A. CUP	vs WATFORD	WON
1984-85	F.A. CUP	vs MANCHESTER UNITED	LOST
1984-85	EUROPEAN CUP WINNERS' CUP	vs RAPID VIENNA	WON
1985-86	F.A. CUP	vs LIVERPOOL	LOST
1988-89	F.A. CUP	vs LIVERPOOL	LOST
1994-95	F.A. CUP	vs MANCHESTER UNITED	WON

LEAGUE CUP FINAL 1983-84
EVERTON V LIVERPOOL

In 1983-84 Everton reached the League Cup Final for only the second time in their history. Facing them were their great rivals from across Stanley Park. The first ever all-Merseyside Wembley Cup Final was a very tight affair. It was a game that both sides were determined not to lose and a stalemate resulted. Nevertheless it was a great occasion enjoyed by a capacity crowd.

Liverpool, the winners of the previous three League Cup Finals, started the game as the favourites, with Ian Rush hungry to complete the job of scoring in every round. However, it was Everton who almost drew first blood when a shot by Adrian Heath appeared to be handled by Alan Hansen. The penalty appeal was rejected by referee Alan Robinson – to the chagrin of the blue half of the stadium.

Kevin Sheedy, Kevin Richardson and Peter Reid all had opportunities to put the Toffeemen ahead in the first half, while Neville Southall did well to keep out Rush. It was a game in which the defences held sway, with Kevin Ratcliffe and

Derek Mountfield both being outstanding for Everton. Sheedy damaged his ankle in this match and was side-lined for the remainder of the season.

EVERTON 0-0 LIVERPOOL (AET)

Date: 25th March 1984

Manager: Howard Kendall

Team: Neville Southall, Gary Stevens, John Bailey, Kevin Ratcliffe, Derek Mountfield, Peter Reid, Alan Irvine, Adrian Heath, Graeme Sharp, Kevin Richardson, Kevin Sheedy (sub. Alan Harper)

Attendance: 100,000 (Wembley Stadium)

Clubs defeated en route to the Final: Chesterfield, Coventry City, West Ham United, Oxford United and Aston Villa

LEAGUE CUP FINAL REPLAY 1983-84 EVERTON V LIVERPOOL

The Milk Cup Final replay took place at Maine Road, on the Wednesday evening following the initial goalless encounter at Wembley. Sheedy's place in the Everton side went to Alan Harper, with Andy King taking the seat on the bench.

Howard Kendall's side fought extremely hard, but were undone by a powerful strike by Graeme Souness in the first half. Bruce Grobbelaar had denied Peter Reid when the game was still goalless and, near the end, Reid and Adrian Heath got in each other's way and an excellent chance to force extra-time went begging.

The League Cup remains a competition which Everton have not won. On the other occasion that they reached the Final (in 1976-77) they lost to Aston Villa (in a second replay). Everton fans took home two consolations from this defeat. Firstly, their side had prevented Ian Rush netting in every round of the Milk Cup. And, more importantly, with an F.A. Cup semi-final against Southampton still to come, there was a very good chance that their boys would be in another Cup Final later in the season. That day did materialise and it was to prove a joyful occasion for Evertonians.

EVERTON 0-1 LIVERPOOL

Date: 28th March 1984

Manager: Howard Kendall

Team: Neville Southall, Gary Stevens, John Bailey, Kevin Ratcliffe, Derek Mountfield, Peter Reid, Alan Irvine (sub. Andy King), Adrian Heath, Graeme Sharp, Kevin Richardson, Alan Harper

Attendance: 52,089 (Maine Road)

F.A. CUP FINAL 1983-84
EVERTON V WATFORD

Everton reached their eighth F.A. Cup Final by edging past Southampton in a Highbury semi-final courtesy of a single goal by Adrian Heath in extra-time. Unlike in the Milk Cup Final, eight weeks earlier, Everton walked on to the hallowed turf as the favourites. Their opponents were Wembley debutants Watford, who had finished four places below them in the First Division table.

Watford, with their fedora-wearing chairman Elton John in attendance, had the better of the early exchanges. John Barnes wasted a good chance with only Neville Southall to beat, while skipper Les Taylor and Mo Johnston also both went close. The Toffees rose to their task though and went ahead seven minutes before the break. Trevor Steven's mis-hit shot fell kindly for Graeme Sharp and the Scot neatly swivelled and fired in via a post.

Kendall's side doubled their lead early in the second half when the excellent Steven crossed for Andy Gray to head home. The Hornets never looked like replying and it was not long before there were buckets full of Evertonian tears of joy. Kevin Ratcliffe became the first Everton captain to hold the F.A. Cup aloft for 18 years. It was a particularly sweet moment for Kendall, an F.A. Cup Final loser as a player in 1964 and 1968, whose job was so much on the line earlier in the 1983-84 campaign.

EVERTON 2-0 WATFORD

Date: 19th May 1984

Manager: Howard Kendall

Team: Neville Southall, Gary Stevens, John Bailey, Kevin Ratcliffe, Derek Mountfield, Peter Reid, Trevor Steven, Adrian Heath, Graeme Sharp, Andy Gray, Kevin Richardson

Scorers: Sharp and Gray

Attendance: 100,000 (Wembley Stadium)

Clubs defeated en route to the Final: Stoke City, Gillingham, Shrewsbury Town, Notts County and Southampton

EUROPEAN CUP WINNERS' CUP FINAL 1984-85
EVERTON V RAPID VIENNA

With their first League Championship crown in 15 years wrapped up and an F.A. Cup Final appearance to come, Everton travelled to Rotterdam in a bid to secure the second part of what could have been an historic treble. The Final was Everton's ninth match in the competition that long campaign. Everton started as favourites, with Only Bayern Munich (in the semi-final second leg) previously breaching their formidable defence.

The Toffees edged the first half and got the ball in the net through Andy Gray just before the break; however, it was ruled out for offside. It was a warning that the Austrians failed to heed and Gray got a legitimate goal 12 minutes into the second half, after good work by Graeme Sharp. With Vienna leaving gaps at the back, Everton doubled their advantage in the 72nd minute when Trevor Steven let fly with a fierce shot. Hans Krankl pulled a goal back, but the two-goal advantage was quickly restored when Sharp set up Kevin Sheedy to fire home.

Everton's first piece of European silverware was secured in front of around 25,000 of their own fans. It was a memorable display by a side filled with confidence and talent.

EVERTON 3-1 RAPID VIENNA

Date: 15th May 1985

Manager: Howard Kendall

Team: Neville Southall, Gary Stevens, Pat Van den Hauwe, Kevin Ratcliffe, Derek Mountfield, Peter Reid, Trevor Steven, Graeme Sharp, Andy Gray, Paul Bracewell, Kevin Sheedy

Attendance: 45,000 (Rotterdam)

Clubs defeated en route to the Final: UC Dublin, Inter Bratislava, Fortuna Sittard and Bayern Munich

F.A. CUP FINAL 1984-85
EVERTON V MANCHESTER UNITED

Just three days after winning the European Cup Winners' Cup Final in Rotterdam, Everton walked out to do battle with Manchester United in the F.A. Cup Final. Howard Kendall's side were just one win away from an historic treble, having secured the League title earlier in May. Everton started as favourites, having finished 14 points in front of fourth place United in the table, but were never in danger of allowing complacency to set in.

As a spectacle this Final was a very turgid affair. Defences held sway and what little action there was was mainly predictable. Everton came closest to scoring in the first half when a goalbound shot from Peter Reid was deflected around the post by former Everton defender John Gidman. Andy Gray fired wide in the second half, while at the other end Neville Southall dived bravely at Norman Whiteside's feet. The talking point of the second period, though, was the sending-off of United defender Kevin Moran after 77 minutes for a lunging tackle on Reid. When referee Peter Willis pointed towards the dressing-room Moran became the first man to be dismissed in an F.A. Cup Final.

Despite having a man advantage, Everton could not squeeze out a winner. The match went into extra-time with Paul Bracewell and Pat Van den Hawue going close. The Toffeemen went closer still when United skipper Bryan Robson headed against his own crossbar. Unfortunately, when the goal did arrive it was in Southall's net. Whiteside was the scorer with a curling cross-shot, with only ten minutes of extra-time remaining.

Undoubtedly fatigue played it's part in Everton's downfall at Wembley. The lush turf took its toll as the game progressed with the same eleven men doing battle that had performed so heroically in Rotterdam the previous Wednesday. Nevertheless 1984-85 had been a glorious campaign for the Blue half of Merseyside.

EVERTON 0-1 MANCHESTER UNITED (AET)

Date: 18th May 1985

Manager: Howard Kendall

Team: Neville Southall, Gary Stevens, Pat Van den Hauwe, Kevin Ratcliffe, Derek Mountfield, Peter Reid, Trevor Steven, Greame Sharp, Andy Gray, Paul Bracewell, Kevin Sheedy

Attendance: 100,000 (Wembley Stadium)

Clubs defeated en route to the Final: Leeds United, Doncaster Rovers, Telford United, Ipswich Town and Luton Town

F.A. CUP FINAL 1985-86
EVERTON V LIVERPOOL

Despite holding a half-time lead, Everton were unable to prevent Liverpool becoming the fifth club to clinch the League and F.A. Cup 'Double' in the same season in 1985-86. In fact it was double heart-break for the Toffeemen who also finished second to the Reds in the League campaign in 1985-86.

Everton dominated the early play and might have had a penalty when Graeme Sharp appeared to be impeded by Steve Nicol. Referee Alan Robinson waved play on – just as he did when Everton had claimed a penalty in the 1984 Milk Cup Final. However, the Toffees did make the breakthrough after good work by Peter Reid just before the half-hour mark. Bruce Grobbelaar blocked Gary Lineker's first shot but the determined striker was successful with his follow-up effort.

Trevor Steven and Kevin Sheedy both might have doubled the lead before the course of the Final changed in the 57th minute. Gary Stevens gave the ball away and in a flash Ronnie Whelan and Jan Molby had set up Ian Rush. The Welsh striker side-stepped Bobby Mimms (deputising for the injured Neville Southall) and the scores were level. Liverpool edged ahead six minutes later when Craig Johnston converted a Rush cross. 'Man of the Match' Rush sealed his side's victory with the game's fourth goal in the 84th minute. Howard Kendall's men kept plugging away, but the better side on the day lifted the trophy.

EVERTON 1-3 LIVERPOOL

Date: 10th May 1986

Manager: Howard Kendall

Team: Bobby Mimms, Gary Stevens (sub. Adrian Heath), Pat Van den Hauwe, Kevin Ratcliffe, Derek Mountfield, Peter Reid, Trevor Steven, Gary Lineker, Graeme Sharp, Paul Bracewell, Kevin Sheedy

Scorer: Lineker

Attendance: 98,000 (Wembley Stadium)

Clubs defeated en route to the Final: Exeter City, Blackburn Rovers, Tottenham Hotspur, Luton Town and Sheffield Wednesday

F.A. CUP FINAL 1988-89
EVERTON V LIVERPOOL

Everton's eleventh F.A. Cup Final finished the way of their tenth, with them being the bridesmaids to their great local rivals. Substitute Stuart McCall twice equalised; but Liverpool were unshakeable in their quest for the trophy. The Final came just eight weeks after the Hillsborough Disaster, which cost 96 Liverpool supporters their lives. Prior to the kick-off the crowd joined Gerry Marsden in an emotional rendition of 'You'll Never Walk Alone.'

On a baking afternoon it was Liverpool who made the early pace and they took the lead in the fourth minute through John Aldridge's first-time shot. The Reds had a clear edge in midfield and only some fine goalkeeping by Neville Southall stopped them from running away with the game. McCall's introduction (for the ineffective Paul Bracewell) breathed life in Everton. With the clock ticking down, the Scottish midfielder slid in the rebound at the far post after Bruce Grobbelaar had parried a shot from Dave Watson.

Liverpool regained the lead six minutes into extra-time through a shot by substitute Ian Rush. However, Everton showed their battling qualities and equalised again through a dipping McCall shot six minutes later. McCall had become the first sub to score twice in an F.A. Cup Final. Sadly, for the blue half of Merseyside, another substitute emulated this feat three minutes later. A header by Rush ended the game's scoring, leaving Everton with only one victory from their four F.A. Cup visits to Wembley in six seasons of the 1980s.

EVERTON 2-3 LIVERPOOL
(AET: 1-1 AFTER 90 MINUTES)

Date: 20th May 1989

Manager: Colin Harvey

Team: Neville Southall, Neil McDonald, Pat Van den Hauwe, Kevin Ratcliffe, Dave Watson, Paul Bracewell (sub. Stuart McCall), Pat Nevin, Trevor Steven, Graeme Sharp, Tony Cottee, Kevin Sheedy (sub. Ian Wilson)

Scorer: McCall 2

Attendance: 82,800 (Wembley Stadium)

Clubs defeated en route to the Final: West Bromwich Albion, Plymouth Argyle, Barnsley, Wimbledon and Norwich City

F.A. CUP FINAL 1994-95
EVERTON V MANCHESTER UNITED

Exactly six years to the day after their previous F.A. Cup appearance, Everton were back at Wembley Stadium to meet Manchester United. Having just done enough to secure their Premiership status, the Toffees set about enjoying themselves against the hot favourites Manchester United.

Everton were also the under-dogs in the semi-final, held at Elland Road. However, they soundly put Spurs (including Jurgen Klinsmann) in place with a 4-1 hiding, with substitute Daniel Amokachi netting a late brace. Amokachi was again on the bench at Wembley, along with fans' favourite Duncan Ferguson.

Manchester United had the bulk of the early possession, but were caught out by a counter-attack one third of the way into the game. Graham Stuart shot against the bar and Paul Rideout responded quickest and headed home the rebound. The Toffees stuck to their task in the second half with the midfield, in which Barry Horne was outstanding, fighting like tigers. Skipper Dave Watson gave a 'Man of the Match' display at the back and Neville Southall made a pulsating double-save from substitute Paul Scholes. Having lost their Premiership crown to Blackburn Rovers, Manchester United finished 1994-95 empty-handed. For Evertonians, though, it was deep joy with Watson becoming the fifth Everton captain – after Jack Taylor, Dixie Dean, Brian Labone and Kevin Ratcliffe – to hold aloft the F.A. Cup.

EVERTON 1-0 MANCHESTER UNITED

Date: 20th May 1995

Manager: Joe Royle

Team: Neville Southall, Matt Jackson, Gary Ablett, Joe Parkinson, Dave Watson, David Unsworth, Anders Limpar (sub. Daniel Amokachi), Barry Horne, Graham Stuart, Paul Rideout (sub. Duncan Ferguson), Andy Hinchcliffe

Scorer: Rideout

Attendance: 79,592 (Wembley Stadium)

Clubs defeated en route to the Final: Derby County, Bristol City, Norwich City, Newcastle United and Tottenham Hotspur

1977-78

1	Aug	20	(h)	Nottingham F	L	1-3	Pearson	38,001
2		23	(a)	Arsenal	L	0-1		32,954
3		27	(a)	Aston Villa	W	2-1	McKenzie 2	37,806
4	Sep	3	(h)	Wolves	D	0-0		36,636
5		10	(a)	Leicester C	W	5-1	Latchford, Thomas, King 2, McKenzie	16,425
6		17	(h)	Norwich C	W	3-0	Rioch, McKenzie, Dobson	34,405
7		24	(a)	West Ham U	D	1-1	McKenzie	25,296
8	Oct	1	(h)	Manchester C	D	1-1	Latchford	43,286
9		4	(h)	West Brom A	W	3-1	Higgins, King (pen), Latchford	34,582
10		8	(a)	Q.P.R.	W	5-1	Latchford 4, McKenzie	20,495
11		15	(h)	Bristol C	W	1-0	King	39,230
12		22	(a)	Liverpool	D	0-0		51,668
13		29	(h)	Newcastle U	D	4-4	Pejic, Latchford 2, Lyons	37,647
14	Nov	5	(a)	Derby C	W	1-0	Lyons	29,335
15		12	(h)	Birmingham C	W	2-1	Latchford 2	37,743
16		19	(a)	Ipswich T	D	3-3	Lyons, Pearson, Buckley	22,790
17		26	(h)	Coventry C	W	6-0	Dobson, Latchford 3, Pearson, King	43,309
18	Dec	3	(a)	Chelsea	W	1-0	Latchford	33,890
19		10	(h)	Middlesbrough	W	3-0	Latchford 2, Buckley	38,647
20		17	(a)	Birmingham C	D	0-0		22,177
21		26	(h)	Manchester U	L	2-6	Latchford, Dobson	48,335
22		27	(a)	Leeds U	L	1-3	Dobson	46,727
23		31	(h)	Arsenal	W	2-0	Latchford, King	47,035
24	Jan	2	(a)	Nottingham F	D	1-1	Ross (pen)	44,030
25		14	(h)	Aston Villa	W	1-0	King	40,630
26		21	(a)	Wolves	L	1-3	Ross (pen)	23,777
27	Feb	4	(h)	Leicester C	W	2-0	Latchford 2	33,707
28		18	(h)	West Ham U	W	2-1	McKenzie, Thomas	33,826
29		25	(a)	Manchester C	L	0-1		46,817
30	Mar	4	(h)	Q.P.R.	D	3-3	Ross, Dobson, King	33,861
31		11	(a)	Bristol C	W	1-0	Ross	25,614
32		15	(a)	Norwich C	D	0-0		18,905
33		24	(a)	Newcastle U	W	2-0	Latchford, McKenzie	28,933
34		25	(h)	Leeds U	W	2-0	Latchford, McKenzie	45,020
35		27	(a)	Manchester U	W	2-1	Latchford 2	55,277
36	Apr	1	(h)	Derby Co	W	2-1	Dobson, Latchford	38,213
37		5	(h)	Liverpool	L	0-1		52,759
38		8	(a)	Coventry C	L	2-3	Latchford, Lyons	26,008
39		15	(h)	Ipswich T	W	1-0	Latchford (pen)	33,402
40		22	(a)	Middlesbrough	D	0-0		15,969
41		25	(a)	West Brom A	L	1-3	Telfer	20,247
42		29	(h)	Chelsea	W	6-0	Dobson, Wright, Robinson, Lyons, Latchford 2 (1 pen)	39,500

FINAL LEAGUE POSITION: 3rd in Division One

Appearances

Sub. Appearances

Goals

Wood	Jones	Pejic	Lyons	Kenyon	Higgins	King	Darracott	Pearson	McKenzie	Thomas	Goodlass	Latchford	Rioch	Dobson	Telfer	Buckley	Ross	Seargeant	Wright	Robinson	
1	2	3	4	5	6	7	8*	9	10	11	12										1
1		3	4	5*	12	7	2	8	10	11		9	6								2
1		3	4		5	7	2	8	10	11		9	6								3
1		3	4		5	7	2	8	10	11		9		6							4
1	12	3	4		5	7	2*		10	11		9	6	8							5
1	12	3	4		5	7	2		10	11		9	6*	8							6
1	12	3	4		5	7	2		10	11*		9	6	8							7
1		3	4		5	7	2		10	11		9	6	8							8
1	2	3	4		5	7		6	10	11		9		8							9
1	2	3	4		5	7		6	10	11		9		8							10
1	2	3	4		5	7	12	10				9		8	11	6*					11
1	2	3	4		5	7		10		11		9	6	8							12
1	2	3	4		5	7		10		11		9*	6	8	12						13
1	2*		4		5	7		10		11		9		8		6	3	12			14
1	2	3	4		5	7		10		11		9		8		6					15
1	2	3*	4		5	7		10		11		9		8		6	12				16
1	2	3	4		5	7		10		11		9		8		6					17
1	2	3	4		5	7		10		11		9		8		6					18
1	2	3	4		5	7		10		11		9		8		6					19
1	2	3	4		5	7		10		11		9		8		6					20
1	2	3	4		5	7		10*		11		9		8		6	12				21
1	2	3	4		5	7			10	11		9		8			6				22
1		3	4	5		7	2		10	11		9		8			6				23
1	12	3	4	5*		7	2		10	11		9		8			6				24
1		3	4		5	7	2		10	11		9		8			6				25
1	12	3	4	5		7	2*	8	10	11		9					6				26
1	2	3	4		5	7			10			9		8	11*		6		12		27
1	2	3	4		5	7			10	11		9*		8	12		6				28
1	2	3	4		5	7		9	10					8	11		6				29
1	2*	3	4	5		7		9	10	11				8	12		6				30
1	2	3	4	5		7			10	11		9		8			6				31
1	2	3	4			7	5		10	11		9		8			6				32
1	2	3	4			7	2	12	10*			9		8	11		6				33
1	2	3	4			7	5		10	11		9		8			6				34
1	2	3	4			7	5		10	11		9		8			6				35
1	2	3	4			7	5		10	11		9		8			6				36
1	2	3	4			7	5		10	11		9		8			6				37
1	2	3	4			7	5		10	11		9		8			6				38
1	2	3	4			7			10	11		9		8		6				5	39
1	2		4			7		6		11		9		8	10				5	2	40
1		3	4			7				11		9		8	10	6			5	2	41
1		3	4			7				11		9		8	10	6			5	2	42
42	29	40	42	7	25	42	19	21	28	38		39	8	38	7	12	18		3	4	
	5				1		1	1			1				3		2	1	1		
		1	5		1	8		3	9	2		30	1	7	1	2	4		1	1	

1978-79

1	Aug	19	(a)	Chelsea	W	1-0	King	32,683
2		22	(h)	Derby Co	W	2-1	King, Nulty	40,125
3		26	(h)	Arsenal	W	1-0	Thomas	41,161
4	Sep	2	(a)	Manchester U	D	1-1	King	53,982
5		9	(h)	Middlesbrough	W	2-0	Lyons, Dobson	36,191
6		16	(a)	Aston Villa	D	1-1	Walsh	39,636
7		23	(h)	Wolves	W	2-0	Latchford, King (pen)	38,895
8		30	(a)	Bristol C	D	2-2	Latchford 2	22,502
9	Oct	7	(h)	Southampton	D	0-0		38,769
10		14	(a)	Ipswich T	W	1-0	Latchford	22,830
11		21	(a)	Q.P.R.	D	1-1	Latchford	21,171
12		28	(h)	Liverpool	W	1-0	King	53,141
13	Nov	4	(a)	Nottingham F	D	0-0		35,515
14		11	(h)	Chelsea	W	3-2	King, Dobson 2	38,346
15		18	(a)	Arsenal	D	2-2	Ross, Dobson	39,711
16		21	(h)	Manchester U	W	3-0	Ross, King, Latchford	42,126
17		25	(a)	Norwich C	W	1-0	Lyons	18,930
18	Dec	9	(a)	Birmingham C	W	3-1	Ross (pen), Todd, Latchford	23,391
19		16	(h)	Leeds U	D	1-1	Ross	37,997
20		23	(a)	Coventry C	L	2-3	Lyons, Latchford	22,778
21		26	(h)	Manchester C	W	1-0	Wright	46,996
22		30	(h)	Tottenham H	D	1-1	Lyons	44,572
23	Jan	31	(h)	Aston Villa	D	1-1	Thomas	29,079
24	Feb	3	(a)	Wolves	L	0-1		21,892
25		10	(h)	Bristol C	W	4-1	King 3, Wright	29,116
26		17	(a)	Southampton	L	0-3		20,681
27		24	(h)	Ipswich T	L	0-1		29,031
28	Mar	3	(h)	Q.P.R.	W	2-1	Latchford, Telfer	24,809
29		6	(a)	Middlesbrough	W	2-1	Jack, Latchford	16,084
30		10	(h)	Nottingham F	D	1-1	Telfer	37,745
31		13	(a)	Liverpool	D	1-1	King	52,352
32		24	(a)	Derby Co	D	0-0		20,814
33		30	(h)	Norwich C	D	2-2	Lyons 2	26,825
34	Apr	3	(a)	Bolton W	L	1-3	Ross (pen)	27,263
35		7	(a)	West Brom A	L	0-1		29,593
36		10	(h)	Coventry C	D	3-3	Ross, Latchford, Kidd	25,302
37		14	(a)	Manchester C	D	0-0		39,711
38		16	(h)	Bolton W	W	1-0	Higgins	31,214
39		21	(a)	Leeds U	L	0-1		29,125
40		28	(h)	Birmingham C	W	1-0	King	23,048
41	May	1	(h)	West Brom A	L	0-2		30,083
42		5	(a)	Tottenham H	D	1-1	Kidd	26,077

FINAL LEAGUE POSITION : 4th in Division One

Appearances

Sub. Appearances

Goals

Wood	Darracott	Pejic	Lyons	Higgins	Nulty	King	Dobson	Latchford	Walsh	Thomas	Wright	Todd	Ross	Robinson	Kenyon	Jones	Telfer	Heard	Jack	Barton	Kidd	Eastoe	
1	2	3	4	5	6	7	8	9	10	11													1
1	2	3	4		6	7	8	9	10	11	5												2
1	2	3	4		6	7	8	9	10	11	5												3
1	2	3	4		6	7	8	9	10	11	5												4
1	2	3	4		6	7	8	9	10	11	5												5
1	2	3	4		6	7	8	9	10	11	5												6
1		3	4			7	8	9	10	11	5	2	6										7
1		3	4			7	8	9	10	11	5	2	6										8
1		3	4			7	8	9	10	11	5	2	6										9
1		3	4			7	8	9	10	11	5	2	6										10
1		3	4*		6	7	8	9	10	11	5	2		12									11
1		3			6	7	8	9	10	11	5	2			4								12
1	2	3				7	8	9	10	11	5	4	6										13
1		3	4			7	8	9	10*	11	5	2	6	12									14
1		3	4		12	7	8	9	10	11	5*	2	6										15
1		3	4		12	7	8	9	10*	11	5	2	6										16
1		3	4			7	8	9		11	5	2	6		10								17
1		3	4	10		7	8	9		11	5	2	6										18
1		3	4	10	12	7	8*	9		11	5	2	6										19
1			4	10	6	7	8	9		11	5	2				3							20
1			4	10	6	7	8	9			5	2		12		3*	11						21
1			4		6	7	8	9			5	2		10	3		11						22
1			4	3		7	8	9	10	11	5	2	6										23
1			4	3		7	8	9	10*	11	5	2	6					12					24
1			4	3		10	8	9		11	5	7	6	2									25
1			4	3		10	8	9		11	5	7		2				6					26
1			4	3		7	8	9	12	11*	5	2					10	6					27
1			4			7	8*	9	12	11	5		6	2			10	3					28
1			4	2			8	9		11	5		6				10	3	7				29
1			4	2		7	8	9	12	11	5		6				10*	3					30
1			4			7	8	9		11	5	2	6				10	3					31
1			4	9		7	8			11	5	2	6				10	3					32
1			4	9*		7	8			11	5	2	6				10	3		12			33
1			4			9	8			11		2	6			3	10			5	7		34
1			4			7	8	9		11*		2	6			3				2	10	12	35
1			4			7	8	9*			5		6			3	12			2	10	11	36
1				4	8	9					5	7	6			3*	12			2	10	11	37
1			4	5	7		8				9		6			3				2	10	11	38
1			4	5		7					9		6			3		8		2	10	11	39
1				5	12	7	8	9			6	4				3				2	10	11*	40
1			4	5		7	8	9			6					3				2	10	11	41
1				5		7	8	9			6	4				3				2	10	11	42
42	7	19	37	20	13	40	40	36	18	33	39	29	26	4	3	11	10	9	1	9	9	7	
					4				3					3			2	1		1		1	
			6	1	1	12	4	11	1	2	2	1	6				2		1		2		

1979-80

1	Aug	18	(h)	Norwich C	L	2-4	Ross (pen), Nulty	27,555
2		22	(a)	Leeds U	L	0-2		27,783
3		25	(a)	Derby Co	W	1-0	King	17,820
4	Sep	1	(h)	Aston Villa	D	1-1	Bailey	29,271
5		8	(a)	Stoke C	W	3-2	King, Bailey, Irvine (og)	23,460
6		15	(h)	Wolves	L	2-3	Kidd, Ross (pen)	31,807
7		22	(a)	Ipswich T	D	1-1	Kidd	19,279
8		29	(h)	Bristol C	D	0-0		24,733
9	Oct	6	(a)	Coventry C	L	1-2	King	17,205
10		13	(h)	Crystal Palace	W	3-1	Kidd, Latchford, King	30,645
11		20	(a)	Liverpool	D	2-2	Kidd, King	52,201
12		27	(h)	Manchester U	D	0-0		37,708
13	Nov	3	(a)	Norwich C	D	0-0		18,025
14		10	(h)	Middlesbrough	L	0-2		25,155
15		13	(h)	Leeds U	W	5-1	Latchford 3, Kidd, Hart (og)	23,319
16		17	(a)	Arsenal	L	0-2		33,450
17		24	(h)	Tottenham H	D	1-1	Latchford	31,079
18	Dec	1	(a)	West Brom A	D	1-1	King	21,237
19		8	(h)	Brighton & H.A.	W	2-0	King, Kidd	23,595
20		15	(a)	Southampton	L	0-1		19,850
21		22	(h)	Manchester C	L	1-2	Kidd	26,314
22		26	(a)	Bolton W	D	1-1	McBride	18,220
23		29	(h)	Derby Co	D	1-1	King	22,554
24	Jan	1	(h)	Nottingham F	W	1-0	Kidd	34,622
25		12	(a)	Aston Villa	L	1-2	Eastoe	22,635
26	Feb	2	(a)	Wolves	L	0-0		21,663
27		9	(h)	Ipswich T	L	0-4		31,603
28		19	(a)	Bristol C	L	1-2	Ross	16,317
29		23	(a)	Crystal Palace	D	1-1	Eastoe	23,400
30	Mar	1	(h)	Liverpool	L	1-2	Eastoe	53,018
31		12	(a)	Manchester U	D	0-0		45,515
32		15	(h)	Coventry C	D	1-1	Eastoe	25,970
33		18	(h)	Stoke C	W	2-0	Latchford, Eastoe	23,847
34		22	(a)	Middlesbrough	L	1-2	Hartford	17,587
35		28	(h)	Arsenal	L	0-1		28,184
36	Apr	2	(a)	Manchester C	D	1-1	King	33,437
37		5	(h)	Bolton W	W	3-1	Megson, Eastoe, Kidd	28,037
38		19	(a)	Tottenham H	L	0-3		25,245
39		26	(h)	Southampton	W	2-0	Stanley, Gidman (pen)	23,552
40		28	(h)	West Brom A	D	0-0		20,356
41	May	3	(a)	Brighton & H.A.	D	0-0		21,204
42		9	(a)	Nottingham F	L	0-1		22,122

FINAL LEAGUE POSITION: 19th in Division One

Appearances

Sub. Appearances

Goals

Wood	Barton	Bailey	Lyons	Wright	Ross	Nulty	Todd	King	Kidd	Heard	Eastoe	Higgins	Hartford	Stanley	Latchford	Varadi	Gidman	Hodge	O'Keefe	McBride	Megson	Ratcliffe	Sharp	
1	2	3	4	5	6	7	8	9	10	11*	12													1
1	2	3	4	11	6	7	8	9	10			5												2
1	2	3	4	11	6	7	8	9	10			5												3
1		3	4	2	6			9	10		11	5	7	8										4
1		3	4	2	6			9	10		11	5	7	8										5
1	12	3	4	2	6			9	10		11*	5	7	8										6
1	2	3	4	8	6	9			10		11	5	7											7
1	2*	3	4	12	6			9	10		11	5	7	8										8
1	2	3	4			6		11	10			5	7	8	9*	12								9
1		3	4	2	6	12		11	10			5	7*	8	9									10
1		3	4	2	6	7		11	10			5		8	9									11
1		3	4	8	6	7			10		11	5			9		2							12
1		3	4	8	6			11	10			5		7	9		2							13
1		3	12	4	6			11	10			5	7*	8	9		2							14
		3	12	4	6			11	10			5	7	8	9*		2	1						15
		3	12	4	6			11	10			5	7	8	9*		2	1						16
		3		4	6			11	10			5	7	8	9		2	1						17
		3		4	6			11	10			5	7	8	9		2	1						18
		3		4	6			11	10			5	7	8	9		2	1						19
		3		4	6			11			12	5	7	8	9*	10	2	1						20
		3	5	4	6			11	10				7	8*	9	12	2	1						21
		3	5	4					10				7	8		9	2	1	6	11				22
		3	5	4				6	10				7	8	9		2	1		11				23
		3	5	4				6	10				7	8	9		2	1		11				24
		3	5	4	6*				10		8		7		9		2	1	12	11				25
		3	5	4							8		10	6	9		2	1		11	7			26
		3	5	4							8		10		9		2	1	6	11	7			27
		3	5	4	6				10		8		9				2	1		11	7			28
		3	5	2	6	4			10		8		9					1		11	7			29
1		3	5	8	6	4*		9	10		12		7				2			11				30
		3	5	2				8	10		6				9			1		11	7	4		31
		3	5	4				8			6		10		9		2	1		11	7			32
		3	5	4				8			6		10		9		2	1		11	7			33
		3	5	4				8			6		10		9		2	1		11	7			34
		3	5	4	12			8			6		10		9		2	1		11	7*			35
		3	5	4	11			8	9		6		10				2	1			7			36
		3	5	4	11			8	9		6		10				2	1			7			37
		3*	5	2	11				9		8		10				4	1		12	7	6		38
1		3	5	4	6						7		10	8	9		2			11				39
1		3	5	4	6						7		10	8	9		2			11				40
1		3	5	4	6						7		10	8	9*		2			11			12	41
1		3	5	4	6						7		10	8			2		11				9	42
19	6	42	35	40	31	9	3	29	31	1	23	19	35	24	26	2	29	23	3	17	12	2	1	
	1		3	1	1	1					3					2			1	1			1	
		2			3	1		9	9		6		1	1	6		1			1	1			

1980-81

1	Aug	16	(a)	Sunderland	L 1-3	Eastoe	32,005
2		19	(h)	Leicester C	W 1-0	Eastoe	23,337
3		23	(h)	Nottingham F	D 0-0		25,981
4		30	(a)	Ipswich T	L 0-4		20,879
5	Sep	6	(h)	Wolves	W 2-0	Eastoe, Wright	21,820
6		13	(a)	Aston Villa	W 2-0	Lyons, Eastoe	25,673
7		20	(h)	Crystal Palace	W 5-0	Latchford 3, Gidman (pen), Eastoe	26,950
8		27	(a)	Coventry C	W 5-0	Eastoe, Latchford 2, McBride 2	14,810
9	Oct	4	(h)	Southampton	W 2-1	McBride 2 (2 pens)	36,544
10		7	(a)	Brighton & H.A.	W 3-1	McMahon, Lyons, McBride	16,523
11		11	(a)	Leeds U	L 0-1		25,601
12		18	(h)	Liverpool	D 2-2	Hartford, McBride	52,565
13		21	(h)	West Brom A	D 1-1	Eastoe	24,046
14		25	(a)	Manchester U	L 0-2		54,260
15	Nov	1	(h)	Tottenham H	D 2-2	Eastoe, McMahon	26,174
16		8	(a)	Norwich C	L 1-2	Latchford	14,557
17		12	(a)	Leicester C	W 1-0	Eastoe	15,511
18		15	(h)	Sunderland	W 2-1	O'Keefe, Hartford	24,099
19		22	(a)	Arsenal	L 1-2	Wright	30,911
20		29	(h)	Birmingham C	D 1-1	O'Keefe	22,258
21	Dec	6	(a)	Stoke C	D 2-2	McBride, Varadi	15,650
22		13	(h)	Brighton & H.A.	W 4-3	Eastoe 2, McMahon, Varadi	19,157
23		26	(h)	Manchester C	L 0-2		36,194
24		27	(a)	Middlesbrough	L 0-1		20,210
25	Jan	10	(h)	Arsenal	L 1-2	O'Keefe	29,360
26		17	(h)	Ipswich T	D 0-0		25,516
27		31	(a)	Nottingham F	L 0-1		25,611
28	Feb	7	(h)	Aston Villa	L 1-3	Ross (pen)	31,434
29		21	(h)	Coventry C	W 3-0	Ross, McMahon, Eastoe	26,731
30		28	(a)	Crystal Palace	W 3-2	Eastoe, McMahon, Varadi	14,594
31	Mar	14	(h)	Leeds U	L 1-2	Varadi	23,014
32		17	(a)	Southampton	L 0-3		20,829
33		21	(a)	Liverpool	L 0-1		49,743
34		28	(h)	Manchester U	L 0-1		25,854
35		31	(a)	West Brom A	L 0-2		14,833
36	Apr	4	(a)	Tottenham H	D 2-2	Hartford, Varadi	27,208
37		11	(h)	Norwich C	L 0-2		16,254
38		18	(h)	Middlesbrough	W 4-1	Hartford 2 (1 pen), Megson, Eastoe	15,706
39		20	(a)	Manchester C	L 1-3	Varadi	34,434
40		25	(h)	Stoke C	L 0-1		15,352
41	May	2	(a)	Birmingham C	D 1-1	Eastoe	12,863
42		4	(a)	Wolves	D 0-0		16,269

FINAL LEAGUE POSITION: 15th in Division One

Appearances

Sub. Appearances

Goals

McDonagh	Gidman	Ratcliffe	Wright	Lyons	Megson	McMahon	Sharp	Latchford	Hartford	McBride	Eastoe	Stanley	O'Keefe	Bailey	Ross	Higgins	Varadi	Hodge	Lodge	Telfer	Barton	
1	2	3	4	5	6*	7	8	9	10	11	12											1
1	2	3	4	5		7		9	10	11	8	6										2
1	2	3	4	5		7		9	10	11	8	6										3
1	2	3	4	5		7		9	8	11	10	6*	12									4
1	2		4	5		7		9*	10	11	8	6	12	3								5
1	2		4	5		7		9	1	11	8*	6	12	3								6
1	2		4	5		7		9	10	11	8	6		3								7
1	2		4	5		7		9	10*	11	8	6	12	3								8
1	2		4	5	10	7		9		11	8	6		3	2							9
1	2		4	5		7		9	10	11	8*	6	12	3								10
1	2		4	5		7		9	10	11	8	6*	12	3								11
1	2*		4	5		7		9	10	11	8	6	12	3								12
1			4	5		7		9	10	11	8	6		3								13
1	2		4	5		7		9	10	11	8	6*	12	3								14
1	2		4	5		7		9*	10	11	8	6	12	3								15
1	2		4	5*		7		9	10	11	8	6	12	3								16
1	2		4			7		9	10	11	8	5	6	3								17
1	2		4		12	7		9*	10	11	8	5	6	3								18
1	2		4		6	7			10	11	8	5	9	3								19
1	2		4		6	7		·	10	11	8	5	9	3								20
1			2			7			10	11	8	4	6	3		5	9					21
1			2	12		7			10	11	8	4	6*	3		5	9					22
1	2	5	4	12		7			10	11*	8		6	3			9					23
1	2	5	4	12		7			10	11	8			3	6		9*					24
1	2	5	4			7			10		8		11	3	6		9					25
1		2	4	5		7			10	12	8		11*	3	6		9					26
		2	4	5		7			10	12	8		11*	3	6		9	1				27
		2	4	5	7				10		8		11*	3	6		9	1	12			28
1	2*	3	4	5		7			10		8		11		6		9		12			29
1	2	3	4	5		7			10		8		11		6*		9		12			30
1	2		4	5		7			10	11	8			3	6		9					31
1	2	3	4	5*		7			10	12	8	6			11		9					32
1	2		4			7				12	8	5	11	3	6		9*		10			33
1	2	12	4			7					8	5	11	3*	6		9		10			34
1	2	3	4			7*			10		8	5			6		12		11	9		35
1	2		4	6					10		8	5		3	7		9*		11	12		36
1	2	3	4	5	12				10		8*	6			7		9		11			37
1	2	3	4	5	7		12		10		8	6*					9		11			38
1	2	3	4	5	7		12		10	11	8*						9		6			39
1		4		5	7		9		10	11*	8			3			12		6		2	40
1	6	4	7	5					10		8			3	11		9				2	41
1	6	4	7	5				12	10		8*			3	11		9				2	42
40	35	20	41	30	8	34	2	18	39	27	41	28	15	31	17	2	20	2	8	1	3	
		1		3	2		2	1		4	1		10				2		3	1		
	1		2	2	1	5		6	5	7	15		3		2		6					

1981-82

1	Aug	29	(h)	Birmingham C	W 3-1	Ainscow, Eastoe, Biley	33,045
2	Sep	2	(a)	Leeds U	D 1-1	Biley	26,502
3		5	(a)	Southampton	L 0-1		21,624
4		12	(h)	Brighton & H.A.	D 1-1	Wright	27,352
5		19	(a)	Tottenham H	L 0-3		31,219
6		22	(h)	Notts Co	W 3-1	Eastoe, Ross, O'Keefe	22,175
7		26	(h)	West Brom A	W 1-0	Lyons	23,873
8	Oct	3	(a)	Stoke C	L 1-3	McBride	16,007
9		10	(a)	West Ham U	D 1-1	McMahon	31,608
10		17	(h)	Ipswich T	W 2-1	Ferguson, Stevens	25,146
11		24	(a)	Middlesbrough	W 2-0	Ferguson 2	13,423
12		31	(h)	Manchester C	L 0-1		31,305
13	Nov	7	(a)	Liverpool	L 1-3	Ferguson	48,861
14		21	(h)	Sunderland	L 1-2	Eastoe	19,759
15		24	(a)	Notts Co	D 2-2	Biley, Sharp	7,771
16		28	(a)	Arsenal	L 0-1		25,860
17	Dec	5	(h)	Swansea C	W 3-1	Sharp, O'Keefe 2	23,860
18		19	(h)	Aston Villa	W 2-0	Lyons, Eastoe	16,538
19		28	(h)	Coventry C	W 3-2	Higgins 2, Sharp	23,895
20	Jan	6	(a)	Manchester U	D 1-1	Sharp	40,451
21		19	(h)	Southampton	D 1-1	Richardson	22,355
22		23	(a)	Wolves	W 3-0	Richardson, Irvine 2	11,784
23		30	(h)	Tottenham H	D 1-1	Sharp	30,717
24	Feb	6	(a)	Brighton & H.A.	L 1-3	Heath	16,148
25		13	(h)	Stoke C	D 0-0		20,656
26		20	(a)	West Brom A	D 0-0		14,819
27		27	(h)	West Ham U	D 0-0		28,618
28	Mar	6	(a)	Ipswich T	L 0-3		19,360
29		13	(h)	Middlesbrough	W 2-0	Higgins, Sharp	15,807
30		20	(a)	Manchester C	D 1-1	Heath	33,002
31		27	(h)	Liverpool	L 1-3	Sharp	51,847
32	Apr	3	(a)	Nottingham F	W 1-0	McMahon	17,323
33		6	(a)	Birmingham C	W 2-0	Heath, Ainscow	12,273
34		10	(h)	Manchester U	D 3-3	Sharp, Lyons, Heath	29,317
35		13	(a)	Coventry C	L 0-1		11,858
36		17	(a)	Sunderland	L 1-3	Irvine	18,359
37		20	(h)	Nottingham F	W 2-1	Sharp 2	15,460
38		24	(h)	Arsenal	W 2-1	Wright, Heath	19,136
39	May	1	(a)	Swansea C	W 3-1	Heath, Sharp 2 (1 pen)	16,243
40		4	(h)	Leeds U	W 1-0	Sharp	17,137
41		8	(h)	Wolves	D 1-1	Eastoe	20,124
42		15	(a)	Aston Villa	W 2-1	Sharp 2	20,446

FINAL LEAGUE POSITION: 8th in Division One

Appearances

Sub. Appearances

Goals

Arnold	Wright	Bailey	Walsh	Lyons	Thomas	Ainscow	Eastoe	Biley	Hartford	Ross	Ratcliffe	McMahon	Ferguson	O'Keefe	McBride	Sharp	Stevens	Higgins	Southall	Lodge	Richardson	Kendall	Irvine	Heath	Borrows	Rimmer S				
1	2	3	4	5	6	7	8	9	10	11																				1
1	2		4	5	6	11	8	9	10		3	7																		2
1	2		4	5	6	11	8	9	10		3	7*	12																	3
1	2		4	5	6	11	8	9	10		3	7																		4
1	2		4	5	6	11	8	9	10		3	7*		12																5
1	2		4	5	6	11	8	9*	10	7	3			12																6
1	2		4	5	6			9	10	7	3	8*		11	12															7
1	2	3*	4	5	6			9		10		7		8	11	12														8
1		3		5	6			8*		10		7	9	12	11		2	4												9
		3	4	5	6*			12		10		7	9	8	11		2		1											10
1		3		5		10*		12				7	9	8	11		2	4		6										11
1		3		5		10*						7	9	8	11	12	2	4		6										12
1		3		5		10*		12				7	9	8	11		2	4		6										13
1		3	4	5		10	8*	9				7			11		2			6	12									14
1			4	5		11*		10			3	7				9	2			6	12	8								15
1			4	5				10		8	3	7		11		9	2			6										16
1			4	5				10		8	3	7		11		9	2					6								17
				5			10			8	3					9	2	4	1	11		6	7							18
				5			10			8	3	7				9	2	4	1			6	11							19
				5			10				3	7				9	2	4	1	11	8		6							20
				5			10				3					9	2	4	1	11	6		7	8						21
				5			10				3					9	2	4	1	11	6		7	8						22
				5			10				3					9	2	4	1	11	6		7	8						23
				5			10				3					9	2	4	1	11	6		7	8						24
	5									11	3		10			9		4	1		6		7	8	2					25
	5	3						10		11						9		4	1		6		7	8	2					26
	5	3						10		11						9		4	1		6		7	8	2					27
	5	3						10*		11		12				9		4	1		6		7	8	2					28
	5	3				12				11		10*				9		4	1		6		7	8	2					29
	5									11	3	10				9		4	1		6		7	8	2					30
	5									11	3	10				9		4	1		6		7	8	2					31
	5					12	10			11	3	6				9*		4	1				7	8	2					32
	5*					10	12			11	3	6				9		4	1				7	8	2					33
				5		10				11	3	6				9		4	1*	12			7	8	2					34
				5		10				11	3	6				9		4	1				7	8	2					35
	5			12		10					3	6	9					4	1		11		7*	8	2					36
	5									11	3	6				9		4	1		10		7	8	2					37
	5		3							11		6				9	2	4	1		10		7	8						38
	5		3							11		6				9	2	4	1		12		7	8		10*				39
	5		3				12			11		6				9	2	4	1				7	8		10*				40
	5		3				10			11		6				9		4	1				7	8	2					41
	5		3				10			11		6				9		4	1				7	8	2					42
16	24	12	18	26	10	15	17	16	7	27	25	31	7	8	7	27	19	29	26	12	15	4	25	22	15	2				
				1		2	2	3				1	1	3	1	2				1	3									
	2			3		2	5	3		1		2	4	3	1	15	1	3			2		3	6						

1982-83

1	Aug	28	(a)	Watford	L	0-2		19,630
2		31	(h)	Aston Villa	W	5-0	Heath 2, King, Sharp 2 (1 pen)	24,026
3	Sep	4	(h)	Tottenham H	W	3-1	Sheedy, Wright, McMahon	30,553
4		8	(a)	Manchester U	L	1-2	King	43,186
5		11	(a)	Notts Co	L	0-1		9,197
6		18	(h)	Norwich C	D	1-1	Irvine	20,281
7		25	(a)	Coventry C	L	2-4	Heath, King	9,319
8	Oct	2	(h)	Brighton & H.A.	D	2-2	Heath, Wright	17,539
9		9	(h)	Manchester C	W	2-1	King, McMahon	25,158
10		16	(a)	Swansea C	W	3-0	Stevenson (og), Richardson, McMahon	11,183
11		23	(h)	Sunderland	W	3-1	Johnson, Sharp, Richardson	20,360
12		30	(a)	Southampton	L	2-3	Wright, King	18,141
13	Nov	6	(h)	Liverpool	L	0-5		52,741
14		13	(a)	Arsenal	D	1-1	King	23,067
15		20	(h)	West Brom A	D	0-0		16,001
16		27	(a)	West Ham U	L	0-2		21,424
17	Dec	4	(h)	Birmingham C	D	0-0		13,707
18		11	(a)	Ipswich T	W	2-0	Sheedy, Richardson	17,512
19		18	(h)	Luton T	W	5-0	Bailey, Sheedy, Curran, Heath 2	14,982
20		27	(a)	Stoke C	L	0-1		25,427
21		28	(h)	Nottingham F	W	3-1	Sharp 2 (1 pen), McMahon	25,147
22	Jan	1	(a)	West Brom A	D	2-2	Sharp, Higgins	15,194
23		3	(a)	Tottenham H	L	1-2	Sharp	28,455
24		15	(h)	Watford	W	1-0	Johnson	19,233
25		22	(a)	Norwich C	W	1-0	Ratcliffe	14,180
26	Feb	5	(h)	Notts Co	W	3-0	King, Heath, Sheedy	14,541
27		12	(a)	Aston Villa	L	0-2		21,117
28		26	(h)	Swansea C	D	2-2	King 2	17,112
29	Mar	2	(a)	Manchester C	D	0-0		22,253
30		5	(a)	Sunderland	L	1-2	Sharp	16,051
31		15	(h)	Southampton	W	2-0	Heath, Sheedy	15,002
32		19	(a)	Liverpool	D	0-0		44,737
33		26	(h)	Arsenal	L	2-3	Ainscow, Heath	16,318
34	Apr	2	(a)	Nottingham F	L	0-2		14,815
35		4	(h)	Stoke C	W	3-1	Sheedy 2, Sharp	15,360
36		9	(a)	Brighton & H.A.	W	2-1	Sheedy 2	14,534
37		19	(h)	Manchester U	W	2-0	Sharp, Heath	21,707
38		23	(a)	Birmingham C	L	0-1		11,045
39		30	(h)	West Ham U	W	2-0	Sharp 2	16,355
40	May	2	(h)	Coventry C	W	1-0	Sharp (pen)	12,972
41		7	(a)	Luton T	W	5-1	Johnson, Sheedy 2, Sharp 2 (1 pen)	12,447
42		14	(h)	Ipswich T	D	1-1	Wark (og)	17,420

FINAL LEAGUE POSITION: 7th in Division One

Appearances

Sub. Appearances

Goals

Southall	Borrows	Bailey	Higgins	Wright	Heath	McMahon	Johnson	Sharp	King	Sheedy	Richardson	Irvine	Ainscow	Walsh	Ratcliffe	Ross	Keeley	Arnold	Stevens	Curran	Reid	Mountfield	
1	2	3	4	5	6	7*	8	9	10	11	12												1
1	2	3	4	5	8	6		9	10	11	12	7*											2
1	2	3	4	5	8	6		9	10	11			7										3
1	2	3	4	5	8	6		9	10	11	12		7*										4
1	2	3	4	5	8	6		9	10	11			7										5
1	2			5	8	6		9	10	11		7*		3	4	12							6
1			4	5	8	6		9	10	11	2	12		3		7*							7
1	2	3	4	5	7	6	8	9	10	11													8
1	2	3	4	5	7	6	8	9	10	11													9
1	2	3	4	5		6	8	9	10	11	7												10
1	2	3	4	5	7*	6	8	9	10	11	12												11
1	2	3	4	5		6	8*	9	10	11	7	12											12
1	2	3		5	7	6	8*	9	10	11	12						4						13
			4	5	7	6	8	9	10		11*	12			3			1	2				14
			4	5	7	6	8	9	10			11			3			1	2				15
			4	5	8*	6	12	9	10	11		7			3			1	2				16
		3	4	5	8	6		9	10	11								1	2	7			17
		3	5		8	6	9			11	10				4			1	2	7			18
		3	5		8	6	9*	12		11	10				4			1	2	7			19
		3	5		8	6	9	12		11	10				4			1	2*	7			20
		3	5		12	6	9*	8		11					4			1	2	7	10		21
		3	5			6	9	8		11					4			1	2	7	10		22
		3	5			6	9	8		11					4			1	2	7	10		23
		3	5		7	6	12	8	9	11					4			1	2		10*		24
		3	5		8	6		9	7	11					4			1	2		10		25
		3	5		7*		12	8	9	11	6				4			1	2		10		26
		3	5		7		12	8	9	11	6				4			1	2		10*		27
		3	5		10		12	9	8	11	6	7*			4			1	2				28
		3	5		10		7	9	8	11	6				4			1	2				29
		3	5		10		7	9	8*	11	6	12			4			1	2				30
		3	5		10	8		9		11	6	7			4			1	2				31
		3	5		10	8		9		11	6	7*	12		4			1	2				32
		3	5		10	8		9		11	6	12	7		4			1	2*				33
		3	5		10	8	12	9		11	6*		7		4			1	2				34
		3	5		10	6	8	9		11	2		7		4			1					35
		3	5		10		8	9		11	6		7		4			1	2				36
		3	5		10	7	8	9		11	6				4			1	2				37
		3			10	7*	8	9		11	6		12		4			1	2			5	38
1		3	5		10		8	9		11	6		7		4				2				39
1		3	5		10	7	8*	9		11	6	12			4				2				40
1		3	5		10	7	8	9		11	6				4				2				41
1		3	5		10		8	9		11	6*	12	7		4				2				42
17	12	37	39	17	37	34	25	39	24	40	24	7	9	2	29	1	1	25	28	7	7	1	
					1		6	2			5	7	2			1							
		1	1	3	10	4	3	15	9	11	3	1	1		1					1			

1983-84

1	Aug	27	(h)	Stoke C	W 1-0	Sharp	22,658
2		29	(h)	West Ham U	L 0-1		20,375
3	Sep	3	(a)	Coventry C	D 1-1	Sheedy	12,532
4		6	(a)	Ipswich T	L 0-3		16,543
5		10	(h)	West Brom A	D 0-0		15,548
6		17	(a)	Tottenham H	W 2-1	Reid, Sheedy	29,125
7		24	(h)	Birmingham C	D 1-1	Sharp (pen)	15,253
8	Oct	1	(a)	Notts Co	W 1-0	Reid	7,949
9		15	(h)	Luton T	L 0-1		14,325
10		22	(h)	Watford	W 1-0	Johnson	13,571
11		29	(a)	Leicester C	L 0-2		10,953
12	Nov	6	(a)	Liverpool	L 0-3		40,875
13		12	(h)	Nottingham F	W 1-0	Heath	17,546
14		19	(a)	Arsenal	L 1-2	King (pen)	24,330
15		26	(h)	Norwich C	L 0-2		14,106
16	Dec	3	(a)	Manchester U	W 1-0	Sheedy	43,664
17		10	(h)	Aston Villa	D 1-1	Gray	15,810
18		17	(a)	Q.P.R.	L 0-2		11,608
19		26	(h)	Sunderland	D 0-0		18,683
20		27	(a)	Wolves	L 0-3		12,761
21		31	(h)	Coventry C	D 0-0		13,659
22	Jan	2	(a)	Birmingham C	W 2-0	Stevens, King	10,004
23		14	(a)	Stoke C	D 1-1	Heath	7,945
24		21	(h)	Tottenham H	W 2-1	Heath 2	18,003
25	Feb	4	(h)	Notts Co	W 4-1	Heath 3, Sheedy (pen)	13,016
26		11	(a)	West Brom A	D 1-1	Mountfield	10,313
27		25	(a)	Watford	D 4-4	Sharp 2, Gray, Heath	16,982
28	Mar	3	(h)	Liverpool	D 1-1	Harper	51,245
29		13	(a)	Nottingham F	L 0-1		13,647
30		17	(h)	Ipswich T	W 1-0	Mountfield	18,013
31		20	(h)	Leicester C	D 1-1	Richardson	15,142
32		31	(h)	Southampton	W 1-0	Gray	20,244
33	Apr	7	(a)	Luton T	W 3-0	Mountfield, Heath 2 (1 pen)	9,224
34		9	(h)	Arsenal	D 0-0		21,174
35		17	(a)	Southampton	L 1-3	Richardson	16,978
36		21	(a)	Sunderland	L 1-2	Heath	15,876
37		23	(h)	Wolves	W 2-0	Gray, Steven	17,185
38		28	(a)	Norwich C	D 1-1	Gray	13,624
39	May	5	(h)	Manchester U	D 1-1	Wakenshaw	28,817
40		7	(a)	Aston Villa	W 2-0	Richardson, Sharp	16,792
41		12	(h)	Q.P.R.	W 3-1	Heath, Sharp 2	20,679
42		14	(a)	West Ham U	W 1-0	Richardson	25,452

FINAL LEAGUE POSITION: 7th in Division One

Appearances

Sub. Appearances

Goals

Arnold	Harper	Bailey	Mountfield	Higgins	Richardson	Steven	Heath	Sharp	King	Sheedy	Johnson	Ratcliffe	Curran	Reid	Southall	Irvine	Gray	Stevens	Hughes	Rimmer S	Wakenshaw	Bishop	
1	2	3	4	5	6	7	8	9	10	11													1
1	2	3	4	5	6*	7	8	9	10	11	12												2
1	2	3		5	6	7	8*	9	10	11	12	4											3
1	2	3*		5	6	8		9		11	10	4	7	12									4
1	2	3		5	12	6	8	9		11	10	4	7*										5
1	2	3		5	12	7	8	9		11	10	4		6*									6
1	2	3		5		7*	8	9	12	11	10	4		6									7
	2	3		5		7	8	9		11		4		6	1	10							8
	2	3		5		7	8	9	10	11		4		6	1								9
	2	3		5	6	7*		9	10	11	8	4			1	12							10
	2	3		5	6	7	8	9	10	11*		4			1	12							11
	2	3		5		6	8	9	10	11		4			1	7							12
	2	3		5			8		10	11		4		6	1	7	9						13
	2	3	5				8		10	11		4		6	1	7	9						14
	2	3	5				8*		10	11		4		6	1	7	9	12					15
			4	5				9	8	11		3		6	1	7	10	2					16
	12	3	5				8		10*	11		4		6	1	7	9	2					17
	3		5				8		10	11	9	4		6	1	7		2					18
	3		5				8			11	10	4		6	1	7	9	2					19
			5		8	12				11*		4		6	1	7	9	2	3	10			20
		3	5		12		8*		10	11		4		6	1	7	9	2					21
		3	5				8		10	11		4		6	1	7	9	2					22
		3	5		2		8	9		11		4		6	1	7	10						23
	3		5		10		8	9		11		4		6	1	7		2					24
		3	5		10		8			11		4		6	1	7	9	2					25
		3	5		10		8			11		4		6	1	7	9	2					26
		3	5				8	9		11		4		6	1	7	10	2					27
	12	3	5			7*	8	9		11		4		6	1		10	2					28
	11	3	5		8			9				4		6	1	7	10	2					29
	3		5		11	12	8	9*				4		6	1	7	10	2					30
		3	5		11	7	8		10			4		6	1		9	2					31
	7*	3	5		11	12	8	9				4		6	1		10	2					32
	4	3	5		11	10	8	9					7	6	1			2					33
		3	5		11	12	8	9*				4	7	6	1		10	2					34
	3		5		11	10	8					4	7	6	1		9	2					35
	12	3	5		11	10	8	9				4	7	6*	1			2					36
		3	5		11	10	8					4	7	6	1		9	2					37
		3	5		11	10	8	12				4	7*	6	1		9	2					38
	4	3	5		11	10		9	8					6	1			2			7*	12	39
		3	5		11	10	8	9	7			4		6	1			2					40
	3		5		11	7	8	9				4		6	1		10	2					41
	3		5		11	7	8	9	10			4		6	1			2					42
7	26	33	31	14	25	23	36	27	19	28	7	38	8	34	35	19	23	26	1	1	1		
	3				3	4		1	1		2			1		2		1				1	
	1		3		4	1	12	7	2	4	1			2			5	1			1		

1984-85

1	Aug	25	(h)	Tottenham H	L 1-4	Heath (pen)	35,630
2		27	(a)	West Brom A	L 1-2	Heath (pen)	13,464
3	Sep	31	(a)	Chelsea	W 1-0	Richardson	17,734
4		4	(h)	Ipswich T	D 1-1	Heath	22,314
5		8	(h)	Coventry C	W 2-1	Sharp, Steven	20,013
6		15	(a)	Newcastle U	W 3-2	Gray, Sheedy, Steven	26,944
7		22	(h)	Southampton	D 2-2	Mountfield, Sharp	22,354
8		29	(a)	Watford	W 5-4	Heath 2, Mountfield, Sharp, Steven	18,335
9	Oct	6	(a)	Arsenal	L 0-1		37,049
10		13	(h)	Aston Villa	W 2-1	Heath, Sharp	25,089
11		20	(a)	Liverpool	W 1-0	Sharp	45,545
12		27	(h)	Manchester U	W 5-0	Heath, Sharp, Sheedy 2, Stevens	40,769
13	Nov	3	(h)	Leicester C	W 3-0	Heath, Sheedy, Steven	27,784
14		10	(a)	West Ham U	W 1-0	Heath	24,089
15		17	(h)	Stoke C	W 4-0	Heath 2, Reid, Steven	26,705
16		24	(a)	Norwich C	L 2-4	Sharp, Sheedy	16,925
17	Dec	1	(h)	Sheffield W	D 1-1	Sharp (pen)	35,440
18		8	(a)	Q.P.R.	D 0-0		14,338
19		15	(h)	Nottingham F	W 5-0	Reid, Sharp 2, Sheedy, Steven	22,487
20		22	(h)	Chelsea	L 3-4	Bracewell, Sharp 2 (1 pen)	29,887
21		26	(a)	Sunderland	W 2-1	Mountfield 2	19,714
22		29	(a)	Ipswich T	W 2-0	Sharp 2	16,045
23	Jan	1	(h)	Luton T	W 2-1	Steven 2	31,682
24		12	(h)	Newcastle U	W 4-0	Mountfield, Sharp, Sheedy 2	32,156
25	Feb	2	(h)	Watford	W 4-0	Sheedy, Stevens 2, Steven	34,026
26		23	(a)	Leicester C	W 2-1	Gray 2	17,345
27	Mar	2	(a)	Manchester U	D 1-1	Mountfield	51,150
28		16	(a)	Aston Villa	D 1-1	Richardson	22,625
29		23	(h)	Arsenal	W 2-0	Gray, Sharp	36,389
30		30	(a)	Southampton	W 2-1	Richardson 2	18,754
31	Apr	3	(a)	Tottenham H	W 2-1	Gray, Steven	48,108
32		6	(h)	Sunderland	W 4-1	Gray 2, Sharp, Steven	35,978
33		16	(h)	West Brom A	W 4-1	Atkins, Sharp 2 (1 pen), Sheedy	29,750
34		20	(a)	Stoke C	W 2-0	Sharp, Sheedy	18,285
35		27	(h)	Norwich C	W 3-0	Bracewell, Mountfield, Steven	32,085
36	May	4	(a)	Sheffield W	W 1-0	Gray	37,381
37		6	(h)	Q.P.R.	W 2-0	Mountfield, Sharp	50,514
38		8	(h)	West Ham U	W 3-0	Gray, Mountfield 2	32,657
39		11	(a)	Nottingham F	L 0-1		18,784
40		23	(h)	Liverpool	W 1-0	Wilkinson	51,045
41		26	(a)	Coventry C	L 1-4	Wilkinson	21,224
42		28	(a)	Luton T	L 0-2		11,509

FINAL LEAGUE POSITION: 1st in Division One

Appearances

Sub. Appearances

Goals

Southall	Stevens	Bailey	Ratcliffe	Mountfield	Reid	Steven	Heath	Sharp	Bracewell	Richardson	Gray	Curran	Sheedy	Van Den Hauwe	Harper	Atkins	Wilkinson	Oldroyd	Wakenshaw	Hughes	Morrissey	Danskin	Walsh	Rimmer N	
1	2	3	4	5	6	7	8	9	10	11*	12														1
1	2	3	4	5	6	10	8	9		11		7													2
1	2	3	4	5	6	7	8	9	10	11															3
1	2	3	4	5	6	7	8	9	10	11*		12													4
1	2	3	4	5	6	7	8	9	10	11*		12													5
1	2	3	4	5	6	7	8		10		9		11												6
1	2	3	4	5	6	7	8	9	10				11												7
1	2	3	4	5	6	7	8	9	10			12	11*												8
1	2		4	5	6	7	8	9	10	11				3											9
1	2		4	5	6	7	8	9	10					3	11										10
1	2		4	5	6	7	8	9	10					3	11										11
1	2		4	5	6	7	8	9	10		12		11*	3											12
1	2		4	5	6	7	8	9*	10		12		11	3											13
1	2		4	5	6	7	8	9	10				11	3											14
1	2		4	5	6	7	8	9	10				11	3											15
1	2		4	5	6	7	8	9	10		12		11	3*											16
1	2		4	5	6	7	8*	9	10		12		11	3											17
1	2		4	5	6	7		9	10		8		11	3											18
1	2		4	5	6	7		9	10		8*	12	11	3											19
1	2	3	4	5	6	7		9	10		8		11												20
1		3	4	5	6	7		9	10		8		11			2									21
1		3	4	5	6	7		9	10			8	11	2											22
1		2	4	5	6	7		9	10			8	11	3											23
1	2		4	5	6	7		9	10		8		11	3											24
1	2		4	5	6	7*		9	10		8	12	11	3											25
1	2		4	5	6	7			10		9		11	3	8										26
1	2		4	5	6	7			10		9	8	11	3											27
1	2		4	5		7		8	10	6	9			3	11										28
1	2		4	5	6	7		8		11	9			3	10										29
1	2		4	5	6	7		8*	10	11	9			3			12								30
1	2		4	5	6	7		8	10		9*		11	3	12										31
1	2	3	4	5	6	7		8	10		9		11*		12										32
1	2		4		6	7		8	10		9		11	3	12	5*									33
1	2		4		6	7		8	10		9		11	3		5									34
1	2		4	5		7		8	10	6	9			3	11										35
1	2		4	5	6	7		8	10		9		11	3											36
1	2		4	5	6	7		8	10		9		11	3											37
1	2			5	6	7		8	10	12	9*		11	3		4									38
1	2		4	5		7				6			11	3	8*	10	9	12							39
1	2	3	4							6	9		11	5	7	10*	8		12						40
1			4			7		9	10	6			11	3	2		8			5					41
1		3								6				5	4		9*		8	2	7	10	11	12	42
42	37	15	40	37	36	40	17	36	37	14	21	4	29	31	10	6	4		1	2	1	1	1		
										1	5	5			3		1	1	1					1	
	3			10	2	12	11	21	2	4	9		11			1	2								

1985-86

1	Aug	17	(a)	Leicester C	L	1-3	Mountfield	16,932
2		20	(h)	West Brom A	W	2-0	Heath 2	26,788
3		24	(h)	Coventry C	D	1-1	Sharp	27,691
4		26	(a)	Tottenham H	W	1-0	Lineker	29,720
5		31	(h)	Birmingham C	W	4-1	Lineker 3, Steven (pen)	28,066
6	Sep	3	(a)	Sheffield W	W	5-1	Mountfield, Lineker 2, Steven, Heath	30,065
7		7	(a)	Q.P.R.	L	0-3		16,544
8		14	(h)	Luton T	W	2-0	Sheedy, Sharp	26,419
9		21	(h)	Liverpool	L	2-3	Sharp, Lineker	51,509
10		28	(a)	Aston Villa	D	0-0		22,048
11	Oct	5	(h)	Oxford U	W	2-0	Sharp, Bracewell	24,553
12		12	(a)	Chelsea	L	1-2	Sheedy	27,634
13		19	(h)	Watford	W	4-1	Heath, Sharp 2, Bracewell	26,425
14		26	(a)	Manchester C	D	1-1	Heath	28,807
15	Nov	2	(a)	West Ham U	L	1-2	Steven	23,844
16		9	(h)	Arsenal	W	6-1	Lineker 2, Heath 2, Steven (pen), Sharp	28,620
17		16	(a)	Ipswich T	W	4-3	Heath, Sharp, Sheedy, Steven (pen)	13,910
18		23	(h)	Nottingham F	D	1-1	Bracewell	27,860
19		30	(a)	Southampton	W	3-2	Lineker, Heath, Steven	16,917
20	Dec	7	(a)	West Brom A	W	3-0	Sheedy, Van Den Hauwe, Lineker	12,206
21		14	(h)	Leicester C	L	1-2	Richardson	23,347
22		21	(a)	Coventry C	W	3-1	Lineker 2, Sharp	11,059
23		26	(h)	Manchester U	W	3-1	Sharp 2, Lineker	42,551
24		28	(h)	Sheffield W	W	3-1	Stevens, Lineker 2	41,536
25	Jan	1	(a)	Newcastle U	D	2-2	Steven, Sharp (pen)	27,820
26		11	(h)	Q.P.R.	W	4-3	Sharp 2 (1 pen), Lineker, Wilkinson	26,015
27		18	(a)	Birmingham C	W	2-0	Lineker 2	10,502
28	Feb	1	(h)	Tottenham H	W	1-0	Reid	33,178
29		11	(h)	Manchester C	W	4-0	Lineker 3, Sharp	30,006
30		22	(a)	Liverpool	W	2-0	Ratcliffe, Lineker	45,445
31	Mar	1	(h)	Aston Villa	W	2-0	Sharp, Lineker	32,133
32		16	(h)	Chelsea	D	1-1	Sheedy	30,145
33		22	(a)	Luton T	L	1-2	Richardson	10,949
34		29	(h)	Newcastle U	W	1-0	Richardson	41,116
35		31	(a)	Manchester U	D	0-0		51,189
36	Apr	12	(a)	Arsenal	W	1-0	Heath	28,251
37		15	(a)	Watford	W	2-0	Lineker, Sharp	18,960
38		19	(h)	Ipswich T	W	1-0	Sharp	39,055
39		26	(a)	Nottingham F	D	0-0		30,171
40		30	(a)	Oxford U	L	0-1		13,939
41	May	3	(h)	Southampton	W	6-1	Mountfield, Steven, Lineker 3, Sharp	33,057
42		5	(h)	West Ham U	W	3-1	Lineker 2, Steven (pen)	40,073

FINAL LEAGUE POSITION: 2nd in Division One

Appearances

Sub. Appearances

Goals

Southall	Stevens	Van Den Hauwe	Ratcliffe	Mountfield	Reid	Steven	Lineker	Sharp	Bracewell	Sheedy	Heath	Marshall	Harper	Atkins	Richardson	Bailey	Mimms	Pointon	Wilkinson	Billinge	Aspinall	
1	2	3	4	5	6	7	8	9	10	11*	12											1
1	2	3	4			7	8		10	11	9	5	6									2
1	2	3				7	8	9	10	11*	6	5	4	12								3
1	2	3	4			7	8	12	10	11	9*	5	6									4
1	2	3	4	5	6	7	8		10	11	9											5
1	2	3	4	5	6*	7	8	9	10	11	12											6
1	2	3	4	5	6	7	8	9	10		11											7
1	2	3	4	5		7	8	12	10	11	9*		6									8
1	2	3	4	5		7	8	9	10	11	12	5*	6									9
1	2	3	4			7	8	9	10	11		5	6									10
1	2	3	4			7	8	9	10	11		5	6									11
1	2	5	4			7	8	9	10	11	12				6*	3						12
1	2	3	4			7	8	9	10	11	6	5*	12									13
	2	5	4			7	8	9	10	11*	6		3		12		1					14
1	2	5	4			7	8	9	10	11	6		3									15
1	5		4			7	8	9	10	11	6		2					3				16
1	5	3	4			7	8	9	10	11	6		2									17
1	5	3	4			7	8	9	10	11	6		2									18
1	5	3	4			7	8		10	11	6		2						9			19
1	5	3	4			7	8		10*	11	6		2					12	9			20
1	2		4			7	8	9	10		6	5			11			3				21
1	2	5	4			7	8	9	10	11	6							3				22
1	2	5	4			7	8	9	10	11	6							3				23
1	2	5	4			7	8	9	10	11	6*		12					3				24
1	2	5	4			7	8	9	10*	11	6		12					3				25
1	2	5	4				8	9		11*	6		7		10			3	12			26
1	2	5	4			7	8	9			11		6		10			3				27
1	2	5	4		6	7	8	9	10						11			3				28
1	2	5	4		6	7	8	9	10	11*					12			3				29
1	2	5	4		6	7	8	9	10*				12		11			3				30
1	2	5	4		6	7	8	9			10				11			3				31
1	2	4		5		7	8	9	10	11	12				6*			3				32
1		4		5		7	8	9	10	11*		12	2		6			3				33
	2	3*	4	5	6	7	8	9	10		12				11		1					34
	2	3	4	5	6	7	8*	9	10		12				11		1					35
	2	3	4	5	6	7	8*	9	10		12				11		1					36
	2	3	4	5	6	7	8*	9	10		12				11		1					37
	2	3	4	5	6	7		9	10		8				11		1					38
	2	3	4	5	6	7	8	9	10	11*	12						1					39
	2	3	4	5		7	8	9	10	11	12				6*		1					40
	2	3	4	5	6	7	8	9	10*	11	12						1					41
	2	3	4			7	8*			11	10				6		1		9	5	12	42
32	41	40	39	15	15	41	41	35	38	31	24	8	17		16	1	10	14	3	1		
								2			12	1	4	1	2			1	1		1	
	1	1	1	3	1	9	30	19	3	5	10				3				1			

1986-87

1	Aug	23	(h)	Nottingham F	W	2-0	Sheedy 2	35,198
2		25	(a)	Sheffield W	D	2-2	Sharp, Langley	33,007
3		30	(a)	Coventry C	D	1-1	Marshall	13,504
4	Sep	2	(h)	Oxford U	W	3-1	Steven (pen), Harper, Langley	26,018
5		6	(h)	Q.P.R.	D	0-0		30,173
6		13	(a)	Wimbledon	W	2-1	Sheedy, Sharp	11,708
7		21	(h)	Manchester U	W	3-1	Sharp, Sheedy, Heath	25,843
8		27	(a)	Tottenham H	L	0-2		28,007
9	Oct	4	(h)	Arsenal	L	0-1		30,007
10		11	(a)	Charlton Ath	L	2-3	Sheedy 2	10,564
11		18	(a)	Southampton	W	2-0	Steven (pen), Wilkinson	18,009
12		25	(h)	Watford	W	3-2	Mountfield 2, Steven (pen)	28,577
13	Nov	2	(a)	West Ham U	L	0-1		19,094
14		8	(h)	Chelsea	D	2-2	Steven (pen), Sheedy	29,727
15		15	(a)	Leicester C	W	2-0	Heath, Sheedy	13,450
16		23	(h)	Liverpool	D	0-0		48,247
17		29	(a)	Manchester C	W	3-1	Heath 2, Power	27,097
18	Dec	6	(h)	Norwich C	W	4-0	Power, Steven (pen), Pointon, Heath	26,746
19		13	(a)	Luton T	L	0-1		11,151
20		20	(h)	Wimbledon	W	3-0	Steven, Sheedy, Heath	25,553
21		26	(a)	Newcastle U	W	4-0	Power, Steven 2, Heath	35,079
22		28	(h)	Leicester C	W	5-1	Heath 2, Wilkinson, O'Neill (og), Sheedy	39,730
23	Jan	1	(h)	Aston Villa	W	3-0	Harper, Steven, Sheedy	40,203
24		3	(a)	Q.P.R.	W	1-0	Sharp	19,297
25		17	(h)	Sheffield W	W	2-0	Steven (pen), Watson	33,011
26		25	(a)	Nottingham F	L	0-1		17,009
27	Feb	7	(h)	Coventry C	W	3-1	Stevens, Steven (pen), Heath	30,402
28		14	(a)	Oxford U	D	1-1	Wilkinson	11,878
29		28	(a)	Manchester U	D	0-0		47,421
30	Mar	8	(a)	Watford	L	1-2	Heath	14,014
31		14	(h)	Southampton	W	3-0	Wright (og), Power, Watson	26,564
32		21	(h)	Charlton Ath	W	2-1	Steven (pen), Stevens	27,291
33		28	(a)	Arsenal	W	1-0	Clarke	36,218
34	Apr	4	(a)	Chelsea	W	2-1	McLaughlin (og), Harper	21,914
35		11	(h)	West Ham U	W	4-0	Clarke, Reid, Stevens, Watson	35,731
36		18	(a)	Aston Villa	W	1-0	Sheedy	31,218
37		20	(h)	Newcastle U	W	3-0	Clarke 3	43,576
38		25	(a)	Liverpool	L	1-3	Sheedy	44,827
39	May	2	(h)	Manchester C	D	0-0		37,541
40		4	(a)	Norwich C	W	1-0	Van Den Hauwe	23,489
41		9	(h)	Luton T	W	3-1	Steven 2 (2 pens), Sharp	44,092
42		11	(h)	Tottenham H	W	1-0	Mountfield	28,287

FINAL LEAGUE POSITION: 1st in Division One

Appearances

Sub. Appearances

Goals

Mimms	Harper	Power	Ratcliffe	Watson	Langley	Steven	Heath	Sharp	Richardson	Sheedy	Wilkinson	Marshall	Adams	Mountfield	Aspinall	Southall	Pointon	Stevens	Reid	Snodin	Van Den Hauwe	Clarke	
1	2	3	4	5	6	7	8	9	10*	11	12												1
1	2	3	4	5	6	7	8	9		11	10												2
1	2	3	4	5	6*	7	8	9		11		12	10										3
1	2	3	4	5	6	7	8	9		11			10										4
1	2	3	4	5	6	7	8	9		11		12	10*										5
1	2	3	4	5	6	7	8*	9		11	12			10									6
1		3	4	5	6	7	8	9		11*	10		12	2									7
1		3	4	5	6	7	8	9		11*	10		12	2									8
1		3	4	5	6	7		9		11	10		8	2*	12								9
1	2	3	4	5	6*	8	10	9		11	12		7										10
1	2	3	4	5*	11	7	8	9			10			6	12								11
	2	3	4		6	10	8	9			11		7	5		1							12
	2	3	4		6*	7	8	9		11	10			5	12	1							13
	2	3	4		6	7	8	9		11	10			5		1							14
	2	3	4		6	7*	8	9		11			10	5	12	1							15
	2	3	4		6*	7	8	9		11	12		10	5		1							16
	2	6*	4			7	8	9		11	12		10	5		1	3						17
	10	6	4	5		7	8	9*		11	12					1	3	2					18
	10	6	4	5		7	8	9		11	12					1	3*	2					19
	10	6	4	5		7	8	9		11						1	3*	2	12				20
	10	6	4	5		7	8	9*		11	12					1	3	2					21
	10	6*	4	5		7	8			11	9				12	1	3	2					22
	10	6*	4	5		7	8			11	9				12	1	3	2					23
	10	6	4	5		7	8	9		11						1	3	2					24
	10	6	4	5*		7	8	9		11						1	3	2		12			25
	10	3*	4			7	8			11	9			5		1	12	2		6			26
	12	11	4	5		7	8	9*								1		2	6	10	3		27
	12	11	4	5		7	8				9					1		2	6	10	3*		28
	8	11	4	5		7	8				12					1		2	6*	10	3		29
		11	4	5		7	8				12					1		2	6	10	3*	9	30
	12	11	4	5		7	8									1		2	6*	10	3	9	31
	12	11	4	5		7	8									1		2	6	10	3*	9	32
	12	11	4	5		7	8									1		2	6	10	3	9*	33
	10	3	4	5		7	8			11*						1	12	2	6			9	34
	10	3	4	5		7	8			11						1		2	6			9	35
	12	3	4	5		7	8			11*						1		2	6	10		9	36
	6	11	4	5		7	8									1	3	2		10		9	37
		3	4	5		7	8			11						1		2	6	10		9	38
	12	11	4	5		7	8									1		2	6*	10	3	9	39
		11	4	5		7	8	9								1		2	6	10	3		40
	11		4	5		7	8	9								1		2	6	10	3		41
	7		4	5			8*	9					11	12		1		2	6	10	3		42
11	29	40	42	35	16	41	41	27	1	28	12		10	12		31	10	25	15	15	10	10	
	7										10	2	2	1	6		2		1	1			
	3	4		3	2	14	11	5		13	3	1		3			1	3	1		1	5	

1987-88

1	Aug	15	(h)	Norwich C	W 1-0	Power	31,728
2		18	(a)	Wimbledon	D 1-1	Sharp	7,763
3		22	(a)	Nottingham F	D 0-0		20,445
4		29	(h)	Sheffield W	W 4-0	Clarke 2, Steven 2 (1 pen)	29,649
5	Sep	2	(a)	Q.P.R.	L 0-1		15,380
6		5	(h)	Tottenham H	D 0-0		32,389
7		12	(a)	Luton T	L 1-2	Pointon	8,124
8		19	(h)	Manchester U	W 2-1	Clarke 2	38,439
9		26	(h)	Coventry C	L 1-2	Clarke	28,153
10	Oct	3	(a)	Southampton	W 4-0	Sharp 4	15,719
11		10	(h)	Chelsea	W 4-1	Sharp 2, Heath 2	32,004
12		17	(a)	Newcastle U	D 1-1	Snodin	20,266
13		24	(h)	Watford	W 2-0	Heath, Sharp	28,501
14	Nov	1	(a)	Liverpool	L 0-2		44,760
15		14	(h)	West Ham U	W 3-1	Watson, Reid, Sharp	29,405
16		21	(a)	Portsmouth	W 1-0	Sharp	17,724
17		28	(h)	Oxford U	D 0-0		25,443
18	Dec	5	(a)	Charlton Ath	D 0-0		7,208
19		12	(h)	Derby Co	W 3-0	Snodin, Steven (pen), Heath	26,224
20		19	(a)	Arsenal	D 1-1	Watson	34,857
21		26	(h)	Luton T	W 2-0	Heath 2	32,242
22		28	(a)	Manchester U	L 1-2	Watson	47,024
23	Jan	1	(a)	Sheffield W	L 0-1		26,443
24		3	(h)	Nottingham F	W 1-0	Clarke	21,680
25		16	(a)	Norwich C	W 3-0	Sharp 2, Heath	15,750
26	Feb	13	(h)	Q.P.R.	W 2-0	Parker (og), Pointon	24,724
27		27	(h)	Southampton	W 1-0	Power	20,764
28	Mar	5	(h)	Newcastle U	W 1-0	Clarke	25,674
29		9	(a)	Tottenham H	L 1-2	Fenwick (og)	18,662
30		12	(a)	Chelsea	D 0-0		17,390
31		20	(h)	Liverpool	W 1-0	Clarke	44,162
32		26	(a)	Watford	W 2-1	Sheedy, Clarke	13,503
33		29	(h)	Wimbledon	D 2-2	Steven (pen), Pointon	20,351
34	Apr	4	(a)	West Ham U	D 0-0		21,195
35		9	(h)	Portsmouth	W 2-1	Heath, Steven	21,292
36		19	(a)	Coventry C	W 2-1	Sharp, Heath	15,641
37		23	(a)	Oxford U	D 1-1	Clarke	7,619
38		30	(h)	Charlton Ath	D 1-1	Steven (pen)	20,372
39	May	2	(a)	Derby Co	D 0-0		17,974
40		7	(h)	Arsenal	L 1-2	Watson	22,445

FINAL LEAGUE POSITION: 4th in Division One

Appearances
Sub. Appearances
Goals

Mimms	Van Den Hauwe	Pointon	Ratcliffe	Watson	Harper	Steven	Clarke	Sharp	Adams	Power	Marshall	Mountfield	Reid	Snodin	Sheedy	Heath	Southall	Wilson	Stevens	Jones	
1	2	3	4	5	6	7	8	9	10	11											1
1	2	3	4	5	6		8	9	7	11	10*	12									2
1	2	3	4	5	7		8	9*		11	12		6	10							3
1		3	4	5	2	7	8	9		11*			6	10	12						4
1		3	4	5	2	7	8*	9		11†		12	6	10	14						5
1	3	11	4	5	2	7	8*	9					6	10		12					6
	3	11*	4	5	2	7			9†		14	12	6	10		8	1				7
	3	11	4	5	2	7	9						6	10		8	1				8
	2*	3	4	5	6†	7	8	9				14		10		12	1	11			9
	3		4	5	12	7	8†	9					6	10		14	1	11*	2		10
1	3		4	5		7		9					6	10		8		11	2		11
1	3		4	5	12	7		9					6	10		8		11	2*		12
		3	4	5		7		9					6	10		8	1	11	2		13
	3		4	5		7	8*	9				12	6	10			1	11	2		14
	3		4	5	12	7*		9					6	10	11†	8	1	14	2		15
	3	12	4	5	7		14	9					6	10	11†	8*	1		2		16
	3		4	5		7		9					6	10*	11	8	1	12	2		17
		3	4	5		7		9	12				6	10	11	8*	1		2		18
		3	4	5		7		9					6	10	11	8	1		2		19
		3	4	5		7		9					6	10	11*	8	1	12	2		20
		3	4	5		7		9					6	10		8	1	11	2		21
		3	4	5		7	12	9					6	10		8	1	11*	2		22
		3	4	5		7	12	9					6	10		8*	1	11	2		23
	3		4	5		7	9						6	10		8	1	11	2		24
	4	3		5	12	7		9					6*	10		8	1	11	2		25
	4	3		5	12	7†		9		11	14		6	10*		8	1		2		26
		3		5	4		8	9	7*	11				10		6	1		2	12	27
	4	3		5	6	7	8	9	10						11		1		2		28
	4	3		5	6	7	8	9	10†	14					11	12	1		2*		29
	4	3		5	6	7	8	9		10					11		1		2		30
	4	3		5	10	7	8*	9		14			6		11†	12	1		2		31
	4	3			6	7	8	9		10		5			11		1		2		32
		3			4	7	8			10		5	6		11	9	1		2		33
	4	3			10	7	8*					5	6	12	11	9	1		2		34
	4	3		5	10	7							6	8	11	9	1		2		35
	4	3		5		7	8	9					6	10*		12	1	11	2		36
	4	3		5	14	7	8	9					6	12		10†	1	11*	2		37
	4	3		5	10	7	9		11				6			8	1		2		38
		3		5	8	7	9			11		4	6	10			1		2		39
	4	3		5	12	7	8*	9		11			6	10†	14		1		2		40
8	28	32	24	37	21	36	24	32	7	12	1	4	32	29	14	23	32	13	31		
		1			7		3		1	2	3	5		2	3	6		3		1	
		3		4		6	10	13		2			1	2	1	9					

1988-89

1	Aug	27	(h)	Newcastle U	W	4-0	Cottee 3, Sharp	41,560
2	Sep	3	(a)	Coventry C	W	1-0	Cottee	18,625
3		10	(h)	Nottingham F	D	1-1	Heath	34,003
4		17	(a)	Millwall	L	1-2	McLeary (og)	17,507
5		24	(h)	Luton T	L	0-2		26,017
6	Oct	1	(a)	Wimbledon	L	1-2	Heath	6,367
7		8	(h)	Southampton	W	4-1	Cottee 2, Watson, Steven	25,356
8		22	(a)	Aston Villa	L	0-2		26,636
9		30	(h)	Manchester U	D	1-1	Cottee	27,005
10	Nov	5	(a)	Sheffield W	D	1-1	Steven (pen)	21,761
11		12	(a)	Charlton Ath	W	2-1	Sharp, Reid	8,627
12		19	(h)	Norwich C	D	1-1	Steven (pen)	28,118
13		26	(a)	West Ham U	W	1-0	Steven	22,176
14	Dec	3	(h)	Tottenham H	W	1-0	Cottee	29,657
15		11	(a)	Liverpool	D	1-1	Clarke (pen)	42,372
16		17	(a)	Q.P.R.	D	0-0		10,067
17		26	(h)	Middlesbrough	W	2-1	Steven, Cottee	32,651
18		31	(h)	Coventry C	W	3-1	Sheedy 2, Bracewell	30,790
19	Jan	2	(a)	Nottingham F	L	0-2		26,008
20		14	(h)	Arsenal	L	1-3	Watson	34,825
21		21	(a)	Luton T	L	0-1		9,013
22	Feb	4	(h)	Wimbledon	D	1-1	Sharp (pen)	23,365
23		11	(a)	Southampton	D	1-1	Sheedy	15,845
24		14	(h)	Aston Villa	D	1-1	Cottee	20,142
25		25	(a)	Derby Co	L	2-3	Sharp, Clarke	17,103
26	Mar	11	(h)	Sheffield W	W	1-0	Cottee	22,542
27		22	(a)	Newcastle U	L	0-2		20,933
28		25	(h)	Millwall	D	1-1	Sheedy	27,062
29		27	(a)	Middlesbrough	D	3-3	Cottee, Sheedy, Nevin	31,351
30	Apr	1	(h)	Q.P.R.	W	4-1	Clarke, Sheedy (pen), Cottee, Steven	23,028
31		8	(a)	Arsenal	L	0-2		37,608
32		10	(h)	Charlton Ath	W	3-2	Sharp, Sheedy, Nevin	16,316
33		22	(a)	Tottenham H	L	1-2	McDonald	28,568
34	May	3	(h)	Liverpool	D	0-0		45,994
35		6	(a)	Norwich C	L	0-1		13,239
36		10	(a)	Manchester U	W	2-1	Sharp 2	26,722
37		13	(h)	West Ham U	W	3-1	Sheedy, Watson, Bracewell	21,694
38		15	(h)	Derby Co	W	1-0	Wilson	17,826

FINAL LEAGUE POSITION: 8th in Division One

Appearances

Sub. Appearances

Goals

Southall	McDonald	Pointon	Snodin	Watson	Reid	Steven	McCall	Sharp	Cottee	Nevin	Sheedy	Heath	Wilson	Clarke	Van Den Hauwe	Ratcliffe	Bracewell	Ebbrell	
1	2	3	4	5	6	7*	8	9	10	11	12								1
1	2	3	4	5	6		8	9	10	7	11								2
1	2	3	4	5	6		8	9	10	7*	11†	12	14						3
1	2	3	4	5	6		8*	9	10		11†	7		12	14				4
1	2*		4	5	6		8	9	10		11	7	3	12					5
1	2	3	4		6		8	9	10		11	7			5				6
1			2	5	6	11	8	9	10			7			3	4			7
1		12	2	5	6	11†	8	9	10			7	14		3*	4			8
1			2	5	6	11	8	9	10			7*	12		3	4			9
1			2	5	6	7	8	9	10				11		3	4			10
1			2	5	6	7	8	9	10				11		3	4			11
1			2	5	6	7	8	9	10				11		3	4			12
1			2	5	6	7	8	9	10				11		3	4			13
1			2	5		7	8	9*	10				11	12	3	4	6		14
1			2	5	12	7	8		10				11	9	3	4	6*		15
1			2	5		7	8		10	11*	12			9	3	4	6		16
1		3	2	5	14	7	8		10*	9	11†			12	4		6		17
1		12	2	5	8	7			10	9	11				3*	4	6		18
1		3	2	5	8	7			10	9*	11		12			4	6		19
1	14	3	2	5	8*		12		10	7	11†			9		4	6		20
1	14	3	2	5			8†		10	7*	11		12	9		4	6		21
1	2			5		6	8	9	10	7			11*		3	4		12	22
1	2			5		7	8	9	10†	14	11		6*	12	3	4			23
1	2			5		7	8	9	10	12	11				3*	4	6		24
1	2	3	6	5		7	8	9*		12	11			10		4			25
1	14	3	2†	5		7	8		10	12	11*			9		4	6		26
1	2	3				7	8*	9	10†	14	11			12	5	4	6		27
1	2	3				7	14	9	12	8	11†			10*	5	4	6		28
1	2	3				7			10*	8	11		12	9	5	4	6		29
1	2	3		5		7			10	8	11			9		4	6		30
1	2	3				7*	5		10	8	11			9	4		6	12	31
1	2	3					8	9		7*	11			10	5	4	6	12	32
1	2			5		8	14	9	10	7	11†			12	3	4	6*		33
1	2			5		8	12	9	10	7	11*				3	4	6		34
1	2	3		5		8	7		10		11			9		4	6		35
1	2	12		5		8	6	9	10	7			11		3*	4			36
1	2	3		5		8		9	10	7	11*		12			4	6		37
1	2	3		5			6	9*	10	7			11	12		4		8	38
38	22	20	23	32	16	29	29	26	35	20	24	6	11	12	24	30	20	1	
	3	3			2		4		1	5	2	1	7	8	1			3	
	1			3	1	6		7	13	2	8	2	1	3			2		

1989-90

1	Aug	19	(a)	Coventry C	L 0-2		17,981
2		22	(h)	Tottenham H	W 2-1	Newell, Sheedy	34,402
3		26	(h)	Southampton	W 3-0	Whiteside, Newell, McCall	27,807
4		30	(a)	Sheffield W	D 1-1	Sheedy	19,657
5	Sep	9	(h)	Manchester U	W 3-2	Newell, Nevin, Sharp	37,916
6		16	(a)	Charlton Ath	W 1-0	Newell	11,491
7		23	(h)	Liverpool	L 1-3	Newell	42,453
8		30	(a)	Crystal Palace	L 1-2	Newell	15,943
9	Oct	14	(h)	Millwall	W 2-1	Sheedy (pen), Whiteside	26,125
10		21	(h)	Arsenal	W 3-0	Nevin 2, McDonald	32,917
11		28	(a)	Norwich C	D 1-1	Cottee	18,627
12	Nov	5	(a)	Aston Villa	L 2-6	Cottee, McGrath (og)	17,637
13		11	(h)	Chelsea	L 0-1		33,737
14		18	(h)	Wimbledon	D 1-1	Sheedy (pen)	21,561
15		25	(a)	Nottingham F	L 0-1		20,709
16	Dec	2	(h)	Coventry C	W 2-0	McCall, Watson	21,171
17		9	(a)	Tottenham H	L 1-2	Cottee	29,374
18		17	(h)	Manchester C	D 0-0		21,737
19		26	(a)	Derby Co	W 1-0	McCall	21,314
20		30	(a)	Q.P.R.	L 0-1		11,683
21	Jan	1	(h)	Luton T	W 2-1	Whiteside, Sharp	21,743
22		13	(a)	Southampton	D 2-2	Whiteside 2	19,381
23		20	(h)	Sheffield W	W 2-0	Sheedy 2	25,545
24	Feb	3	(a)	Liverpool	L 1-2	Sharp	38,370
25		10	(h)	Charlton Ath	W 2-1	Cottee, Whiteside	21,442
26	Mar	3	(a)	Wimbledon	L 1-3	Sheedy	6,512
27		14	(a)	Manchester U	D 0-0		37,398
28		17	(h)	Crystal Palace	W 4-0	Sharp, Cottee 2, Whiteside	19,274
29		21	(a)	Millwall	W 2-1	Pointon, Cottee	11,495
30		24	(h)	Norwich C	W 3-1	Cottee 2, Sharp	21,707
31		31	(a)	Arsenal	L 0-1		35,223
32	Apr	4	(h)	Nottingham F	W 4-0	Cottee 2, Whiteside 2	17,795
33		7	(h)	Q.P.R.	W 1-0	Cottee (pen)	19,887
34		14	(a)	Luton T	D 2-2	Cottee, Sharp	9,538
35		16	(h)	Derby Co	W 2-1	Atteveld, Sharp	23,933
36		21	(a)	Manchester C	L 0-1		32,144
37		28	(a)	Chelsea	L 1-2	Nevin	18,879
38	May	5	(h)	Aston Villa	D 3-3	Cascarino (og), Newell, Sheedy (pen)	29,551

FINAL LEAGUE POSITION : 6th in Division One

Appearances

Sub. Appearances

Goals

Southall	Snodin	Pointon	Ratcliffe	Watson	Whiteside	Nevin	McCall	Sharp	Newell	Sheedy	Cottee	Ebbrell	Keown	McDonald	Rehn	Beagrie	Atteveld	Wright	
1	2	3	4	5	6	7	8	9	10*	11	12								1
1	2	3	4	5	6	7	8	9	10	11									2
1	2	3	4	5	6	7	8	9*	10	11		12							3
1	2	3	4	5*	6	7	8		9	11	10†		12	14					4
1	2	3	4	5	6*	7	8	9	10	11				12					5
1	2	3	4	5		7*	8	9	10	11				12	6				6
1	2	3*	4	5	6†	7	8	9	10	11				12	14				7
1	2		4	5	6*	7	8	9	10	11				3	12				8
1	2†			5	6	7		12	9	11	10	8	4	3	14*				9
1				5	6	7	8		9	11	10	2	4	3					10
1				5	6	7	8		9	11	10	2	4	3					11
1				5†	6*	7	8	12	9	11	10	2	4	3		14			12
1		3				7	8	12	9	11	10*	2	4	5		6			13
1	7	3					8	9	10	11		2	4	5		6			14
1	6	3†		5			8	9	10	11	12	14	4	2		7*			15
1			4	5			8	9		11	10	6		3		7	2		16
1			4	5			8	9	12	11	10	6*		3		7	2		17
1			4	5			8	9	12	11	10	6*		3		7	2		18
1	2		4	5		14	8	9	12	11	10*			3		7	6†		19
1	2		4	5		14	8	9	12	11	10*			3		7	6†		20
1	2		4	5	6	7	8	9	10					3		11*	12		21
1	2		4		6	12	8	9	10	11			5	3		7*			22
1	2		4		6	7	8	9	10	11			5	3					23
1	2		4	5	6	7*	8	9	12	11			10	3					24
1	2		4	12	6	7	8	9		11	10		5	3*					25
1	2		4	5	12		8	9	14	11	10†		7	3*			6		26
1	2	3	4		6		8	9		11*	10		5			12	7		27
1	2	3	4		6	12	8	9		11	10		5				7*		28
1	2	3	4		6		8	9		11	10		5			12	7*		29
1	2	3	4†		6	14	8	9		11*	10		5			12	7		30
1	2	3		5	6	7	8	9		11*	10		4†	14		12			31
1	2†	3*		5	6	14	8	9		12	10			4		11	7		32
1					6	7*	8	9		12	10	3		4		11	2	5	33
1				5		7	8	9		6	10	3		4		11	2		34
1				5	6	7	8	9		12	10	3		4		11*	2		35
1		3		5	6	7	8	9*		11	10	12		4			2		36
1		3		5	6†	14	8		9	11	10	12	4	2			7*		37
1		3	4	5†		7	8		9	12	10	11*	2	6			14		38
38	25	19	24	28	26	23	37	30	20	33	25	13	19	26	1	14	16	1	
				1	1	7		3	6	4	2	4	1	5	3	5	2		
		1		1	9	4	3	6	7	9	13			1			1		

1990-91

1	Aug	25	(h)	Leeds U	L	2-3	Nevin, Ebbrell	34,412
2		29	(a)	Coventry C	L	1-3	Nevin	12,902
3	Sep	1	(a)	Manchester C	L	0-1		31,456
4		8	(h)	Arsenal	D	1-1	Newell	29,919
5		15	(a)	Sunderland	D	2-2	Sharp, Newell	25,004
6		22	(h)	Liverpool	L	2-3	Hinchcliffe, McCall	39,847
7		29	(h)	Southampton	W	3-0	Cottee 2, Ebbrell	23,093
8	Oct	7	(a)	Nottingham F	L	1-3	McDonald	25,790
9		20	(h)	Crystal Palace	D	0-0		24,504
10		27	(a)	Luton T	D	1-1	Nevin	10,047
11	Nov	3	(h)	Q.P.R.	W	3-0	Newell, Nevin, McDonald	22,352
12		10	(a)	Sheffield U	D	0-0		21,447
13		18	(h)	Tottenham H	D	1-1	McCall	28,716
14		24	(a)	Wimbledon	L	1-2	Sheedy (pen)	6,411
15	Dec	1	(h)	Manchester U	L	0-1		32,400
16		8	(h)	Coventry C	W	1-0	McCall	17,472
17		16	(a)	Leeds U	L	0-2		27,775
18		22	(a)	Norwich C	L	0-1		14,294
19		26	(h)	Aston Villa	W	1-0	Sharp	27,804
20		29	(h)	Derby Co	W	2-0	Newell, Nevin	25,361
21	Jan	1	(a)	Chelsea	W	2-1	Sharp, Cundy (og)	18,351
22		13	(h)	Manchester C	W	2-0	Beagrie, Sheedy	22,774
23		19	(a)	Arsenal	L	0-1		35,349
24	Feb	2	(h)	Sunderland	W	2-0	Sheedy, Beagrie	23,124
25		9	(a)	Liverpool	L	1-3	Nevin	25,116
26		23	(h)	Sheffield U	L	1-2	Cottee	28,148
27	Mar	2	(a)	Manchester U	W	2-0	Newell, Watson	45,656
28		16	(a)	Southampton	W	4-3	Watson, Milligan, Newell, Cottee	15,410
29		23	(h)	Nottingham F	D	0-0		23,078
30		30	(a)	Aston Villa	D	2-2	Warzycha 2	27,660
31	Apr	1	(h)	Norwich C	W	1-0	Newell	20,485
32		10	(h)	Wimbledon	L	1-2	Cottee	14,590
33		13	(h)	Chelsea	D	2-2	Cottee, Ebbrell	19,526
34		20	(a)	Crystal Palace	D	0-0		16,439
35		24	(a)	Tottenham H	D	3-3	Nevin, Stewart (og), Cottee	21,675
36	May	4	(h)	Luton T	W	1-0	Cottee	19,809
37		8	(a)	Derby Co	W	3-2	Cottee 2, Sheedy	12,403
38		11	(a)	Q.P.R.	D	1-1	Nevin	12,508
FINAL LEAGUE POSITION: 9th in Division One								Appearances
								Sub. Appearances
								Goals

Southall	McDonald	Hinchcliffe	Keown	Watson	Milligan	Nevin	McCall	Sharp	Newell	Ebbrell	Sheedy	Atteveld	Ratcliffe	Whiteside	Cottee	Beagrie	Snodin	Youds	Warzycha	Barlow	Jenkins	
1	2	3	4	5	6	7	8*	9	10	11	12											1
1	2*	3	4	5	8	7		9	10	6		11†	12	14								2
1		3	2	5	6	7		9	10	8	11*	12	4									3
1		3		5	6	7	8*	9	10	11		2	4		12							4
1		3		5	6	7	8	9	10	11		2	4									5
1	14	3		5	6†	7	8	9	10*	11		2	4		12							6
1	6	3		5		7	8	9*	12	11		2	4		10							7
1	6	3		5		7*	8	9	12	11		2	4		10							8
1	6	3†	14	5		7	8	9	12	11		2	4*		10							9
1	6		3	5		7	8	9		11		2	4		10							10
1	6		3	5		7	8		9	10		2	4			11						11
1	6		3	5		7	8		9	11	10*	2	4			12						12
1	6†		5			14	8	9	12	3	11	2	4		10		7*					13
1	2		5			14	8	9*	10	3	11	7	4	6†	12							14
1	2		5			7	8	12	9	3*	11	6	4		10							15
1	2		3	5	6	7	8	12	9	14	11†		4		10*							16
1	2		3	5		14	8	9†	10	6*		7	4		12	11						17
1	2	11	3†	5		7		12	9	6		8	4		10*			14				18
1	8	3	14	5		7*		9	12	6	10		4			11†		2				19
1	2	3		5		7	8	9	12	6	10		4			11*						20
1	2	3		5		7	8	9		6	10		4			11						21
1	2	3		5		7	8	9		6	10		4		12	11*						22
1	2		14	5†	6*	7	8	9		3	10		4		12	11						23
1	2			5	6*	7	8	9		3	10		4		12	11						24
1	2			5	6	7	8	9		3	10		4		12	11*						25
1	2	3	6	5	7	14	8	9*	12	11			4†		10							26
1	2	3	6	5		7†	8	9*	10	11		14	4		12							27
1	2		6	5	11	7*	8		9	3		14	4		10†	12						28
1	14		2	5†	6	11*		9	12	3	8		4		10				7			29
1	2	3	5		6	12	8	9			11*		4		10				7			30
1	2	3	5		6	12	8		9	14	11†				10			4	7*			31
1	2†	3		5	6*	9	8						4		10	11		14	7	12		32
1			4	5		7	8		9*	6	11		3		10			2		12		33
1			4	5†		7	8		9	6	11		3		10*	14		2	12			34
1		3	5			9	8			6	12		4		10	11		2*	7			35
1		3		5			8		9	2		6	4		10	11			7			36
1				5		9	8		12	3	6	2	4		10	11			7*			37
1				5†	12	7	8		9	2	6		4		10*	11		14			3	38
38	27	21	21	32	16	31	33	24	20	34	20	17	35	1	20	14	1	5	7		1	
	2		3		1	6		3	9	2	2	3	1	1	9	3		3	1	2		
	2	1		2	1	8	3	3	7	3	4				10	2			2			

1991-92

1	Aug	17	(a)	Nottingham F	L 1-2	Pearce (og)	24,422
2		20	(h)	Arsenal	W 3-1	Ward 2, Cottee	31,200
3		24	(h)	Manchester U	D 0-0		36,085
4		28	(a)	Sheffield W	L 1-2	Watson	28,690
5		31	(a)	Liverpool	L 1-3	Newell	39,072
6	Sep	3	(h)	Norwich C	D 1-1	Ward	19,197
7		7	(h)	Crystal Palace	D 2-2	Warzycha, Beardsley	21,065
8		14	(a)	Sheffield U	L 1-2	Beardsley	19,817
9		17	(a)	Manchester C	W 1-0	Beardsley	27,509
10		21	(h)	Coventry C	W 3-0	Beardsley 3 (1 pen)	20,542
11		28	(a)	Chelsea	D 2-2	Ebbrell, Beardsley	19,038
12	Oct	5	(h)	Tottenham H	W 3-1	Cottee 3 (1 pen)	29,505
13		19	(h)	Aston Villa	L 0-2		27,688
14		26	(a)	Q.P.R.	L 1-3	Cottee	10,002
15	Nov	2	(a)	Luton T	W 1-0	Warzycha	8,022
16		16	(h)	Wimbledon	W 2-0	Cottee (pen), Watson	18,762
17		23	(h)	Notts Co	W 1-0	Cottee	24,230
18		30	(a)	Leeds U	L 0-1		30,043
19	Dec	7	(h)	West Ham U	W 4-0	Cottee, Beagrie, Beardsley, Johnston	21,563
20		14	(a)	Oldham Ath	D 2-2	Sheedy, Nevin	14,955
21		21	(a)	Arsenal	L 2-4	Warzycha, Johnston	29,684
22		26	(h)	Sheffield W	L 0-1		30,788
23		28	(h)	Liverpool	D 1-1	Johnston	37,681
24	Jan	1	(a)	Southampton	W 2-1	Ward, Beardsley	16,546
25		11	(a)	Manchester U	L 0-1		46,619
26		19	(h)	Nottingham F	D 1-1	Watson	17,717
27	Feb	2	(a)	Aston Villa	D 0-0		17,451
28		8	(h)	Q.P.R.	D 0-0		18,212
29		23	(h)	Leeds U	D 1-1	Jackson	19,248
30		29	(a)	West Ham U	W 2-0	Johnston, Ablett	20,976
31	Mar	7	(h)	Oldham Ath	W 2-1	Beardsley 2	21,014
32		10	(a)	Wimbledon	D 0-0		3,569
33		14	(h)	Luton T	D 1-1	Johnston	16,707
34		17	(a)	Notts Co	D 0-0		7,480
35		21	(a)	Norwich C	L 3-4	Johnston 2, Beardsley	11,900
36	Apr	1	(h)	Southampton	L 0-1		15,201
37		4	(a)	Crystal Palace	L 0-2		14,338
38		11	(h)	Sheffield U	L 0-2		18,285
39		18	(a)	Coventry C	W 1-0	Beagrie	14,669
40		20	(h)	Manchester C	L 1-2	Nevin	21,101
41		25	(a)	Tottenham H	D 3-3	Beardsley 2, Unsworth	34,630
42	May	2	(h)	Chelsea	W 2-1	Beardsley (pen), Beagrie	20,163

FINAL LEAGUE POSITION: 13th in Division One

Appearances

Sub. Appearances

Goals

Southall	Harper	Ebbrell	Ratcliffe	Watson	Keown	Warzycha	Sheedy	Beardsley	Cottee	Ward	McDonald	Nevin	Newell	Hinchcliffe	Atteveld	Jackson	Beagrie	Johnston	Ablett	Barlow	Jenkins	Unsworth	
1	2	3	4	5	6	7†	8	9	10	11*	12	14											1
1	2	3	4	5	6	7	8	9	10	11*		12											2
1	2	3	4	5	6	7*	8	9	10†	11		12	14										3
1	2	3	4	5	6	7*	8	9	10†	11	12		14										4
1	2	3	12	5	6*	14	11	8	10†	7	4		9										5
1	2	6	4	5		7	10	8		11			9	3									6
1	2†	3	4	5	6	7*	10	8		11		12	9	14									7
1		4		5	6	7	10	8	12	11*			9	3	2								8
1		4		5	6	7*	10	8		11	12		9	3	2								9
1		4		5	6	7	10*	8		11	12		9	3	2								10
1		4		5	6	7*	10	8	12			11	9	3	2								11
1	2	4	3	5	6	7	10†	8	9	11*			12		14								12
1	10	4	3*	5	6	7	11†	8	9				12		14	2							13
1		4		5	6	7*	10	8	9	11†			12	3	14	2							14
1		4		5	6	14		8	12			7*	9	3	10	2†	11						15
1	10	4		5	6			8	9	7				3		2	11						16
1	14	4		5	6	12		8	10	7				3		2	11*	9†					17
1	3	4		5	6	12		8	10	7*					9	2	11						18
1		4		5	6	12		8	10	7*				3		2	11	9					19
1	12	4		5	6	7†	10*	8				14		3		2	11	9					20
1	3	4		5		7	10*	8	12			14			2	6	11†	9					21
1	3	4		5	6	7*		8	10	11						2	12	9					22
1	3	4		5	6	7*		8		10		12				2	11	9					23
1	3	4		5	6	7*		8		10		12			14	2	11†	9					24
1	3	4		5	6	7†		8	12	10					14	2	11*	9					25
1	10	4		5	6	7*		8	12	11						2†	14	9	3				26
1		4		5	6	12		8*	10	11		7				2	9		3				27
1	10*	4		5	6	12		8		7		14				2	11	9†	3				28
1		4		5	6	7†		8	10*	11				14		2	12	9	3				29
1	14	4		5	6			8	10†	7				11		2*	12	9	3				30
1	10	4		5	6*			8		7				11		2	12	9	3				31
1	14	4		5	6	10†		8		7				11		2	12	9*	3				32
1	10	4		5	6	12		8		7				14		2†	11	9*	3				33
1	10	4		5†	6	12		8		7				11*		2	14	9	3				34
1	10	4			6	7		8		11					5	2		9	3*	12			35
1	3	4			6	7*		8	12	10						2	11	9	5				36
1	3	4			6	7*		8		10						2	11	9	5	12			37
1	2	4			6*			8	10†	7		14				5	11	9	3	12			38
1	10			5	6			8		4		7				2	11	9*	3	12			39
1	3	4			6	12		8		10		7*				2†	11		5	9	14		40
1	4					2		8		10		7				6	11		5	9	3*	12	41
1	4†				6	12		8		10		7				2	11		5	9*	14	3	42
42	29	39	8	35	39	26	16	42	17	37	1	7	8	15	8	30	20	21	17	3	1	1	
	4		1			11			7		4	10	5	3	5		7			4	2	1	
		1		3		3	1	15	8	4		2	1			1	3	7	1			1	

1992-93

1	Aug	15	(h)	Sheffield W	D 1-1	Horne	27,687
2		19	(a)	Manchester U	W 3-0	Beardsley, Warzycha, Johnston	31,901
3		22	(a)	Norwich C	D 1-1	Beardsley	14,150
4		25	(h)	Aston Villa	W 1-0	Johnston	22,372
5		29	(h)	Wimbledon	D 0-0		18,118
6	Sep	5	(a)	Tottenham H	L 1-2	Beardsley	26,503
7		12	(h)	Manchester U	L 0-2		30,002
8		15	(a)	Blackburn R	W 3-2	Cottee 2, Ebbrell	19,563
9		19	(h)	Crystal Palace	L 0-2		18,080
10		26	(a)	Leeds U	L 0-2		27,915
11	Oct	4	(a)	Oldham Ath	L 0-1		13,013
12		17	(h)	Coventry C	D 1-1	Beagrie	17,587
13		24	(a)	Arsenal	L 0-2		28,052
14		31	(h)	Manchester C	L 1-3	Brightwell (og)	20,242
15	Nov	7	(a)	Nottingham F	W 1-0	Rideout	20,941
16		21	(h)	Chelsea	L 0-1		17,418
17		28	(a)	Ipswich T	L 0-1		18,034
18	Dec	7	(h)	Liverpool	W 2-1	Johnston, Beardsley	35,826
19		12	(a)	Sheffield U	L 0-1		16,266
20		19	(h)	Southampton	W 2-1	Beardsley (pen), Rideout	14,051
21		26	(h)	Middlesbrough	D 2-2	Rideout, Beardsley (pen)	24,391
22		28	(a)	Q.P.R.	L 2-4	Barlow 2	14,802
23	Jan	9	(a)	Crystal Palace	W 2-0	Jackson, Beardsley	13,227
24		16	(h)	Leeds U	W 2-0	Cottee 2	21,031
25		26	(a)	Wimbledon	W 3-1	Cottee 2, Snodin	3,039
26		30	(h)	Norwich C	L 0-1		20,301
27	Feb	6	(a)	Sheffield W	L 1-3	Cottee	24,979
28		10	(h)	Tottenham H	L 1-2	Sansom	16,164
29		20	(a)	Aston Villa	L 1-2	Beardsley (pen)	32,913
30		27	(h)	Oldham Ath	D 2-2	Beardsley (pen), Barlow	18,025
31	Mar	3	(h)	Blackburn R	W 2-1	Hendry (og), Cottee	18,086
32		7	(a)	Coventry C	W 1-0	Ward	11,285
33		10	(a)	Chelsea	L 1-2	Kenny	12,739
34		13	(h)	Nottingham F	W 3-0	Cottee 2, Hinchcliffe	21,271
35		20	(a)	Liverpool	L 0-1		44,619
36		24	(h)	Ipswich T	W 3-0	Barlow, Jackson, Cottee	15,638
37	Apr	10	(a)	Middlesbrough	W 2-1	Watson, Radosavljevic	16,627
38		12	(h)	Q.P.R.	L 3-5	Cottee, Barlow, Radosavljevic	19,057
39		17	(a)	Southampton	D 0-0		16,911
40	May	1	(h)	Arsenal	D 0-0		19,044
41		4	(h)	Sheffield U	L 0-2		15,197
42		8	(a)	Manchester C	W 5-2	Jackson, Beagrie 2, Beardsley, Radosavljevic	25,180

FINAL LEAGUE POSITION: 13th in Premier League

Appearances

Sub. Appearances

Goals

Southall	Jackson	Hinchcliffe	Ebbrell	Watson	Ablett	Ward	Beardsley	Rideout	Horne	Beagrie	Warzycha	Harper	Johnston	Barlow	Cottee	Unsworth	Radosavljevic	Keown	Kenny	Snodin	Jenkins	Kearton	Sansom	Holmes	Moore					
1	2	3	4	5	6	7	8	9	10*	11	12																			1
1		3	4	5	6	11	8	9*	10	12	7†	2	14																	2
1		3	4†	5	6	11	8	9	10	12	7*	2	14																	3
1		3	4	5	6	7	8	9*	10	12		2	11																	4
1		3	4	5	6	11*	8	9†	10	12	7	2	14																	5
1		3	4	5	6	11	8		10	12	7*	2	9†	14																6
1		3	4*	5	6	11	8		10	12	7	2	9																	7
1	14	3	11	5	6	7*	8	9†	4		12	2			10															8
1	12	3	4	5	6		8*	9†	11	7		2	14		10															9
1		3	4	5	6				8	12	7†	2	14		10	9*	11													10
1		3	4	5	6			9	8	12	7	2	10†		14		11*													11
1		3		5	6		8		10*	11	2†				9		14	4	7	12										12
1		3*		5	6		8	12	10	11	7	14			9			4		2†										13
1	2			5	3			9	10*	11	7			8			12	6	4											14
1	2		11	5	3		8	9	10		12	7*						6		4										15
1	2	11		5	3		8	9	10†		12	7*		14				6		4										16
1		11		5	3		8	12			14	2		9	10†			6	7	4*										17
1				5	3		8	14	2	12			10	9		11*		6	7	4†										18
1	2†			5	3		8	14	7	12			10*	9			11	6		4										19
1				5	3		8	9	4	11	7							6	10	2										20
1				5	6		8	9	4	11	7†			14		3	12		10	2*										21
1				5	3		8	9	4	11†	7*			14				6	10		2	12								22
1	2		11	5	3		8	9*						12			7	6	10	4										23
1	2		4	5	3		8		10	11†		14		12	9*		7	6												24
1	2			5	3		8		10					12	9		11*	6		4										25
1	2			5	6		8	14	10			7		12	9		7†		11	4†										26
1	2			5	6		8				7*	3		12	9		11†		10	4		14	3							27
1	4			5	6		8	10	11						9		12		7*				3							28
	2			5	6		8		11		7†	2†	14	14	9		12			4		1	3							29
	2			5	6		8	12	10				10*	11*	9				7	4		1	3							30
1	2		11	5	6	7	8		10					12	9				4*				3							31
1	2		11	5	6	7	8		10						9		12			4*			3							32
1	2	3		5	6	7	8		10					11	9		12		4*											33
1	2	3		5	6	7	8							12	9		11†		10	4*			14							34
1	2	3	11	5	6	7	8							14	9		12		10†	4										35
1	6	3	10	5		7†	8	14		12				11	9					4*				2						36
1	2	3	11	5	6	7	8	10†	4					14*	9		12													37
1	2†	3	11	5	6	7*	8		4					14	9		12			10										38
1	6	3	4	5		11	8							10*	9		7		12					2						39
1	2	3	10	5	6	11*	8		4					12	9		7													40
1	5	3	4		6		8		10†	11				12	9		7*							2	14					41
1†	5	3	4		6	7	8			11				12	9		10*					14		2						42
40	25	25	24	40	40	19	39	17	34	11	15	16	7	8	25	3	13	13	16	19	1	2	6	4						
	2							7		11	5	2	6	18	1		10		1	1		3	1		1					
	3	1	1	1		1	10	3	1	3	1		3	5	12		3		1	1			1							

1993-94

1	Aug	14	(a)	Southampton	W	2-0	Beagrie, Ebbrell	14,051
2		17	(h)	Manchester C	W	1-0	Rideout	26,025
3		21	(h)	Sheffield U	W	4-2	Cottee 3, Ebbrell	24,177
4		25	(a)	Newcastle U	L	0-1		34,490
5		28	(a)	Arsenal	L	0-2		29,063
6		31	(h)	Aston Villa	L	0-1		24,067
7	Sep	11	(a)	Oldham Ath	W	1-0	Cottee	13,666
8		18	(h)	Liverpool	W	2-0	Ward, Cottee	38,157
9		25	(h)	Norwich C	L	1-5	Rideout	20,631
10	Oct	3	(a)	Tottenham H	L	2-3	Rideout, Cottee (pen)	27,487
11		16	(a)	Swindon T	D	1-1	Beagrie	14,437
12		23	(h)	Manchester U	L	0-1		35,455
13		30	(a)	Ipswich T	W	2-0	Barlow, Whelan (og)	15,078
14	Nov	6	(a)	Coventry C	L	1-2	Rideout	11,550
15		20	(h)	Q.P.R.	L	0-3		17,326
16		23	(h)	Leeds U	D	1-1	Cottee	17,102
17		27	(a)	Wimbledon	D	1-1	Barlow	6,934
18	Dec	4	(h)	Southampton	W	1-0	Cottee	13,265
19		8	(a)	Manchester C	L	0-1		20,513
20		11	(a)	Sheffield U	D	0-0		15,135
21		18	(h)	Newcastle U	L	0-2		25,362
22		27	(h)	Sheffield W	L	0-2		16,471
23		29	(a)	Blackburn R	L	0-2		22,061
24	Jan	1	(h)	West Ham U	L	0-1		19,602
25		3	(a)	Chelsea	L	2-4	Cottee, Barlow	18,338
26		15	(h)	Swindon T	W	6-2	Ebbrell, Cottee 3 (1 pen), Ablett, Beagrie	20,760
27		22	(a)	Manchester U	L	0-1		44,750
28	Feb	5	(h)	Chelsea	W	4-2	Ebbrell, Rideout 2, Angell	18,201
29		12	(h)	Ipswich T	D	0-0		19,641
30		19	(h)	Arsenal	D	1-1	Cottee	19,760
31	Mar	5	(h)	Oldham Ath	W	2-1	Radosavljevic, Stuart	18,881
32		13	(a)	Liverpool	L	1-2	Watson	44,281
33		21	(a)	Norwich C	L	0-3		16,432
34		26	(h)	Tottenham H	L	0-1		23,460
35		29	(a)	Aston Villa	D	0-0		36,044
36	Apr	2	(a)	Sheffield W	L	1-5	Cottee	24,080
37		4	(h)	Blackburn R	L	0-3		27,463
38		9	(a)	West Ham U	W	1-0	Cottee	20,243
39		16	(a)	Q.P.R.	L	1-2	Cottee	13,330
40		23	(h)	Coventry C	D	0-0		23,352
41		30	(a)	Leeds U	L	0-3		35,487
42	May	7	(h)	Wimbledon	W	3-2	Stuart 2 (1 pen), Horne	31,233

FINAL LEAGUE POSITION: 17th in Premiership

Appearances

Sub. Appearances

Goals

Southall	Holmes	Jackson	Snodin	Watson	Ablett	Ward	Ebbrell	Cottee	Rideout	Beagrie	Radosavljevic	Barlow	Hinchcliffe	Stuart	Horne	Angell	Warzycha	Unsworth	Moore	Limpar	Rowett	
1	2	3	4	5	6	7	8	9	10	11												1
1	2	3	4*	5†	6	7	8	9	10	11	12	14										2
1	2	5			6	7	4	9	10	11*	12	14	3	8†								3
1	2†	5			6	7	4	9	10	11*	12	14	3	8								4
1	2	5			6	7	4	9†	10		12	14	3	8*	11							5
1		5			6	7	4	9	10†	11	12	14	3	8*	2							6
1	2	5			6	7	4	9	10†	11	8*	14	3		12							7
1	2	5			6	7	4	9	10	11*	12		3		8							8
1	2†	5			6	7*	4	9	10	11	12		3		8	14						9
1	2	5			6	7	4	9†	10	11*	12	14	3		8							10
1		2		5	6	7	4	9	10†	11	12	14*	3		8							11
1	2	14		5	6	7†	4	9		11	12	10*	3		8							12
1	2		12	5	6	7	4	9		11*		10	3		8							13
1	2			5	6	7*	4	9	10	11		12	3		8							14
1	2	3		5	6	7	4	9		11†	8*	10		14	12							15
1		2	11†	5	6	7	4	9			10*	12	3	14	8							16
1		2	11	5	6	7	4	9			12	10†	3	14	8*							17
1		2	6	5	3	7*	4	9		11				10	8		12					18
1		2	6	5	3	7	4	9		11				10	8*		12					19
1		2	6	5	3	7	4	9		11				8			10					20
1		2	6	5	3	7	4	9			12	10		8			11*					21
1		2	6	5*	3	7	4			11	12†	10		9	8		14					22
1		5	2		6	7	4	9		11			3		8		12	10*				23
1	2	5	3		6	7†	4	9*	10	11		12		14	8							24
1	2	5†	6		3	7		9	10*	11		12		8	4			14				25
1		5	2		6	7	4	9*		11		12	3		8	10						26
1		2	6		3		4	9*		11		12	14	8		10	7†		5			27
1		2	5		6		4		9	11	7		3	8		10						28
1		2	6	14			4	12	9*	11	7†		3	8		10			5			29
1		2	4	5				12	9*	11	7†		3	8	14	10			6			30
1		2	6	5		14		9	12	11	7†		3	8	4	10*						31
1		2	6	5			4	9	12	11	7†		3	8	14	10*						32
1		2	6	5			4	9	10	11	7*		3	8		12						33
1		2	6	5			4	9	10*				3	7	8	12				11		34
1		2	6	5			4						3	7	8	10		9		11		35
1		2	6	5			4	12						7	8	10†		3	9*	11	14	36
1		2	6	5			4	9				12		7	8	10*		3		11		37
1		2	3	5	6		4	9	12					7	8	10*				11		38
1		2	3	5	6		4	9						7	8	10				11		39
1		2		5			4	9			12		3	7	8*	10		6		11		40
1			3	5	6		4	9	10					7	8			2		11*	12	41
1			3	5	6		4*	9	10			12		7	8			2		11		42
42	15	37	28	27	32	26	39	36	21	29	9	6	25	26	28	13	3	7	4	9		
		1	1	1		1		3	3		14	16	1	4	4	3	4	1			2	
				1	1	1	4	16	6	3	1	3		3	1	1						

1994-95

1	Aug	20	(h)	Aston Villa	D 2-2	Stuart, Rideout	35,552
2		24	(a)	Tottenham H	L 1-2	Rideout	24,553
3		27	(a)	Manchester C	L 0-4		19,867
4		30	(h)	Nottingham F	L 1-2	Rideout	26,689
5	Sep	10	(a)	Blackburn R	L 0-3		26,548
6		17	(h)	Q.P.R.	D 2-2	Amokachi, Rideout	27,291
7		24	(h)	Leicester C	D 1-1	Ablett	28,015
8	Oct	1	(a)	Manchester U	L 0-2		43,803
9		8	(a)	Southampton	L 0-2		15,163
10		15	(h)	Coventry C	L 0-2		28,219
11		22	(a)	Crystal Palace	L 0-1		15,026
12		29	(h)	Arsenal	D 1-1	Unsworth	32,005
13	Nov	1	(h)	West Ham U	W 1-0	Ablett	28,353
14		5	(a)	Norwich C	D 0-0		18,377
15		21	(h)	Liverpool	W 2-0	Ferguson, Rideout	39,866
16		26	(a)	Chelsea	W 1-0	Rideout	28,115
17	Dec	5	(h)	Leeds U	W 3-0	Rideout, Ferguson, Unsworth (pen)	25,906
18		10	(a)	Aston Villa	D 0-0		29,678
19		17	(h)	Tottenham H	D 0-0		32,813
20		26	(h)	Sheffield W	L 1-4	Ferguson	37,089
21		31	(h)	Ipswich T	W 4-1	Ferguson, Rideout 2, Watson	25,667
22	Jan	2	(a)	Wimbledon	L 1-2	Rideout	9,506
23		14	(a)	Arsenal	D 1-1	Watson	34,743
24		21	(h)	Crystal Palace	W 3-1	Ferguson 2, Rideout	23,734
25		24	(a)	Liverpool	D 0-0		39,505
26	Feb	1	(a)	Newcastle U	L 0-2		34,465
27		4	(h)	Norwich C	W 2-1	Stuart, Rideout	23,295
28		13	(a)	West Ham U	D 2-2	Rideout, Limpar	21,081
29		22	(a)	Leeds U	L 0-1		30,793
30		25	(h)	Manchester U	W 1-0	Ferguson	40,011
31	Mar	4	(a)	Leicester C	D 2-2	Limpar, Samways	20,447
32		8	(a)	Nottingham F	L 1-2	Barlow	24,526
33		15	(h)	Manchester C	D 1-1	Unsworth (pen)	28,485
34		18	(a)	Q.P.R.	W 3-2	Barlow, McDonald (og), Hinchcliffe	14,488
35	Apr	1	(h)	Blackburn R	L 1-2	Stuart	37,905
36		14	(h)	Newcastle U	W 2-0	Amokachi 2	34,628
37		17	(a)	Sheffield W	D 0-0		27,880
38		29	(h)	Wimbledon	D 0-0		31,567
39	May	3	(h)	Chelsea	D 3-3	Hinchcliffe, Ablett, Amokachi	33,180
40		6	(h)	Southampton	D 0-0		36,851
41		9	(a)	Ipswich T	W 1-0	Rideout	14,940
42		14	(a)	Coventry C	D 0-0		21,787

FINAL LEAGUE POSITION: 15th in F.A. Carling Premiership

Appearances

Sub. Appearances

Goals

Southall	Jackson	Ablett	Ebbrell	Watson	Unsworth	Samways	Stuart	Cottee	Rideout	Limpar	Parkinson	Angell	Hinchcliffe	Burrows	Amokachi	Snodin	Holmes	Rowett	Barlow	Durrant	Ferguson	Horne	Kearton	Grant	Barrett					
1	2	3	4	5*	6	7	8	9	10	11	12																			1
1	2	3	4	5	6	7	8	9	10*		11†	12	14																	2
1	2	3	4	5	6	7	8	9*	10	12	11																			3
1	2		4	5	6	7	8		10	11		9	3																	4
1	2		4	5	6	7	8		10	11				3	9															5
1	2		4	5	6	7	8		10	11*				3	9	12														6
1		4		5	6	7	8					10		3	9	11	2													7
1				5	6	7	8*				4		11	3	9	2		10	12											8
1	2*			5†	6	7	12		10		4		11	3	9			8		14										9
1	2	5			6	7	12				4*			3	9					11	10	8								10
1	2	5			6	7*	8				12			3	9					11	10	4								11
1	2	5			6*		8		12	14	4			3	9					11†	10	7								12
1	2	6		5			8†		12	14	4			3	9*					11	10	7								13
1	2	4		5	6*		8		10	12	11			3							9	7								14
1	2*	3	4	5	6				12	14	8		11		9†						10	7								15
1	2	4		5	6				10	11	8		3								9	7								16
1	2	3*	4	5	6		12		10		8		11								9	7								17
	2		4	5	6				10	7	8		11	3							9		1							18
1	2		4	5	6				10	12	8*		11	3					9			7								19
1	2		4	5	6		12		10	7			11	3*							9	8								20
1	2		4	5	6				10		8		11	3							9	7								21
1	2		4	5	6				10		8		11	3*					12		9	7								22
1	2		4	5	6				10		8		11	3							9	7								23
1	2		4	5	6				10		8		11	3							9	7								24
1	2		4	5	6				10		8		11	3							9	7								25
1	2		4	5	6	12	9			7†	10			11*								8		14	3					26
1		3	4	5	6	12	9		10		8*		11									7			2					27
1		3*	4	5	6		8		10	12			11								9	7			2					28
1		6	4	5			12		10*	11	8		3								9	7			2					29
1			4*	5	6	12				11	8		3						10		9	7			2					30
1	12			5	6	7	14			11†	4		3						10*		9	8			2					31
1		3		5	6	7	12			11	4*								10		9	8			2					32
1		6†	4	5	12		14			11	8*		3						10		9	7			2					33
1	12	6	4	5						11		10†	3		14				9			7		8*	2					34
1	2	6		5			8				11		3		9				10*			7		12	4					35
1		3		5	6		8			7	4		11		9*							10		12	2					36
1	12	3		5	6				10	7	4		11*								9†	8		14	2					37
1		3		5	6		10		12	7*	4		11		9							8			2					38
1		3		5	6		8*		10		4		11		9				12			7			2					39
1		3	4*	5	6	12			10	14	8		11†		9							7			2					40
1		3	4	5	6	12			10	7*			11		9†				14			8			2					41
1	5	3	4		6	7*	8			11	10				9						12				2					42
41	26	26	26	38	37	14	20	3	25	19	32	3	28	19	17	2	1	2	7	4	22	31	1	1	17					
	3				1	5	8		4	8	2	1	1		1	1			4	1	1			4						
		3		2	3	1	3		14	2			2		4				2		7									

1995-96

1	Aug	19	(a)	Chelsea	D 0-0		30,189
2		23	(h)	Arsenal	L 0-2		36,047
3		26	(h)	Southampton	W 2-0	Limpar, Amokachi	33,676
4		30	(a)	Manchester C	W 2-0	Parkinson, Amokachi	28,432
5	Sep	9	(h)	Manchester U	L 2-3	Limpar, Rideout	39,496
6		17	(a)	Nottingham F	L 2-3	Rideout 2	24,786
7		23	(a)	West Ham U	L 1-2	Samways	21,085
8	Oct	1	(h)	Newcastle U	L 1-3	Limpar	33,026
9		14	(a)	Bolton W	D 1-1	Rideout	20,427
10		22	(h)	Tottenham H	D 1-1	Stuart	33,629
11		28	(a)	Aston Villa	L 0-1		32,792
12	Nov	5	(h)	Blackburn R	W 1-0	Stuart	30,097
13		18	(a)	Liverpool	W 2-1	Kanchelskis 2	40,818
14		22	(h)	Q.P.R.	W 2-0	Stuart, Rideout	30,009
15		25	(h)	Sheffield W	D 2-2	Kanchelskis, Amokachi	35,898
16	Dec	2	(a)	Tottenham H	D 0-0		32,894
17		11	(h)	West Ham U	W 3-0	Stuart, Unsworth (pen), Ebbrell	31,778
18		16	(a)	Newcastle U	L 0-1		36,557
19		23	(a)	Coventry C	L 1-2	Rideout	16,638
20		26	(h)	Middlesbrough	W 4-0	Short, Stuart 2, Kanchelskis	40,091
21		30	(h)	Leeds U	W 2-0	Wetherall (og), Kanchelskis	40,009
22	Jan	1	(a)	Wimbledon	W 3-2	Ebbrell, Ferguson 2	11,121
23		13	(h)	Chelsea	D 1-1	Unsworth (pen)	34,968
24		20	(a)	Arsenal	W 2-1	Stuart, Kanchelskis	38,275
25	Feb	3	(a)	Southampton	D 2-2	Stuart, Horne	15,126
26		10	(h)	Manchester C	W 2-0	Parkinson, Hinchcliffe (pen)	37,354
27		21	(a)	Manchester U	L 0-2		42,459
28		24	(h)	Nottingham F	W 3-0	Kanchelskis, Watson, Ferguson	33,163
29	Mar	2	(a)	Middlesbrough	W 2-0	Grant, Hinchcliffe (pen)	29,805
30		9	(h)	Coventry C	D 2-2	Ferguson 2	34,517
31		17	(a)	Leeds U	D 2-2	Stuart, Kanchelskis	29,422
32		23	(h)	Wimbledon	L 2-4	Short, Kanchelskis	31,282
33		30	(a)	Blackburn R	W 3-0	Amokachi, Kanchelskis 2	29,468
34	Apr	6	(h)	Bolton W	W 3-0	Hottiger, Kanchelskis, Amokachi	37,974
35		8	(a)	Q.P.R.	L 1-3	Ebbrell	18,349
36		16	(h)	Liverpool	D 1-1	Kanchelskis	40,120
37		27	(a)	Sheffield W	W 5-2	Amokachi, Ebbrell, Kanchelskis 3	32,724
38	May	5	(h)	Aston Villa	W 1-0	Parkinson	40,127

FINAL LEAGUE POSITION: 6th in F.A. Carling Premiership

Appearances

Sub. Appearances

Goals

Southall	Barrett	Hinchcliffe	Unsworth	Watson	Ablett	Limpar	Horne	Ferguson	Rideout	Parkinson	Samways	Amokachi	Barlow	Kanchelskis	Holmes	Short	Grant	Stuart	Ebbrell	Jackson	O'Connor	Branch	Hottiger	
1	2	3	4	5	6	7*	8	9	10	11	12													1
1	2	3	4	5	6	7*	8	9	10	11†		12	13											2
1	2		4	5	3	11	8		10	6		9		7										3
1	2	12	4	5	3	11*	8		10	6		9		7										4
1		12	4	5	3	11	8		10	6		9		7*	2									5
1	2	11		5	3†	7*	8		10	4		9	12			6	13							6
1	2	3		5		12	8		10†	4	7	9				6	11*	13						7
1	2	3	4	5		12	7		10	11*							8	9	6					8
1	2	3			6*	12	8		10			9	13	7†		5		11		4				9
1		11*		5	3	12	8		10		4			7		6		9		2				10
1		3*	13	5	6	12			10		11	9†		7				8	4	2				11
1				5	3	11			10	8		12		7		6		9*	4	2				12
1			12	5	3*	11			10	8				7		6		9	4	2				13
1			3	5		11			10	8				7		6		9	4	2				14
1		3	6	5		11			10*	8		12		7				9	4	2				15
1		12	3	5		11				8		9		7		6*		10	4	2				16
1			3	5		11*		12		8		9		7		6		10	4	2				17
1			3	5		11	12	13		8*		9		7		6		10	4	2†				18
1			3	5		11*			12	8		9		7		6		10	4	2				19
1			3	5		11	8		10	4				7		6		9	2					20
1		12	3	5			8	9*	10	4				7		6		11	2					21
1		12	3	5			8	9	10	4				7*				11	2	6				22
1		3*	4		6	11	8		10			12		7		5		9	2					23
1			12	5	3		8	9		4		10*		7		6		11	2					24
1		3		5		11*	8	9	12	4				7		6		10		2				25
1		11	3	5		7	8	9		4						6		10		2				26
1		3	6	5			8					9		7			11*	10	4		2	12		27
1		3	6	5				9*		8		12		7			11	10	4		2			28
1		3	6	5				9		8				7			11	10	4		2			29
1		3	6					9		8*		12		7		5†	11	10	4		13		2	30
1		3	6			11	8	9						7		5		10	4				2	31
1		3		5		11	8	9	12			13		7		6		10†	4*				2	32
1		3	4	5		11*	8	9	12†			13		7		6	10						2	33
1		3	6	5			8	9		4		10		7			11*		12				2	34
1		3	6*	5		11°	8†	9		10				7		12	13		4			14	2	35
1		3	6	5			8	9				10*		7			11	12	4				2	36
1			3	5					12			9		7		6	8	11	4			10*	2	37
1		3	6	5		12	8		13	4		9†		7			11*	10					2	38
38	8	23	28	34	13	22	25	16	19	28	3	17		32	1	22	11	27	24	14	3	1	9	
		5	3			6	1	2	6		1	8	3			1	2	2	1		1	2		
		2	2	1		3	1	5	6	3	1	6		16		2	1	9	4				1	

1996-97

1	Aug	17	(h)	Newcastle U	W 2-0	Unsworth (pen), Speed	40,117
2		21	(a)	Manchester U	D 2-2	Ferguson 2	54,943
3		24	(a)	Tottenham H	D 0-0		29,669
4	Sep	4	(h)	Aston Villa	L 0-1		39,115
5		7	(a)	Wimbledon	L 0-4		13,684
6		14	(h)	Middlesbrough	L 1-2	Short	39,250
7		21	(a)	Blackburn R	D 1-1	Unsworth	27,091
8		28	(h)	Sheffield W	W 2-0	Kanchelskis, Stuart	34,160
9	Oct	12	(h)	West Ham U	W 2-1	Stuart, Speed	36,541
10		28	(a)	Nottingham F	W 1-0	Short	19,892
11	Nov	4	(h)	Coventry C	D 1-1	Stuart (pen)	31,477
12		16	(h)	Southampton	W 7-1	Stuart, Kanchelskis 2, Speed 3, Barmby	35,669
13		20	(a)	Liverpool	D 1-1	Speed	40,751
14		23	(a)	Leicester C	W 2-1	Hinchcliffe, Unsworth	20,975
15		30	(h)	Sunderland	L 1-3	Ferguson	40,087
16	Dec	7	(a)	Chelsea	D 2-2	Branch, Kanchelskis	27,920
17		16	(a)	Derby Co	W 1-0	Barmby	17,252
18		21	(h)	Leeds U	D 0-0		36,954
19		26	(a)	Middlesbrough	L 2-4	Unsworth (pen), Ferguson	29,673
20		28	(h)	Wimbledon	L 1-3	Stuart	36,733
21	Jan	1	(h)	Blackburn R	L 0-2		30,427
22		11	(a)	Sheffield W	L 1-2	Ferguson	24,175
23		19	(a)	Arsenal	L 1-3	Ferguson	38,095
24		29	(a)	Newcastle U	L 1-4	Speed	36,143
25	Feb	1	(h)	Nottingham F	W 2-0	Ferguson, Barmby	32,567
26		22	(a)	Coventry C	D 0-0		19,452
27	Mar	1	(h)	Arsenal	L 0-2		36,980
28		5	(a)	Southampton	D 2-2	Ferguson, Speed	15,134
29		8	(a)	Leeds U	L 0-1		32,055
30		15	(h)	Derby Co	W 1-0	Watson	32,140
31		22	(h)	Manchester U	L 0-2		40,079
32	Apr	5	(a)	Aston Villa	L 1-3	Unsworth	39,339
33		9	(h)	Leicester C	D 1-1	Branch	30,368
34		12	(h)	Tottenham H	W 1-0	Speed	36,380
35		16	(h)	Liverpool	D 1-1	Ferguson	40,177
36		19	(a)	West Ham U	D 2-2	Branch, Ferguson	24,525
37	May	3	(a)	Sunderland	L 0-3		22,052
38		11	(h)	Chelsea	L 1-2	Barmby	38,321

FINAL LEAGUE POSITION: 15th in F.A. Carling Premiership

Appearances

Sub. Appearances

Goals

Southall	Barrett	Hinchcliffe	Unsworth	Watson	Parkinson	Kanchelskis	Stuart	Ferguson	Ebbrell	Speed	Short	Grant	Rideout	Branch	Limpar	Hottiger	Barmby	Gerrard	Allen	Hills	Phelan	Dunne	Thomsen	Ball	Cadamarteri	
1	2	3	4	5*	6	7	8	9	10	11	12															1
1	2	3	4		6	7*	8	9	10	11	5	12														2
1	2	3	4		6	7	8*	9		11	5	10	12													3
1	2	3	4		6	7	8*	9		11	5	10	12													4
1	2	3	4		6	7	8	9		11	5	10*		12												5
1	2	3	4		6	7	12	9	8	11	5			10*												6
1	2	3	4		6	7		9		8	5	12	10		11*											7
1	2	3	4		6	7	8		10	11	5			9												8
1	2	3	4		6*	7	9		8†	11	5	12		10		13										9
1	2	3	4	5	8	7	9			11	6	12		10*												10
1	2	3	4*	5	6†	7	8			11	10	13		12			9									11
1°	2	3	4	5	6	7	8			11		10					9	14								12
1	2	3	4	5	6	7*	8	12		11		10					9									13
1	2	3	4	5	6		8	9		11	12	10*					7									14
1	2	3†	4	5	6	7°	8	12		11	13	10*		14			9									15
1	2	3	4	5	6	7	12	9		11		10		8*												16
1	2	3	4	5	6	7	12	9		11				10*			8									17
1	2	3†	12	5	6	7		9		11	4*	10		13			8									18
1	2		4	5†	6		8	9		3		10	12	11*		14	7		13°							19
1	5		4				8	9	6†	3		11	10*	12		2	7			13						20
1	4			5		7*	10	9	6	11				13	12	2	8†				3					21
1	2		12	5		7	10†	9		11		13	4	14			8				3°	6*				22
1	2		4	5		7*	10	9		11				12			8				3		6			23
	2		4	5	8		7	9		11	6*	12†	13					1			3		10			24
	2		4	5	6		7	9		11							8	1			3		10			25
	2		4	5			7	9		11	6						8	1			3		10			26
1	2		4*	5	6		7	9		11	12			13			8†				3		10			27
1	2		4	5	8		12	9		11	6			13			7†				3		10*			28
1	2		4	5	8*		12	9		11	6°		14	13			7†				3		10			29
1	2		4	5	8		12	9			6			11*		13	7				3		10†			30
	2		4	5	6		8	9		11			12				7	1			3		10*			31
1			4†	5	8		7	9		11	6			12		2*					3	13	10			32
1			4	5	6†		7	9		11	2			10		12	8*				3		13			33
1	2			5			7	9		11			4	8*			12				3†	6	10	13		34
1	2		3	5			7	9		11	4†			8			12					6	10*	13		35
1	2		3	5			7	9		11				8			12					6	10	4*		36
1	2			5			7†	9		11				10			8			12	3*	6	4	13		37
1	2			5				9		11						4	8			7		6	10*	3	12	38
34	36	18	32	29	28	20	29	31	7	37	19	11	4	13	1	4	22	4		1	15	6	15	2		
			2				6	2			4	7	6	12	1	4	3	1	1	2		1	1	3	1	
		1	5	1		4	5	10		9	2			3			4									

1997-98

1	Aug	9	(h)	Crystal Palace	L	1-2	Ferguson	35,716
2		23	(h)	West Ham U	W	2-1	Speed, Stuart	34,356
3		27	(h)	Manchester U	L	0-2		40,479
4	Sep	1	(a)	Bolton W	D	0-0		23,131
5		13	(a)	Derby Co	L	1-3	Stuart	27,828
6		20	(h)	Barnsley	W	4-2	Speed 2 (1 pen), Cadamarteri, Oster	32,659
7		24	(a)	Newcastle U	L	0-1		36,705
8		27	(h)	Arsenal	D	2-2	Ball, Cadamarteri	35,457
9	Oct	4	(a)	Sheffield W	L	1-3	Cadamarteri	24,483
10		18	(h)	Liverpool	W	2-0	Ruddock (og), Cadamarteri	40,112
11		25	(a)	Coventry C	D	0-0		18,755
12	Nov	2	(h)	Southampton	L	0-2		29,565
13		8	(a)	Blackburn R	L	2-3	Speed, Ferguson	25,397
14		22	(a)	Aston Villa	L	1-2	Speed (pen)	36,389
15		26	(a)	Chelsea	L	0-2		32,736
16		29	(h)	Tottenham H	L	0-2		36,670
17	Dec	6	(a)	Leeds U	D	0-0		34,872
18		13	(h)	Wimbledon	D	0-0		28,533
19		20	(a)	Leicester C	W	1-0	Speed (pen)	20,628
20		26	(a)	Manchester U	L	0-2		55,167
21		28	(h)	Bolton W	W	3-2	Ferguson 3	37,149
22	Jan	10	(a)	Crystal Palace	W	3-1	Barmby, Ferguson, Madar	23,311
23		18	(h)	Chelsea	W	3-1	Speed, Ferguson, Duberry (og)	32,355
24		31	(a)	West Ham U	D	2-2	Barmby, Madar	25,905
25	Feb	7	(a)	Barnsley	D	2-2	Ferguson, Grant	18,654
26		14	(h)	Derby Co	L	1-2	Thomsen	34,876
27		23	(a)	Liverpool	D	1-1	Ferguson	44,501
28		28	(h)	Newcastle U	D	0-0		37,972
29	Mar	7	(a)	Southampton	L	1-2	Tiler	15,102
30		14	(h)	Blackburn R	W	1-0	Madar	33,423
31		28	(h)	Aston Villa	L	1-4	Madar	36,471
32	Apr	4	(a)	Tottenham H	D	1-1	Madar	35,624
33		11	(h)	Leeds U	W	2-0	Hutchison, Ferguson	37,099
34		13	(a)	Wimbledon	D	0-0		15,131
35		18	(h)	Leicester C	D	1-1	Madar	33,642
36		25	(h)	Sheffield W	L	1-3	Ferguson	35,497
37	May	3	(a)	Arsenal	L	0-4		38,269
38		10	(h)	Coventry C	D	1-1	Farrelly	40,109

FINAL LEAGUE POSITION: 17th in F.A. Carling Premiership

Appearances

Sub. Appearances

Goals

Southall	Thomas	Phelan	Thomsen	Watson	Bilic	Stuart	Farrelly	Ferguson	Oster	Speed	Branch	Barmby	Short	Williamson	Barrett	Hinchcliffe	Cadamarteri	Gerrard	Grant	McCann	Ball	O'Connor	Ward	Tiler	Myhre	Allen	Jeffers	Dunne	Madar	O'Kane	Hutchison	Spencer	Beagrie	
1	2*	3	4†	5	6	7	8	9	10°	11	12	13	14																					1
1		3		5	6	7	10†	9	13	11		8	12	4*	2																			2
1	12	3		5	6	7		9	13	11	14	8†	4°	10	2*																			3
1	2°	3		5*	6	7		9	10	11	13	8†	12	4		14																		4
1					6	7		9	10	11	8†	12	5	4	2*	3	13																	5
				5	6	7	12	9	13	11		8	2	4*		3	10†	1																6
				5	6	7		12	10	11		8°			2	3	9*	1	4†	13	14													7
		3		5	6	7			10	11					2		9	1	8*	12	4													8
	2†			5	6	7			10	11		12	13	4		3	9	1			8*													9
1				5		7		9	10*	11			6	4	2	3	8†			12	13													10
1				5		7		9	10	11		12	6	4	2	3	8*																	11
1		12		5		7		9	10	11	13		6	4	2*	3	8†																	12
1		3			6	7°	12	9	13	10	14		5	4*	2	11	8†																	13
1					6	7	12	9	13	11		8	5	4*	2°	3	10†					14												14
1		3°			6		10†	9	12	11		8	4	7		5*	13				14		2											15
1		3†			6		10*	9	12	11		8	4°	7		13	14						2	5										16
				5			7	9		11		8	4	10		3							2	6	1									17
				5			7		12	11		8	4	10*	13	3	9						2†	6	1									18
				5			7		10*	11		8	4		2	3	9				12			6	1									19
			12	5°			7		10			8	4		2†	3	9				11*			6	1	13	14							20
	2		12				7	9	10*			8				3	11				4			6	1			5						21
	2		14		6		12	9		11		8	4				13†		10*		3			5	1				7†					22
			12		6		13	9		11		8	4*						10		3			5	1	2			7†					23
				5	6		7	9				8					12		10		4		2		1	13			11*	3†				24
			12	5			7	9	13			8*	4				14		10		3		2		1				11°	6†				25
	2		12	5	13		7	9	10				4†				14		8*		3			6	1				11°					26
			8	5	6		7	9	12								10*			13	3		2	4	1				11†					27
					5		7		12				4				9				3		2†	6	1	13			11	8*	10			28
				5	6		7*		10			8					12				3			4	1				9	2	11			29
				5	6				10			8†					12			13	3			4	1				9*	2	11	7		30
				5			7*		10°			8	4†				12				2				1			13	9	3	6	11	14	31
				5				9				8	4							10	3				1			6	7*	2	11	12		32
							12	9†				8*	4							7	3			5	1				13	2	6	10	11	33
							12	9	13			8†	4							6	3			5	1				10*	2	7	14	11°	34
					12		7	9	13				4							6*	3			5	1				10†	2	8	14	11°	35
				12	6			9	13			8	4†							7	3			5*	1	2°			10		11		14	36
				5	6*		12	9	13			8	4								3			7	1				14	2†	10		11°	37
				5			7†	9				8	4				12			13	3			6	1				11*	2	10			38
12	6	8	2	25	2	14	18	28	16	21	1	26	27	15	12	15	15	4	7	5	21		8	19	22	2		2	15	12	11	3	4	
	1	1	6	1	2		8	1	15		5	4	4		1	2	11			6	4	1				3	1	1	2			3	2	
			1			2	1	11	1	7		2					4		1		1			1					6		1			

1998-99

1	Aug	15	(h)	Aston Villa	D 0-0		40,112
2		22	(a)	Leicester C	L 0-2		21,037
3		29	(h)	Tottenham H	L 0-1		39,378
4	Sep	8	(a)	Nottingham F	W 2-0	Ferguson 2	25,610
5		12	(h)	Leeds U	D 0-0		36,687
6		19	(a)	Middlesbrough	D 2-2	Ball (pen), Collins	34,563
7		26	(h)	Blackburn R	D 0-0		36,404
8	Oct	3	(a)	Wimbledon	W 2-1	Cadamarteri, Ferguson	16,054
9		17	(h)	Liverpool	D 0-0		40,185
10		24	(a)	Sheffield W	D 0-0		26,592
11		31	(h)	Manchester U	L 1-4	Ferguson	40,087
12	Nov	8	(a)	Arsenal	L 0-1		38,088
13		15	(a)	Coventry C	L 0-3		19,279
14		23	(h)	Newcastle U	W 1-0	Ball (pen)	30,357
15		28	(a)	Charlton Ath	W 2-1	Cadamarteri 2	20,043
16	Dec	5	(h)	Chelsea	D 0-0		36,430
17		12	(h)	Southampton	W 1-0	Bakayoko	32,073
18		19	(a)	West Ham U	L 1-2	Cadamarteri	25,998
19		26	(h)	Derby Co	D 0-0		39,206
20		28	(a)	Tottenham H	L 1-4	Bakayoko	36,053
21	Jan	9	(h)	Leicester C	D 0-0		32,792
22		18	(a)	Aston Villa	L 0-3		32,488
23		30	(h)	Nottingham F	L 0-1		34,175
24	Feb	7	(a)	Derby Co	L 1-2	Barmby	27,603
25		17	(h)	Middlesbrough	W 5-0	Barmby 2, Dacourt, Materazzi, Unsworth	31,606
26		20	(a)	Leeds U	L 0-1		36,344
27		27	(h)	Wimbledon	D 1-1	Jeffers	32,574
28	Mar	10	(a)	Blackburn R	W 2-1	Bakayoko 2	27,219
29		13	(h)	Arsenal	L 0-2		38,049
30		21	(a)	Manchester U	L 1-3	Hutchison	55,182
31	Apr	3	(a)	Liverpool	L 2-3	Dacourt, Jeffers	44,852
32		5	(h)	Sheffield W	L 1-2	Jeffers	35,270
33		11	(h)	Coventry C	W 2-0	Campbell 2	32,341
34		17	(a)	Newcastle U	W 3-1	Campbell 2, Gemmill	36,775
35		24	(h)	Charlton Ath	W 4-1	Hutchison, Campbell 2, Jeffers	40,089
36	May	1	(a)	Chelsea	L 1-3	Jeffers	34,000
37		8	(h)	West Ham U	W 6-0	Campbell 3, Ball (pen), Hutchison, Jeffers	40,029
38		16	(a)	Southampton	L 0-2		15,254

FINAL LEAGUE POSITION: 14th in F.A. Carling Premiership

Appearances

Sub. Appearances

Goals

Myhre	Cleland	Ball	Short	Materazzi	Tiler	Collins	Barmby	Ferguson	Dacourt	Spencer	Hutchison	Cadamarteri	Unsworth	Watson	Thomas	Farrelly	Oster	Grant	Bakayoko	Ward	Dunne	Milligan	Jeffers	Bilic	Madar	Branch	Farley	Weir	Jevons	O'Kane	Degn	Gemmill	Campbell	
1	2	3	4	5	6	7	8	9	10*	11†	12	13																						1
1	2	3	4	5°	6	7	8†	9	10	11*	13	12	14																					2
1	2*	3	4	5		7	8†	9	10	13	12	11	6																					3
1	2	3		6		7	8*	9†	10		11	12	4	5	13																			4
1	2	3		6		7	8*	9	10		11†	12	4	5		13																		5
1	2	3		6		7	8	9	10		11*	12	4	5																				6
1	2†	3	10	6		7	8*	9			11	12	4	5			13																	7
1		3	2	6		7		9	10		11	8	4	5																				8
1	2	3	4			7		9			11	12	6	5				8*	10†	13														9
1	2	3		6		7		9	10		8	12	4	5					11*															10
1		3	2*	6		7		9	10			8	4	5					11		12													11
1	2*	3		6°		7		9	10		12	13	8	5†					11		4	14												12
1	2†	3	4	5		7		9			10	12	6					8	11*			13												13
1		3	4			7					10	9†	6	5				8	11*		2	12	13											14
1	12	3	4	13		7					10	9	6	5†			14	8°	11*		2													15
1	2	3	4	5		7					10	9						8	11		6													16
1	2	3				7	12		13		10		6					8*	11		4			5	9†									17
1	3			5		12	13		10		11	7	6					8†		2*				4	9°	14								18
1		3		6		7†	12		10		11	8*	4						9		2			5		13								19
1	12	3	4*			7°	8		10		11	13	6				14		9†		2			5										20
1	2	3					12		10		11	7*	6	5			8		9		4													21
1	2	3		6			8		10		11	12		5			4*	7†	9°	13						14								22
1		3		5			8		12		11	9†	6				10	7*	13	2°	4					14								23
1		3					8		10		6		4*	5					9	7	2		11				12							24
1		3		5			8		10		11		6				4†	7	12		2		9*					13						25
1		3		5			8		10		11	12	6				4°	7†	13		2		9*					14						26
1		11		6			8		10			9	3	5			4*						7			12		2						27
1		3	4	5			8°				10		6					12	9*		2					13		7	14	11†				28
1		3		6			8*		10		11	12	4	5				13	9°		2†		14					7						29
1		3	4	5					10		11	12	6					8°	9*				13					2		7†	14			30
1		3	2	6°			8†		10			12	4	5									13			11*		14				7	9	31
1		12	4	5*			8†		10				3					6°	13				11					2			14	7	9	32
1		3	4	6			8		10					5				12					11*					2				7	9	33
1		3	4						10		11	12	6	5					13				8*					2				7	9†	34
1		3	4						10		11		6	5									8					2				7	9	35
1		3	4				8				11	12	6							7*	5†		10					2			13		9	36
1		3	4						10		11		6	5									8					2				7	9	37
1		3	4*						10		11	12	6	5					13				8†					2			14	7°	9	38
38	16	36	22	26	2	19	20	13	28	2	29	11	33	22			6	13	17	4	15		11	4	2	1		11		2		7	8	
	2	1		1		1	4		2	1	4	19	1		1	1	3	3	6	2	1	3	4			6	1	3	1		4			
		3		1		1	3	4	2		3	4	1						4				6									1	9	

1999-2000

1	Aug	8	(h)	Manchester U	D	1-1	Stam (og)	39,141
2		11	(a)	Aston Villa	L	0-3		30,337
3		14	(a)	Tottenham H	L	2-3	Unsworth 2 (2 pens)	34,308
4		21	(h)	Southampton	W	4-1	Gough, Lundekvam (og), Jeffers, Campbell	31,755
5		25	(h)	Wimbledon	W	4-0	Unsworth, Barmby, Jeffers, Campbell	32,818
6		28	(a)	Derby Co	L	0-1		26,550
7	Sep	11	(a)	Sheffield W	W	2-0	Barmby, Gemmill	23,539
8		19	(h)	West Ham U	W	1-0	Jeffers	35,154
9		27	(a)	Liverpool	W	1-0	Campbell	44,802
10	Oct	2	(h)	Coventry C	D	1-1	Jeffers	34,839
11		16	(a)	Arsenal	L	1-4	Collins	38,042
12		24	(h)	Leeds U	D	4-4	Campbell 2, Hutchison, Weir	37,355
13		30	(a)	Middlesbrough	L	1-2	Campbell	33,916
14	Nov	7	(a)	Newcastle U	D	1-1	Campbell	36,164
15		20	(h)	Chelsea	D	1-1	Campbell	38,225
16		27	(h)	Aston Villa	D	0-0		34,750
17	Dec	4	(a)	Manchester U	L	1-5	Jeffers	55,193
18		18	(a)	Watford	W	3-1	Barmby, Hutchison, Unsworth (pen)	17,346
19		26	(h)	Sunderland	W	5-0	Hutchison 2, Jeffers, Pembridge, Campbell	40,017
20		28	(a)	Bradford C	D	0-0		18,276
21	Jan	3	(h)	Leicester C	D	2-2	Hutchison, Unsworth (pen)	30,490
22		15	(h)	Tottenham H	D	2-2	Campbell, Moore	36,144
23		22	(a)	Southampton	L	0-2		15,232
24	Feb	6	(a)	Wimbledon	W	3-0	Campbell 2, Moore	13,172
25		12	(h)	Derby Co	W	2-1	Moore, Ball (pen)	33,260
26		26	(a)	West Ham U	W	4-0	Barmby 3, Moore	26,025
27	Mar	4	(h)	Sheffield W	D	1-1	Weir	32,020
28		11	(a)	Chelsea	D	1-1	Cadamarteri	35,113
29		15	(a)	Coventry C	L	0-1		18,513
30		19	(h)	Newcastle U	L	0-2		32,512
31		25	(a)	Sunderland	L	1-2	Barmby	41,155
32	Apr	1	(h)	Watford	W	4-2	Hughes M, Moore 2, Hughes S	31,960
33		8	(a)	Leicester C	D	1-1	Hutchison	18,705
34		15	(h)	Bradford C	W	4-0	Pembridge, Unsworth (pen), Barmby, Collins	31,646
35		21	(h)	Liverpool	D	0-0		40,052
36		29	(h)	Arsenal	L	0-1		35,919
37	May	8	(a)	Leeds U	D	1-1	Barmby	37,713
38		14	(h)	Middlesbrough	L	0-2		34,663

FINAL LEAGUE POSITION: 13th in F.A. Premiership

Appearances

Sub. Appearances

Goals

Gerrard	Weir	Unsworth	Ward	Watson	Gough	Collins	Barmby	Campbell	Hutchison	Gemmill	Cadamarteri	Phelan	Ball	Jeffers	Pembridge	Dunne	Cleland	Xavier	Johnson	Grant	Moore	Simonsen	Myhre	Hughes S	Hughes M	Jevons	Milligan					
1	2	3	4*	5	6	7	8	9	10†	11	12	13																				1
1	2	5	4*		6	7	8	9	10	11†			3	12	13																	2
1	2	3	4°		6	7	8	9	12	11*	13			10†		5	14															3
1	2	3	12		6	7	8	9	10†	13	14			11°	4*	5																4
1	2	3	7		6		8°	9	10	12	13		14	11†	4*	5																5
1	2	3			6	7	8*	9	10	12	13		14	11†	4°	5																6
1	2	3	7†	5	6	12	8	9	13	11				10*	4°			14														7
1	2	3*			6	7	8	9	10†	12			13	11°		5	14	4														8
1	2				6	7	8	9	10				3	11		5		4														9
1	2				6	7	8*	9	10	13	12		3	11		5†		4														10
1	2	5†			6	7	8	9	10	11*	12		3				13	4														11
1	2	4		5	6	7	8	9	10	11*			3†		12				13													12
1	2	4			6	7	8†	9	10		12		3*		11	5			13													13
1	3	4				7	8	9	10				6*		11	5	2		12													14
1		3			6		8	9	10					7	11	5	2	4														15
1	2	3			6	7	8*	9	10					11	4	5				12												16
1	2	3			6	7	8†	9					12	10	11°	5*	13	4		14												17
1	4	3		12		7	8	9	10						11	5	2*	6														18
1	2	3			6	7	8*	9	10					11†	4	5	12				13											19
1	2	3			6	7*	8		10	13	14			11	4	5	12†				9°											20
1	2	3		5	6	7	8*	9	10	12				11†	4						13											21
1	2	3*		5		7	8	9	10				12	11†	4	6					13											22
1°	2	3*			6	7	8	9	10				12	11	4	5†					13	15										23
	2	3			6			9	10*		8		11		4	5		12			7		1									24
	2				6	12	8	9	10		7*		3		4	5					11		1									25
	2	4	12		5	7	8*	9					3		11			6			10		1									26
	5	4	2*			7	8	9					3		11	12		6			10		1									27
1	2				5	3	8				9				7	4		6			10			11								28
1	2	12			5	3	8†			13	14				7	4		6			9°			11*	10							29
1	2	3			5	7	8*				13		14		4	12		6			9†			11°	10							30
1		3			5	7	8		12		13				4	2		6			9*			11	10†							31
1					5	7	8						3		4	2		6			9			11	10							32
1	2	3			5*	7	8		10		13		14		4	12		6			9†			11°								33
1	2	5*				3	8		10				13	14	4	12		6†						11	9°	7						34
1	5	4	12			7	8*		10				13	14	3†	2		6						11	9°							35
1	5	3				7	8		10				12	13	4°	2*		6						11†	9	14						36
1	5	4	12			7	8		10		13		3		6*	2								11	9†							37
1	5†	4				7	8		10				3	12		2								11	9	6*	13					38
34	35	32	6	5	29	33	37	26	28	6	3		14	16	29	27	3	18			11		4	11	9	2						
		1	4	1		2			3	8	14	1	11	5	2	4	6	2	3	2	4	1				1	1					
	2	6			1	2	9	12	6	1	1		1	6	2						6			1	1							

2000-2001

1	Aug	19	(a)	Leeds U	L 0-2		40,010
2		23	(h)	Charlton Ath	W 3-0	Jeffers, Ferguson 2	36,300
3		26	(h)	Derby Co	D 2-2	Jeffers, Gravesen	34,840
4	Sep	5	(a)	Tottenham H	L 2-3	Jeffers, Nyarko	35,923
5		9	(a)	Middlesbrough	W 2-1	Jeffers 2	30,885
6		16	(h)	Manchester U	L 1-3	Gravesen	38,541
7		24	(a)	Leicester C	D 1-1	Unsworth	18,084
8		30	(h)	Ipswich T	L 0-3		32,597
9	Oct	14	(h)	Southampton	D 1-1	Ball (pen)	29,491
10		21	(a)	Newcastle U	W 1-0	Campbell	51,625
11		29	(a)	Liverpool	L 1-3	Campbell	44,718
12	Nov	5	(h)	Aston Villa	L 0-1		27,670
13		11	(a)	Bradford C	W 1-0	Naysmith	17,276
14		18	(h)	Arsenal	W 2-0	Cadamarteri, Campbell	33,106
15		25	(h)	Chelsea	W 2-1	Cadamarteri, Campbell	33,515
16	Dec	4	(a)	Sunderland	L 0-2		43,736
17		9	(a)	Manchester C	L 0-5		34,516
18		16	(h)	West Ham U	D 1-1	Cadamarteri	31,246
19		23	(a)	Charlton Ath	L 0-1		20,043
20		26	(h)	Coventry C	L 1-2	Gemmill	35,704
21	Jan	1	(a)	Derby Co	L 0-1		27,358
22		13	(h)	Tottenham H	D 0-0		32,290
23		20	(a)	Coventry C	W 3-1	Gemmill, Cadamarteri, Campbell	19,172
24		31	(h)	Middlesbrough	D 2-2	Naysmith, Tal	34,244
25	Feb	3	(a)	Manchester U	L 0-1		67,528
26		7	(h)	Leeds U	D 2-2	Ferguson, Campbell	34,244
27		10	(h)	Leicester C	W 2-1	Jeffers, Campbell	30,409
28		24	(a)	Ipswich T	L 0-2		22,211
29	Mar	3	(h)	Newcastle U	D 1-1	Unsworth (pen)	35,779
30		17	(a)	Southampton	L 0-1		15,251
31		31	(a)	West Ham U	W 2-0	Unsworth (pen), Alexandersson	26,044
32	Apr	8	(h)	Manchester C	W 3-1	Ferguson, Ball, Weir	36,561
33		14	(a)	Aston Villa	L 1-2	Unsworth	31,272
34		16	(h)	Liverpool	L 2-3	Ferguson, Unsworth (pen)	40,260
35		21	(a)	Arsenal	L 1-4	Campbell	38,029
36		28	(h)	Bradford C	W 2-1	Ferguson, Alexandersson	34,256
37	May	5	(a)	Chelsea	L 1-2	Campbell	35,196
38		19	(h)	Sunderland	D 2-2	Tal, Ball (pen)	37,444
FINAL LEAGUE POSITION: 16th in F.A. Premiership							Appearances
							Sub. Appearances
							Goals

Gerrard	Watson	Pistone	Unsworth	Weir	Ball	Nyarko	Gemmill	Jeffers	Hughes M	Hughes S	Gascoigne	Moore	Ferguson	Gravesen	Gough	Alexandersson	Cadamarteri	Cleland	Xavier	Campbell	Dunne	McLeod	Pembridge	Tal	Naysmith	Simonsen	Myhre	Clarke	Jevons	Hibbert	
1	2	3	4	5	6	7	8*	9	10†	11°	12	13	14																		1
1	2	3*	12	5		7		9	10°	11	8†	13	14	4	6																2
1	2		3	5		7		9*	12	11	13	10°		4	6†	8	14														3
1	2		3	5		7		9	10*	11°	4†	12		6		8	13	14													4
1	2			5		7*		9	10†	11	4			6		8		12	3	13											5
1	2		12	5		7	13	9	10°	11*	4†			6		8				14	3										6
1	2		3	5		7		9*	12		11	13		6		8				10†	4										7
1	2		3†	5		7	10		12	13	4	11*		6		8°				9		14									8
1	2			5	3	7			10†	12	8	13		6						9	4		11*								9
1	2		12	5	3	7					8			6					4	9			10†	11*	13						10
1	2			5	3†	7					8	12		6					4	9			10	11*	13						11
1	2*		6°	5			12			11	8†			7			13		4	9			10	14	3						12
1			6	5		7	12			11†		14		2			13		4	9			10*	8°	3						13
1				5	6		7			11							8	2		9		12	4	10*	3						14
1	2		12	5	6		7			11							8†			9		13	4	10*	3						15
1	2			5	6	12	7*			11		13		14			8†			9			4	10°	3						16
1	2		3*	5	6	7	8							4			12			9			10		11						17
1†	2			5	6		7			11				4*		12	8			9			10		3	13					18
	2		12	5	6		7			11*		9°	13	4		8	10†							14	3		1				19
	2		12	5	6	13	7					14	10	4			9°						11†	8*	3		1				20
	2		12	5	6	7*	8					13	10	4†		9°							11	14	3		1				21
	2		3	5†	6					11		10*		4		7°	12	13		9			8	14			1				22
	5		3		6		8									7†	10	2*		9			4	11			1	12	13		23
	2			5	6		7					11*	10	8†	4				12	9				13	3		1				24
1	2		12	5	6		7					10†		8	4		13			9				11°	3*				14		25
1	2		12	5	6		7					11*	10†	8	4					9				13	3						26
1	2		12	5	6		7	10†		11°		14		8	4*		13			9					3						27
1				5	6	7		10*		11				4					2	9		12		8†	3				13		28
1	2		12	5	6	7°	11	10			13			8					4†	9				14	3*						29
1	2	12	13	5	6		10†				14		9	8	4	7°			3				11*								30
1	4		3	5	6	7	11	12					9	8*		10														2	31
1	4	2	3	5	6		11	12					10*	8†		7°				9			13	14							32
1	4	2	3†	5	6	12	11					13		8*		7°				9			10	14							33
1	2*	12	3	5	6	7	8						10		4†	13			11	9											34
1		3		5	6	7†	8					12		4		10*			2	9			11*	13						14	35
1	2		3*	5	6		8						10	12	4†	7				9			11							13	36
1	2		3	5	6		8					10†				7*				9		14	11°	4	12				13		37
1	2		10	5	6		8							7*		12	13			9			11	4†	3						38
32	34	5	17	37	29	19	25	10	6	16	10	8	9	30	9	17	7	2	10	27	3		20	12	17		6			1	
		2	12			3	3	2	3	2	4	13	3	2		3	9	3	1	2		5	1	10	3	1		1	4	2	
			5	1	3	1	2	6					6	2		2	4			9				2	2						

2001-2002

1	Aug	18	(a)	Charlton Ath	W	2-1	Ferguson (pen), Weir	20,451
2		20	(h)	Tottenham H	D	1-1	Ferguson (pen)	29,503
3		25	(h)	Middlesbrough	W	2-0	Campbell, Gemmill	32,829
4	Sep	8	(a)	Manchester U	L	1-4	Campbell	67,534
5		15	(h)	Liverpool	L	1-3	Campbell	39,554
6		22	(a)	Blackburn R	L	0-1		27,732
7		29	(h)	West Ham U	W	5-0	Campbell, Hutchison (og), Gravesen, Watson, Radzinski	32,049
8	Oct	13	(a)	Ipswich T	D	0-0		22,820
9		20	(h)	Aston Villa	W	3-2	Watson, Radzinski, Gravesen	33,352
10		27	(h)	Newcastle U	L	1-3	Weir	37,524
11	Nov	3	(a)	Bolton W	D	2-2	Stubbs, Gascoigne	27,343
12		18	(h)	Chelsea	D	0-0		30,555
13		24	(a)	Leicester C	D	0-0		21,539
14	Dec	2	(h)	Southampton	W	2-0	Radzinski, Pembridge	28,138
15		8	(a)	Fulham	L	0-2		19,338
16		15	(h)	Derby Co	W	1-0	Moore	38,615
17		19	(a)	Leeds U	L	2-3	Moore, Weir	40,201
18		22	(a)	Sunderland	L	0-1		42,486
19		26	(h)	Manchester U	L	0-2		39,948
20		29	(h)	Charlton Ath	L	0-3		31,131
21	Jan	1	(a)	Middlesbrough	L	0-1		27,463
22		12	(h)	Sunderland	W	1-0	Blomqvist	30,736
23		19	(a)	Tottenham H	D	1-1	Weir	36,075
24		30	(a)	Aston Villa	D	0-0		32,460
25	Feb	2	(h)	Ipswich T	L	1-2	Unsworth (pen)	33,069
26		10	(h)	Arsenal	L	0-1		30,859
27		23	(a)	Liverpool	D	1-1	Radzinski	44,371
28	Mar	3	(h)	Leeds U	D	0-0		33,226
29		6	(a)	West Ham U	L	0-1		29,883
30		16	(h)	Fulham	W	2-1	Unsworth, Ferguson	34,639
31		23	(a)	Derby Co	W	4-3	Unsworth, Stubbs, Alexandersson, Ferguson	33,297
32		29	(a)	Newcastle U	L	2-6	Ferguson, Alexandersson	51,921
33	Apr	1	(h)	Bolton W	W	3-1	Pistone, Radzinski, Chadwick	39,784
34		6	(a)	Chelsea	L	0-3		40,545
35		13	(h)	Leicester C	D	2-2	Chadwick, Ferguson	35,580
36		20	(a)	Southampton	W	1-0	Watson	31,785
37		28	(h)	Blackburn R	L	1-2	Chadwick	34,976
38	May	11	(a)	Arsenal	L	3-4	Carsley, Radzinski, Watson	38,240

FINAL LEAGUE POSITION: 15th in F.A. Premiership

Appearances
Sub. Appearances
Goals

Gerrard	Watson	Pistone	Stubbs	Weir	Gravesen	Alexandersson	Gemmill	Campbell	Ferguson	Pembridge	Unsworth	Moore	Tal	Naysmith	Xavier	Gascoigne	Hibbert	Radzinski	Simonsen	Cleland	Cadamarteri	Chadwick	Blomqvist	Clarke	Linderoth	Carsley	Ginola	
1	2	3	4	5	6	7*	8	9	10	11	12																	1
1	2†	3	4	5	6*	7°	8	9	10	11	12	13	14															2
1	2	3	4	5		7†	8	9	10	11*	6		12	13														3
1	2	6	4†	5°		7*	8	9	10	11	3	12	13		14													4
1	2		4	5	8	7°		9	10		6*			3	11†	12	14	13										5
1			4	5	6*	7		9	10		12	13		2	3	8	11†											6
1	2	6		5	11	7		9		12†		14		3	4	8*	13	10°										7
1	2*	4	12	5		7		9	10°	11†	13		14	3	6			8										8
1	2	6		5	8°	7	12	9	13	11*				3	4	14		10†										9
1		2	12	5	8	7	11	9†	13		6°			3	4*	14		10										10
		2	4	5	10	7	11				6			3		8*		9†	1	12	13							11
	10	2	4	5	6	7*	8		12		3			11				9	1									12
	10	2	4	5	6†	7	8			12	3			11*		13		9	1									13
	9	2	4	5	8	7†	11			12	6*			3		13		10	1									14
	2	6	4	5	10†	12	7			11		13		3		8*		9	1									15
	9	2†	4*	5	6°	7	8			11	12	13		3		14		10	1									16
	9	2†		5		7°	8			11*	6	13	14	3	4	12		10	1									17
	2				6*	12	11				4	9	7°	3	5	8		10†	1			13	14					18
	2			5	9†	7°	8		12		6	13		3	4	14		10	1				11*					19
	2			5		7°	8		12		6	9	13	3	4	14		10*	1				11†					20
	2†		4	5		7°	8		10		11	12		3	6		13		1		9*		14					21
			4	5		7*	10	9			6			3		8	2		1	12		13	11†					22
			4	5		7†	11	9	10		6	12		3		8*	2		1					13				23
			4				11	9	10		6	7		3			2†		1	13	8*	12		5				24
			4	5			11	9	10		2*	12		3		8			1				7	6†	13			25
			4	5				9		12	3†	14		11		13			1				7*	2°	8	6	10	26
		3	4	5	12		8	9						11				13	1					2	7*	6	10†	27
		2	4	5	12		8	9			3							10	1				11†		7*	6	13	28
		2	4	5	12	7*	8	9†			3							10	1				11		14	6°	13	29
		2	4	5	8		11		10		3†	12					7	9*	1				13			6		30
			4°	5	7	12	8	13	10		3						2	9†	1				11	14		6*		31
	12	3°	4	5	6	7	8		10		11						2*	9†	1			13	14					32
	2	3	4	5		7	8		10		6							9†	1			12	11*		13			33
	2	3		5	6	7*	8		10									9	1			12	11†	4	13			34
1	2*	3	4	5	6	7	8	12	10		11							9†				13						35
1	2	3	4	5	10		8	9			11							12				7*				6		36
1	2	3	4	5	6	7*	8	9			11†							12				10	13					37
	2		4	5		7*		9		11	3							10	1						8	6	12	38
13	24	25	29	36	22	28	31	21	17	10	28	3	1	23	11	8	7	23	25		2	2	10	5	4	8	2	
	1		2		3	3	1	2	5	4	5	13	6	1	1	10	3	4		3	1	7	5	2	4		3	
	4	1	2	4	2	2	1	4	6	1	3	2				1		6				3	1			1		

Season 1977/78

DIVISION ONE

Nottingham Forest	42	25	14	3	69	24	64
Liverpool	42	24	9	9	65	34	57
Everton	**42**	**22**	**11**	**9**	**76**	**45**	**55**
Manchester City	42	20	12	10	74	51	52
Arsenal	42	21	10	11	60	37	52
West Bromwich Albion	42	18	14	10	62	53	50
Coventry City	42	18	12	12	75	62	48
Aston Villa	42	18	10	14	57	42	46
Leeds United	42	18	10	14	63	53	46
Manchester United	42	16	10	16	67	63	42
Birmingham City	42	16	9	17	55	60	41
Derby County	42	14	13	15	54	59	41
Norwich City	42	11	18	13	52	66	40
Middlesbrough	42	12	15	15	42	54	39
Wolverhampton Wands.	42	12	12	18	51	64	36
Chelsea	42	11	14	17	46	69	36
Bristol City	42	11	13	18	49	53	35
Ipswich Town	42	11	13	18	47	61	35
Queen's Park Rangers	42	9	15	18	47	64	33
West Ham United	42	12	8	22	52	69	32
Newcastle United	42	6	10	26	42	78	22
Leicester City	42	5	12	25	26	70	22

Season 1978/79

DIVISION ONE

Liverpool	42	30	8	4	85	16	68
Nottingham Forest	42	21	18	3	61	26	60
West Bromwich Albion	42	24	11	7	72	35	59
Everton	**42**	**17**	**17**	**8**	**52**	**40**	**51**
Leeds United	42	18	14	10	70	52	50
Ipswich Town	42	20	9	13	63	49	49
Arsenal	42	17	14	11	61	48	48
Aston Villa	42	15	16	11	59	49	46
Manchester United	42	15	15	12	60	63	45
Coventry City	42	14	16	12	58	68	44
Tottenham Hotspur	42	13	15	14	48	61	41
Middlesbrough	42	15	10	17	57	50	40
Bristol City	42	15	10	17	47	51	40
Southampton	42	12	16	14	47	53	40
Manchester City	42	13	13	16	58	56	39
Norwich City	42	7	23	12	51	57	37
Bolton Wanderers	42	12	11	19	54	75	35
Wolverhampton Wands.	42	13	8	21	44	68	34
Derby County	42	10	11	21	44	71	31
Queen's Park Rangers	42	6	13	23	45	73	25
Birmingham City	42	6	10	26	37	64	22
Chelsea	42	5	10	27	44	92	20

Season 1979/80

DIVISION ONE

Liverpool	42	25	10	7	81	30	60
Manchester United	42	24	10	8	65	35	58
Ispwich	42	22	9	11	68	39	53
Arsenal	42	18	16	8	52	36	52
Nottingham Forest	42	20	8	14	63	43	48
Wolverhampton Wands.	42	19	9	14	58	47	47
Aston Villa	42	16	14	12	51	50	46
Southampton	42	18	9	15	65	53	45
Middlesbrough	42	16	12	14	50	44	44
West Bromwich Albion	42	11	19	12	54	50	41
Leeds United	42	13	14	15	46	50	40
Norwich City	42	13	14	15	58	66	40
Crystal Palace	42	12	16	14	41	50	40
Tottenham Hotspur	42	15	10	17	52	62	40
Coventry City	42	16	7	19	56	66	39
Brighton & Hove Albion	42	11	15	16	47	57	37
Manchester City	42	12	13	17	43	66	37
Stoke City	42	13	10	19	44	58	36
Everton	**42**	**9**	**17**	**16**	**43**	**51**	**35**
Bristol City	42	9	13	20	37	66	31
Derby County	42	11	8	23	47	67	30
Bolton Wanderers	42	5	15	22	38	73	25

Season 1980/81

DIVISION ONE

Aston Villa	42	26	8	8	72	40	60
Ipswich Town	42	23	10	9	77	43	56
Arsenal	42	19	15	8	61	45	53
West Bromwich Albion	42	20	12	10	60	42	52
Liverpool	42	17	17	8	62	42	51
Southampton	42	20	10	12	76	56	50
Nottingham Forest	42	19	12	11	62	44	50
Manchester United	42	15	18	9	51	36	48
Leeds United	42	17	10	15	39	47	44
Tottenham Hotspur	42	14	15	13	70	68	43
Stoke City	42	12	18	12	51	60	42
Manchester City	42	14	11	17	56	59	39
Birmingham City	42	13	12	17	50	61	38
Middlesbrough	42	16	5	21	53	61	37
Everton	**42**	**13**	**10**	**19**	**55**	**58**	**36**
Coventry City	42	13	10	19	48	68	36
Sunderland	42	14	7	21	52	53	35
Wolverhampton Wands.	42	13	9	20	43	55	35
Brighton & Hove Albion	42	14	7	21	54	67	35
Norwich City	42	13	7	22	49	73	33
Leicester City	42	13	6	23	40	67	32
Crystal Palace	42	6	7	29	47	83	19

Season 1981/82

DIVISION ONE

Liverpool	42	26	9	7	80	32	87
Ipswich Town	42	26	5	11	75	53	83
Manchester United	42	22	12	8	59	29	78
Tottenham Hotspur	42	20	11	11	67	48	71
Arsenal	42	20	11	11	48	37	71
Swansea City	42	21	6	15	58	51	69
Southampton	42	19	9	14	72	67	66
Everton	**42**	**17**	**13**	**12**	**56**	**50**	**64**
West Ham United	42	14	16	12	66	57	58
Manchester City	42	15	13	14	49	50	58
Aston Villa	42	15	12	15	55	53	57
Nottingham Forest	42	15	12	15	42	48	57
Brighton & Hove Albion	42	13	13	16	43	52	52
Coventry City	42	13	11	18	56	62	50
Notts County	42	13	8	21	61	69	47
Birmingham City	42	10	14	18	53	61	44
West Bromwich Albion	42	11	11	20	46	57	44
Stoke City	42	12	8	22	44	63	44
Sunderland	42	11	11	20	38	58	44
Leeds United	42	10	12	20	39	61	42
Wolverhampton Wands.	42	10	10	22	32	63	40
Middlesbrough	42	8	15	19	34	52	39

Season 1982/83

DIVISION ONE

Liverpool	42	24	10	8	87	37	82
Watford	42	22	5	15	74	57	71
Manchester United	42	19	13	10	56	38	70
Tottenham Hotspur	42	20	9	13	65	50	69
Nottingham Forest	42	20	9	13	62	50	69
Aston Villa	42	21	5	16	62	50	68
Everton	**42**	**18**	**10**	**14**	**66**	**48**	**64**
West Ham United	42	20	4	18	68	62	64
Ipswich Town	42	15	13	14	64	50	58
Arsenal	42	16	10	16	58	56	58
West Bromwich Albion	42	15	12	15	51	49	57
Southampton	42	15	12	15	54	58	57
Stoke City	42	16	9	17	53	64	57
Norwich City	42	14	12	16	52	58	54
Notts County	42	15	7	20	55	71	52
Sunderland	42	12	14	16	48	61	50
Birmingham City	42	12	14	16	40	55	50
Luton Town	42	12	13	17	65	84	49
Coventry City	42	13	9	20	48	59	48
Manchester City	42	13	8	21	47	70	47
Swansea City	42	10	11	21	51	69	41
Brighton & Hove Albion	42	9	13	20	38	68	40

Season 1983/84

DIVISION ONE

Liverpool	42	22	14	6	73	32	80
Southampton	42	22	11	9	66	38	77
Nottingham Forest	42	22	8	12	76	45	74
Manchester United	42	20	14	8	71	41	74
Queen's Park Rangers	42	22	7	13	67	37	73
Arsenal	42	18	9	15	74	60	63
Everton	**42**	**16**	**14**	**12**	**44**	**42**	**62**
Tottenham Hotspur	42	17	10	15	64	65	61
West Ham United	42	17	9	16	60	55	60
Aston Villa	42	17	9	16	59	61	60
Watford	42	16	9	17	68	77	57
Ipswich Town	42	15	8	19	55	57	53
Sunderland	42	13	13	16	42	53	52
Norwich City	42	12	15	15	48	49	51
Leicester City	42	13	12	17	65	68	51
Luton Town	42	14	9	19	53	66	51
West Bromwich Albion	42	14	9	19	48	62	51
Stoke City	42	13	11	18	44	63	50
Coventry City	42	13	11	18	57	77	50
Birmingham City	42	12	12	18	39	50	48
Notts County	42	10	11	21	50	72	41
Wolverhampton Wands.	42	6	11	25	27	80	29

Season 1984/85

DIVISION ONE

Everton	**42**	**28**	**6**	**8**	**88**	**43**	**90**
Liverpool	42	22	11	9	68	35	77
Tottenham Hotspur	42	23	8	11	78	51	77
Manchester United	42	22	10	10	77	47	76
Southampton	42	19	11	12	56	47	68
Chelsea	42	18	12	12	63	48	66
Arsenal	42	19	9	14	61	49	66
Sheffield Wednesday	42	17	14	11	58	45	65
Nottingham Forest	42	19	7	16	56	48	64
Aston Villa	42	15	11	16	60	60	56
Watford	42	14	13	15	81	71	55
West Bromwich Albion	42	16	7	19	58	62	55
Luton Town	42	15	9	18	57	61	54
Newcastle United	42	13	13	16	55	70	52
Leicester City	42	15	6	21	65	73	51
West Ham United	42	13	12	17	51	68	51
Ipswich Town	42	13	11	18	46	57	50
Coventry City	42	15	5	22	47	64	50
Queen's Park Rangers	42	13	11	18	53	72	50
Norwich City	42	13	10	19	46	64	49
Sunderland	42	10	10	22	40	62	40
Stoke City	42	3	8	31	24	91	17

Season 1985/86

DIVISION ONE

Liverpool	42	26	10	6	89	37	88
Everton	**42**	**26**	**8**	**8**	**87**	**41**	**86**
West Ham United	42	26	6	10	74	40	84
Manchester United	42	22	10	10	70	36	76
Sheffield Wednesday	42	21	10	11	63	54	73
Chelsea	42	20	11	11	57	56	71
Arsenal	42	20	9	13	49	47	69
Nottingham Forest	42	19	11	12	69	53	68
Luton Town	42	18	12	12	61	44	66
Tottenham Hotspur	42	19	8	15	74	52	65
Newcastle United	42	17	12	13	67	72	63
Watford	42	16	11	15	69	62	59
Queen's Park Rangers	42	15	7	20	53	64	52
Southampton	42	12	10	20	51	62	46
Manchester City	42	11	12	19	43	57	45
Aston Villa	42	10	14	18	51	67	44
Coventry City	42	11	10	21	48	71	43
Oxford United	42	10	12	20	62	80	42
Leicester City	42	10	12	20	54	76	42
Ipswich Town	42	11	8	23	32	55	41
Birmingham City	42	8	5	29	30	73	29
West Bromwich Albion	42	4	12	26	35	89	24

Season 1986/87

DIVISION ONE

Everton	**42**	**26**	**8**	**8**	**76**	**31**	**86**
Liverpool	42	23	8	11	72	42	77
Tottenham Hotspur	42	21	8	13	68	43	71
Arsenal	42	20	10	12	58	35	70
Norwich City	42	17	17	8	53	51	68
Wimbledon	42	19	9	14	57	50	66
Luton Town	42	18	12	12	47	45	66
Nottingham Forest	42	18	11	13	64	51	65
Watford	42	18	9	15	67	54	63
Coventry City	42	17	12	13	50	45	63
Manchester United	42	14	14	14	52	45	56
Southampton	42	14	10	18	69	68	52
Sheffield Wednesday	42	13	13	16	58	59	52
Chelsea	42	13	13	16	53	64	52
West Ham United	42	14	10	18	52	67	52
Queen's Park Rangers	42	13	11	18	48	64	50
Newcastle United	42	12	11	19	47	65	47
Oxford United	42	11	13	18	44	69	46
Charlton Athletic	42	11	11	20	45	55	44
Leicester City	42	11	9	22	54	76	42
Manchester City	42	8	15	19	36	57	39
Aston Villa	42	8	12	22	45	79	36

Season 1987/88

DIVISION ONE

Liverpool	40	26	12	2	87	24	90
Manchester United	40	23	12	5	71	38	81
Nottingham Forest	40	20	13	7	67	39	73
Everton	**40**	**19**	**13**	**8**	**53**	**27**	**70**
Queen's Park Rangers	40	19	10	11	48	38	67
Arsenal	40	18	12	10	58	39	66
Wimbledon	40	14	15	11	58	47	57
Newcastle United	40	14	14	12	55	53	56
Luton Town	40	14	11	15	57	58	53
Coventry City	40	13	14	13	46	53	53
Sheffield Wednesday	40	15	8	17	52	66	53
Southampton	40	12	14	14	49	53	50
Tottenham Hotspur	40	12	11	17	38	48	47
Norwich City	40	12	9	19	40	52	45
Derby County	40	10	13	17	35	45	43
West Ham United	40	9	15	16	40	52	42
Charlton Athletic	40	9	15	16	38	52	42
Chelsea	40	9	15	16	50	68	42
Portsmouth	40	7	14	19	36	66	35
Watford	40	7	11	22	27	51	32
Oxford United	40	6	13	21	44	80	31

Season 1988/89

DIVISION ONE

Arsenal	38	22	10	6	73	36	76
Liverpool	38	22	10	6	65	28	76
Nottingham Forest	38	17	13	8	64	43	64
Norwich City	38	17	11	10	48	45	62
Derby County	38	17	7	14	40	38	58
Tottenham Hotspur	38	15	12	11	60	46	57
Coventry City	38	14	13	11	47	42	55
Everton	**38**	**14**	**12**	**12**	**50**	**45**	**54**
Queen's Park Rangers	38	14	11	13	43	37	53
Millwall	38	14	11	13	47	52	53
Manchester United	38	13	12	13	45	35	51
Wimbledon	38	14	9	15	50	46	51
Southampton	38	10	15	13	52	66	45
Charlton Athletic	38	10	12	16	44	58	42
Sheffield Wednesday	38	10	12	16	34	51	42
Luton Town	38	10	11	17	42	52	41
Aston Villa	38	9	13	16	45	56	40
Middlesbrough	38	9	12	17	44	61	39
West Ham United	38	10	8	20	37	62	38
Newcastle United	38	7	10	21	32	63	31

Season 1989/90

DIVISION ONE

Liverpool	38	23	10	5	78	37	79
Aston Villa	38	21	7	10	57	38	70
Tottenham Hotspur	38	19	6	13	59	47	63
Arsenal	38	18	8	12	54	38	62
Chelsea	38	16	12	10	58	50	60
Everton	**38**	**17**	**8**	**13**	**57**	**46**	**59**
Southampton	38	15	10	13	71	63	55
Wimbledon	38	13	16	9	47	40	55
Nottingham Forest	38	15	9	14	55	47	54
Norwich City	38	13	14	11	44	42	53
Queen's Park Rangers	38	13	11	14	45	44	50
Coventry City	38	14	7	17	39	59	49
Manchester United	38	13	9	16	46	47	48
Manchester City	38	12	12	14	43	52	48
Crystal Palace	38	13	9	16	42	66	48
Derby County	38	13	7	18	43	40	46
Luton Town	38	10	13	15	43	57	43
Sheffield Wednesday	38	11	10	17	35	51	43
Charlton Athletic	38	7	9	22	31	57	30
Millwall	38	5	11	22	39	65	26

Season 1990/91

DIVISION ONE

Arsenal	38	24	13	1	74	18	83
Liverpool	38	23	7	8	77	40	76
Crystal Palace	38	20	9	9	50	41	69
Leeds United	38	19	7	12	65	47	64
Manchester City	38	17	11	10	64	53	62
Manchester United	38	16	12	10	58	45	60
Wimbledon	38	14	14	10	53	46	56
Nottingham Forest	38	14	12	12	65	50	54
Everton	**38**	**13**	**12**	**13**	**50**	**46**	**51**
Tottenham Hotspur	38	11	16	11	51	50	49
Chelsea	38	13	10	15	58	69	49
Queen's Park Rangers	38	12	10	16	44	53	46
Sheffield United	38	13	7	18	36	55	46
Southampton	38	12	9	17	58	69	45
Norwich City	38	13	6	19	41	64	45
Coventry City	38	11	11	16	42	49	44
Aston Villa	38	9	14	15	46	58	41
Luton Town	38	10	7	21	42	61	37
Sunderland	38	8	10	20	38	60	34
Derby County	38	5	9	24	37	75	24

Arsenal had 2 points deducted
Manchester United had 1 point deducted

Season 1991/92

DIVISION ONE

Leeds United	42	22	16	4	74	37	82
Manchester United	42	21	15	6	63	33	78
Sheffield Wednesday	42	21	12	9	62	49	75
Arsenal	42	19	15	8	81	46	72
Manchester City	42	20	10	12	61	48	70
Liverpool	42	16	16	10	47	40	64
Aston Villa	42	17	9	16	48	44	60
Nottingham Forest	42	16	11	15	60	58	59
Sheffield United	42	16	9	17	65	63	57
Crystal Palace	42	14	15	13	53	61	57
Queen's Park Rangers	42	12	18	12	48	47	54
Everton	**42**	**13**	**14**	**15**	**52**	**51**	**53**
Wimbledon	42	13	14	15	53	53	53
Chelsea	42	13	14	15	50	60	53
Tottenham Hotspur	42	15	7	20	58	63	52
Southampton	42	14	10	18	39	55	52
Oldham Athletic	42	14	9	19	63	67	51
Norwich City	42	11	12	19	47	63	45
Coventry City	42	11	11	20	35	44	44
Luton Town	42	10	12	20	38	71	42
Notts County	42	10	10	22	40	62	40
West Ham United	42	9	11	22	37	59	38

Season 1992/93

F.A. PREMIER LEAGUE

Manchester United	42	24	12	6	67	31	84
Aston Villa	42	21	11	10	57	40	74
Norwich City	42	21	9	12	61	65	72
Blackburn Rovers	42	20	11	11	68	46	71
Queen's Park Rangers	42	17	12	13	63	55	63
Liverpool	42	16	11	15	62	55	59
Sheffield Wednesday	42	15	14	13	55	51	59
Tottenham Hotspur	42	16	11	15	60	66	59
Manchester City	42	15	12	15	56	51	57
Arsenal	42	15	11	16	40	38	56
Chelsea	42	14	14	14	51	54	56
Wimbledon	42	14	12	16	56	55	54
Everton	**42**	**15**	**8**	**19**	**53**	**55**	**53**
Sheffield United	42	14	10	18	54	53	52
Coventry City	42	13	13	16	52	57	52
Ipswich Town	42	12	16	14	50	55	52
Leeds United	42	12	15	15	57	62	51
Southampton	42	13	11	18	54	61	50
Oldham Athletic	42	13	10	19	63	74	49
Crystal Palace	42	11	16	15	48	61	49
Middlesbrough	42	11	11	20	54	75	44
Nottingham Forest	42	10	10	22	41	62	40

Season 1993/94

F.A.PREMIERSHIP

Manchester United	42	27	11	4	80	38	92
Blackburn Rovers	42	25	9	8	63	36	84
Newcastle United	42	23	8	11	82	41	77
Arsenal	42	18	17	7	53	28	71
Leeds United	42	18	16	8	65	39	70
Wimbledon	42	18	11	13	56	53	65
Sheffield Wednesday	42	16	16	10	76	54	64
Liverpool	42	17	9	16	59	55	60
Queen's Park Rangers	42	16	12	14	62	61	60
Aston Villa	42	15	12	15	46	50	57
Coventry City	42	14	14	14	43	45	56
Norwich City	42	12	17	13	65	61	53
West Ham United	42	13	13	16	47	58	52
Chelsea	42	13	12	17	49	53	51
Tottenham Hotspur	42	11	12	19	54	59	45
Manchester City	42	9	18	15	38	49	45
Everton	**42**	**12**	**8**	**22**	**42**	**63**	**44**
Southampton	42	12	7	23	49	66	43
Ipswich Town	42	9	16	17	35	58	43
Sheffield United	42	8	18	16	42	60	42
Oldham Athletic	42	9	13	20	42	68	40
Swindon Town	42	5	15	22	47	100	30

Season 1995/96

F.A. PREMIERSHIP

Manchester United	38	25	7	6	73	35	82
Newcastle United	38	24	6	8	66	37	78
Liverpool	38	20	11	7	70	34	71
Aston Villa	38	18	9	11	52	35	63
Arsenal	38	17	12	9	49	32	63
Everton	**38**	**17**	**10**	**11**	**64**	**44**	**61**
Blackburn Rovers	38	18	7	13	61	47	61
Tottenham Hotspur	38	16	13	9	50	38	61
Nottingham Forest	38	15	13	10	50	54	58
West Ham United	38	14	9	15	43	52	51
Chelsea	38	12	14	12	46	44	50
Middlesbrough	38	11	10	17	35	50	43
Leeds United	38	12	7	19	40	57	43
Wimbledon	38	10	11	17	55	70	41
Sheffield Wednesday	38	10	10	18	48	61	40
Coventry City	38	8	14	16	42	60	38
Southampton	38	9	11	18	34	52	38
Manchester City	38	9	11	18	33	58	38
Queen's Park Rangers	38	9	6	23	38	57	33
Bolton Wanderers	38	8	5	25	39	71	29

Season 1994/95

F.A. PREMIERSHIP

Blackburn Rovers	42	27	8	7	80	39	89
Manchester United	42	26	10	6	77	28	88
Nottingham Forest	42	22	11	9	72	43	77
Liverpool	42	21	11	10	65	37	74
Leeds United	42	20	13	9	59	38	73
Newcastle United	42	20	12	10	67	47	72
Tottenham Hotspur	42	16	14	12	66	58	62
Queen's Park Rangers	42	17	9	16	61	59	60
Wimbledon	42	15	11	16	48	65	56
Southampton	42	12	18	12	61	63	54
Chelsea	42	13	15	14	50	55	54
Arsenal	42	13	12	17	52	49	51
Sheffield Wednesday	42	13	12	17	49	57	51
West Ham United	42	13	11	18	44	48	50
Everton	**42**	**11**	**17**	**14**	**44**	**51**	**50**
Coventry City	42	12	14	16	44	62	50
Manchester City	42	12	13	17	53	64	49
Aston Villa	42	11	15	16	51	56	48
Crystal Palace	42	11	12	19	34	49	45
Norwich City	42	10	13	19	37	54	43
Leicester City	42	6	11	25	45	80	29
Ipswich Town	42	7	6	29	36	93	27

Season 1996/97

F.A. PREMIERSHIP

Manchester United	38	21	12	5	76	44	75
Newcastle United	38	19	11	8	73	40	68
Arsenal	38	19	11	8	62	32	68
Liverpool	38	19	11	8	62	37	68
Aston Villa	38	17	10	11	47	34	61
Chelsea	38	16	11	11	58	55	59
Sheffield Wednesday	38	14	15	9	50	51	57
Wimbledon	38	15	11	12	49	46	56
Leicester City	38	12	11	15	46	54	47
Tottenham Hotspur	38	13	7	18	44	51	46
Leeds United	38	11	13	14	28	38	46
Derby County	38	11	13	14	45	58	46
Blackburn Rovers	38	9	15	14	42	43	42
West Ham United	38	10	12	16	39	48	42
Everton	**38**	**10**	**12**	**16**	**44**	**57**	**42**
Southampton	38	10	11	17	50	56	41
Coventry City	38	9	14	15	38	54	41
Sunderland	38	10	10	18	35	53	40
Middlesbrough	38	10	12	16	51	60	39
Nottingham Forest	38	6	16	16	31	59	34

Middlesbrough had 3 points deducted

Season 1997/98

F.A. PREMIERSHIP

Arsenal	38	23	9	6	68	33	78
Manchester United	38	23	8	7	73	26	77
Liverpool	38	18	11	9	68	42	65
Chelsea	38	20	3	15	71	43	63
Leeds United	38	17	8	13	57	46	59
Blackburn Rovers	38	16	10	12	57	52	58
Aston Villa	38	17	6	15	49	48	57
West Ham United	38	16	8	14	56	57	56
Derby County	38	16	7	15	52	49	55
Leicester City	38	13	14	11	51	41	53
Coventry City	38	12	16	10	46	44	52
Southampton	38	14	6	18	50	55	48
Newcastle United	38	11	11	16	35	44	44
Tottenham Hotspur	38	11	11	16	44	56	44
Wimbledon	38	10	14	14	34	46	44
Sheffield Wednesday	38	12	8	18	52	67	44
Everton	**38**	**9**	**13**	**16**	**41**	**56**	**40**
Bolton Wanderers	38	9	13	16	41	61	40
Barnsley	38	10	5	23	37	82	35
Crystal Palace	38	8	9	21	37	71	33

Season 1999/2000

F.A. PREMIERSHIP

Manchester United	38	28	7	3	97	45	91
Arsenal	38	22	7	9	73	43	73
Leeds United	38	21	6	11	58	43	69
Liverpool	38	19	10	9	51	30	67
Chelsea	38	18	11	9	53	34	65
Aston Villa	38	15	13	10	46	35	58
Sunderland	38	16	10	12	57	56	58
Leicester City	38	16	7	15	55	55	55
West Ham United	38	15	10	13	52	53	55
Tottenham Hotspur	38	15	8	15	57	49	53
Newcastle United	38	14	10	14	63	54	52
Middlesbrough	38	14	10	14	46	52	52
Everton	**38**	**12**	**14**	**12**	**59**	**49**	**50**
Coventry City	38	12	8	18	47	54	44
Southampton	38	12	8	18	45	62	44
Derby County	38	9	11	18	44	57	38
Bradford City	38	9	9	20	38	68	36
Wimbledon	38	7	12	19	46	74	33
Sheffield Wednesday	38	8	7	23	38	70	31
Watford	38	6	6	26	35	77	24

Season 1998/99

F.A. PREMIERSHIP

Manchester United	38	22	13	3	80	37	79
Arsenal	38	22	12	4	59	17	78
Chelsea	38	20	15	3	57	30	75
Leeds United	38	18	13	7	62	34	67
West Ham United	38	16	9	13	46	53	57
Aston Villa	38	15	10	13	51	46	55
Liverpool	38	15	9	14	68	49	54
Derby County	38	13	13	12	40	45	52
Middlesbrough	38	12	15	11	48	54	51
Leicester City	38	12	13	13	40	46	49
Tottenham Hotspur	38	11	14	13	47	50	47
Sheffield Wednesday	38	13	7	18	41	42	46
Newcastle United	38	11	13	14	48	54	46
Everton	**38**	**11**	**10**	**17**	**42**	**47**	**43**
Coventry City	38	11	9	18	39	51	42
Wimbledon	38	10	12	16	40	63	42
Southampton	38	11	8	19	37	64	41
Charlton Athletic	38	8	12	18	41	56	36
Blackburn Rovers	38	7	14	17	38	52	35
Nottingham Forest	38	7	9	22	35	69	30

Season 2000/2001

F.A. PREMIERSHIP

Manchester United	38	24	8	6	79	31	80
Arsenal	38	20	10	8	63	38	70
Liverpool	38	20	9	9	71	39	69
Leeds United	38	20	8	10	64	43	68
Ipswich Town	38	20	6	12	57	42	66
Chelsea	38	17	10	11	68	45	61
Sunderland	38	15	12	11	46	41	57
Aston Villa	38	13	15	10	46	43	54
Charlton Athletic	38	14	10	14	50	57	52
Southampton	38	14	10	14	40	48	52
Newcastle United	38	14	9	15	44	50	51
Tottenham Hotspur	38	13	10	15	47	54	49
Leicester City	38	14	6	18	39	51	48
Middlesbrough	38	9	15	14	44	44	42
West Ham United	38	10	12	16	45	50	42
Everton	**38**	**11**	**9**	**18**	**45**	**59**	**42**
Derby County	38	10	12	16	37	59	42
Manchester City	38	8	10	20	41	65	34
Coventry City	38	8	10	20	36	63	34
Bradford City	38	5	11	22	30	70	26

Season 2001/2002

F.A. PREMIERSHIP

Arsenal	38	26	9	3	79	36	87
Liverpool	38	24	8	6	67	30	80
Manchester United	38	24	5	9	87	45	77
Newcastle United	38	21	8	9	74	52	71
Leeds United	38	18	12	8	53	37	66
Chelsea	38	17	13	8	66	38	64
West Ham United	38	15	8	15	48	57	53
Aston Villa	38	12	14	12	46	47	50
Tottenham Hotspur	38	14	8	16	49	53	50
Blackburn Rovers	38	12	10	16	55	51	46
Southampton	38	12	9	17	46	54	45
Middlesbrough	38	12	9	17	35	47	45
Fulham	38	10	14	14	36	44	44
Charlton Athletic	38	10	14	14	38	49	44
Everton	**38**	**11**	**10**	**17**	**45**	**57**	**43**
Bolton Wanderers	38	9	13	16	44	62	40
Sunderland	38	10	10	18	29	51	40
Ipswich Town	38	9	9	20	41	64	36
Derby County	38	8	6	24	33	63	30
Leicester City	38	5	13	20	30	64	28

EVERTON CUP RESULTS – 1977-78 to 2001-2002

F.A. CUP COMPETITION

1977/78 SEASON

3rd Round

Jan 7 vs Aston Villa (h) 4-1

Att: 46,320 King, Ross (pen), McKenzie, Latchford

4th Round

Jan 28 vs Middlesbrough (a) 2-3

Att: 33,692 Telfer, Lyons

1978/79 SEASON

3rd Round

Jan 10 vs Sunderland (a) 1-2

Att: 28,602 Dobson

1979/80 SEASON

3rd Round

Jan 5 vs Aldershot (h) 4-1

Att: 23,700 Latchford, Hartford, King, Kidd

4th Round

Jan 26 vs Wigan Athletic (h) 3-0

Att: 51,853 McBride, Latchford, Kidd

5th Round

Feb 16 vs Wrexham (h) 5-2

Att: 44,830 Megson, Eastoe 2, Ross (pen), Latchford

6th Round

Mar 8 vs Ipswich Town (h) 2-1

Att: 45,104 Latchford, Kidd

Semi-Final (at Villa Park)

Apr 12 vs West Ham United 1-1

Att: 47,685 Kidd (pen)

Replay (at Elland Road)

Apr 16 vs West Ham United 1-2

Att: 40,720 Latchford

1980/81 SEASON

3rd Round

Jan 3 vs Arsenal (h) 2-0

Att: 34,240 Sansom (og), Lyons

4th Round
Jan 24 vs Liverpool (h) 2-1
Att: 53,084 Cohen (og), Varadi

5th Round
Feb 14 vs Southampton (a) 0-0
Att: 24,152

Replay
Feb 17 vs Southampton (h) 1-0 (aet.)
Att: 49,192 O'Keefe

6th Round
Mar 7 vs Manchester City (h) 2-2
Att: 52,791 Eastoe, Ross (pen)

Replay
Mar 11 vs Manchester City (a) 1-3
Att: 52,532 Eastoe

1981/82 SEASON

3rd Round
Jan 2 vs West Ham United (a) 1-2
Att: 24,431 Eastoe

1982/83 SEASON

3rd Round
Jan 8 vs Newport County (a) 1-1
Att: 9,527 Sheedy

Replay
Jan 11 vs Newport County (h) 2-1
Att: 18,565 Sharp, King

4th Round
Jan 30 vs Shrewsbury Town (h) 2-1
Att: 35,188 Sheedy, Heath

5th Round
Feb 19 vs Tottenham Hotspur (h) 2-0
Att: 42,995 King, Sharp

6th Round
Mar 12 vs Manchester United (a) 0-1
Att: 58,198

1983/84 SEASON

3rd Round
Jan 6 vs Stoke City (a) 2-0
Att: 16,462 Gray, Irvine

4th Round
Jan 28 vs Gillingham (h) 0-0
Att: 22,380

Replay
Jan 31 vs Gillingham (a) 0-0 (aet.)
Att: 15,339

2nd Replay
Feb 6 vs Gillingham (a) 3-0
Att: 17,817 Sheedy 2, Heath

5th Round
Feb 18 vs Shrewsbury Town (h) 3-0
Att: 27,106 Irvine, Reid, Griffin (og)

6th Round
Mar 10 vs Notts County (a) 2-1
Att: 19,534 Richardson, Gray

Semi-Final (at Highbury)
Apr 14 vs Southampton 1-0 (aet.)
Att: 46,587 Heath

FINAL (at Wembley)
May 19 vs Watford 2-0
Att: 100,000 Sharp, Gray

1984/85 SEASON

3rd Round
Jan 5 vs Leeds United (a) 2-0
Att: 21,211 Sharp (pen), Sheedy

4th Round
Jan 26 vs Doncaster Rovers (h) 2-0
Att: 37,537 Steven, Stevens

5th Round
Feb 16 vs Telford United (h) 3-0
Att: 47,402 Reid, Sheedy (pen), Steven

6th Round
Mar 9 vs Ipswich Town (h) 2-2
Att: 36,468 Sheedy, Mountfield

Replay
Mar 13 vs Ipswich Town (a) 1-0
Att: 27,737 Sharp (pen)

Semi-Final (at Villa Park)
Apr 13 vs Luton Town 2-1 (aet.)
(score after 90 minutes 1-1)
Att: 45,289 Sheedy, Mountfield

FINAL (at Wembley)
May 18 vs Manchester United 0-1
Att: 100,000

1985/86 SEASON

3rd Round
Jan 5 vs Exeter City (h) 1-0
Att: 22,726 Stevens

4th Round
Jan 25 vs Blackburn Rovers (h) 3-1
Att: 41,831 Van den Hauwe, Lineker 2

5th Round
Mar 4 vs Tottenham Hotspur (a) 2-1
Att: 23,338 Heath, Lineker

6th Round
Mar 8 vs Luton Town (a) 2-2
Att: 15,529 Donaghy (og), Heath

Replay
Mar 12 vs Luton Town (h) 1-0
Att: 44,264 Lineker

Semi-Final (at Villa Park)
Apr 5 vs Sheffield Wednesday 2-1
Att: 47,711 Harper, Sharp

FINAL (at Wembley)
May 10 vs Liverpool 1-3
Att: 98,000 Lineker

1986/87 SEASON

3rd Round
Jan 10 vs Southampton (h) 2-1
Att: 32,320 Sharp 2

4th Round
Jan 31 vs Bradford City (a) 1-0
Att: 15,519 Snodin

5th Round
Feb 22 vs Wimbledon (a) 1-3
Att: 9,924 Wilkinson

1987/88 SEASON

3rd Round
Jan 9 vs Sheffield Wednesday (a) 1-1
Att: 33,304 Reid

Replay
Jan 13 vs Sheffield Wed. (h) 1-1 (aet.)
Att: 32,935 Chapman

2nd Replay
Jan 25 vs Sheffield Wed. (h) 1-1 (aet.)
Att: 37,414 Chapman

3rd Replay
Jan 27 vs Sheffield Wednesday (a) 5-0
Att: 38,953 Sharp 3, Heath, Snodin

4th Round
Jan 30 vs Middlesbrough (h) 1-1
Att: 36,564 Sharp

Replay
Feb 3 vs Middlesbrough (a) 2-2 (aet.)
Att: 25,235 Watson, Steven

2nd Replay
Feb 9 vs Middlesbrough (h) 2-1
Att: 32,222 Sharp, Mowbray (og)

5th Round
Feb 21 vs Liverpool (h) 0-1
Att: 48,270

1988/89 SEASON

3rd Round
Jan 7 vs West Bromwich Albion (a) 1-1
Att: 31,186 Sheedy (pen)

Replay
Jan 11 vs West Brom. Albion (h) 1-0
Att: 31,697 Sheedy

4th Round
Jan 28 vs Plymouth Argyle (a) 1-1
Att: 27,566 Sheedy (pen)

Replay
Jan 31 vs Plymouth Argyle (h) 4-0
Att: 28,542 Sharp 2, Nevin, Sheedy

5th Round
Feb 18 vs Barnsley (a) 1-0
Att: 32,551 Sharp

6th Round
Mar 19 vs Wimbledon (h) 1-0
Att: 24,562 McCall

Semi-Final (at Villa Park)
Apr 15 vs Norwich City 1-0
Att: 46,533 Nevin

FINAL (at Wembley)
May 20 vs Liverpool 2-3
Att: 82,800 McCall 2

1989/90 SEASON

3rd Round
Jan 6 vs Middlesbrough (a) 0-0
Att: 20,075

Replay
Jan 10 vs Middlesbrough (h) 1-1 (aet.)
Att: 24,352 Sheedy

2nd Replay
Jan 17 vs Middlesbrough (a) 1-0
Att: 23,866 Whiteside

4th Round
Jan 28 vs Sheffield Wednesday (a) 2-1
Att: 31,754 Whiteside 2

5th Round
Feb 17 vs Oldham Athletic (a) 2-2
Att: 19,320 Sharp, Cottee

Replay
Feb 21 vs Oldham Ath. (h) 1-1 (aet.)
Att: 36,663 Sheedy (pen)

2nd Replay
Mar 10 vs Oldham Ath. (a) 1-2 (aet.)
Att: 19,346 Cottee

1990/91 SEASON

3rd Round
Jan 5 vs Charlton Athletic (a) 2-1
Att: 12,234 Ebbrell 2

4th Round
Jan 27 vs Woking (h) 1-0
Att: 34,724 Sheedy

5th Round
Feb 17 vs Liverpool (a) 0-0
Att: 38,323

Replay
Feb 20 vs Liverpool (h) 4-4 (aet.)
Att: 37,766 Cottee 2, Sharp 2

2nd Replay
Feb 27 vs Liverpool (h) 1-0
Att: 40,201 Watson

6th Round
Mar 11 vs West Ham United (a) 1-2
Att: 28,162 Watson

1991/92 SEASON

3rd Round
Jan 4 vs Southend United (h) 1-0
Att: 22,606 Beardsley

4th Round
Jan 26 vs Chelsea (a) 0-1
Att: 21,152

1992/93 SEASON

3rd Round
Jan 2 vs Wimbledon (h) 0-0
Att: 7,818

Replay
Jan 12 vs Wimbledon (a) 1-2
Att: 15,293 Watson

1993/94 SEASON

3rd Round
Jan 8 vs Bolton Wanderers (a) 1-1
Att: 21,702 Rideout

Replay
Jan 19 vs Bolton Wands. (h) 2-3 (aet.)
Att: 34,642 Barlow 2

1994/95 SEASON

3rd Round
Jan 7 vs Derby County (h) 1-0
Att: 29,406 Hinchcliffe

4th Round
Jan 29 vs Bristol City (a) 1-0
Att: 19,816 Jackson

5th Round
Feb 18 vs Norwich City (h) 5-0
Att: 31,616 Limpar, Parkinson, Rideout, Ferguson, Stuart

6th Round
Mar 12 vs Newcastle United (h) 1-0
Att: 35,203 Watson

Semi-Final (at Elland Road)
Apr 9 vs Tottenham Hotspur 4-1
Att: 38,226 Jackson, Stuart, Amokachi 2

FINAL (at Wembley)
May 20 vs Manchester United 1-0
Att: 79,592 Rideout

1995/96 SEASON

3rd Round
Jan 7 vs Stockport County (h) 2-1
Att: 28,921 Ablett, Stuart

4th Round
Jan 27 vs Port Vale (h) 2-2
Att: 33,168 Amokachi, Ferguson

Replay
Feb 14 vs Port Vale (a) 1-2
Att: 19,197 Stuart

1996/97 SEASON

3rd Round
Jan 5 vs Swindon Town (h) 3-0
Att: 20,411 Kanchelskis (pen), Barmby, Ferguson

4th Round
Jan 25 vs Bradford City (h) 2-3
Att: 30,007 O'Brien (og), Speed

1997/98 SEASON

3rd Round
Jan 4 vs Newcastle United (h) 0-1
Att: 20,885

1998/99 SEASON

3rd Round
Jan 2 vs Bristol City (a) 2-0
Att: 19,608 Bakayoko 2

4th Round
Jan 23 vs Ipswich Town (h) 1-0
Att: 28,854 Barmby

5th Round
Feb 13 vs Coventry City (h) 2-1
Att: 33,907 Jeffers, Oster

6th Round
Mar 7 vs Newcastle United (a) 1-4
Att: 36,504 Unsworth

1999/2000 SEASON

3rd Round
Dec 11 vs Exeter City (a) 0-0
Att: 6,045

Replay
Dec 21 vs Exeter City (h) 1-0
Att: 16,869 Barmby

4th Round
Jan 8 vs Birmingham City (h) 2-0
Att: 25,405 Unsworth 2 (2 pens)

5th Round
Jan 29 vs Preston North End (h) 2-0
Att: 37,486 Unsworth, Moore

6th Round
Feb 20 vs Aston Villa (h) 1-2
Att: 35,331 Moore

2000/2001 SEASON

3rd Round
Jan 6 vs Watford (a) 2-1
Att: 15,635 Hughes, Watson

4th Round
Jan 27 vs Tranmere Rovers (h) 0-3
Att: 39,207

2001/2002 SEASON

3rd Round
Jan 5 vs Stoke City (a) 1-0
Att: 28,218 Stubbs

4th Round
Jan 26 vs Leyton Orient (h) 4-1
Att: 35,851 McGhee (og), Ferguson, Campbell 2

5th Round
Feb 17 vs Crewe Alexandra (h) 0-0
Att: 29,399

Replay
Feb 26 vs Crewe Alexandra (a) 2-1
Att: 10,073 Radzinski, Campbell

6th Round
Mar 10 vs Middlesbrough (a) 0-3
Att: 26,950

LEAGUE CUP COMPETITION

1977/78 SEASON

2nd Round
Aug 30 vs Sheffield United (a) 3-0
Att: 18,571 Latchford, McKenzie, King

3rd Round
Oct 25 vs Middlesbrough (h) 2-2
Att: 32,766 King, Telfer

Replay
Oct 31 vs Middlesbrough (a) 2-1
Att: 28,500 Lyons, Pearson

4th Round
Nov 29 vs Sheffield Wednesday (a) 3-1
Att: 36,079 Lyons, Dobson, Pearson

5th Round
Jan 18 vs Leeds United (a) 1-4
Att: 35,020 Thomas

1978/79 SEASON

2nd Round
Aug 29 vs Wimbledon (h) 8-0
Att: 23,137 Latchford 5 (1 pen), Dobson 3

3rd Round
Oct 3 vs Darlington (h) 1-0
Att: 23,682 Dobson

4th Round
Nov 7 vs Nottingham Forest (h) 2-3
Att: 48,503 Burns (og), Latchford

1979/80 SEASON

2nd Round (1st leg)
Aug 28 vs Cardiff City (h) 2-0
Att: 18,061 Kidd 2

2nd Round (2nd leg)
Sep 5 vs Cardiff City (a) 0-1 (agg. 2-1)
Att: 9,698

3rd Round
Sep 25 vs Aston Villa (a) 0-0
Att: 22,635

Replay
Oct 9 vs Aston Villa (h) 4-1
Att: 22,080 Kidd, Latchford 2, Rimmer (og)

4th Round
Oct 30 vs Grimsby Town (a) 1-2
Att: 22,043 Kidd

1980/81 SEASON

2nd Round (1st leg)
Aug 26 vs Blackpool (h) 3-0
Att: 20,156 Eastoe, Latchford, McBride

2nd Round (2nd leg)
Sep 3 vs Blackpool (a) 2-2 (agg. 5-2)
Att: 10,579 Latchford 2

3rd Round
Sep 24 vs West Brom. Albion (h) 1-2
Att: 23,436 Gidman

1981/82 SEASON

2nd Round (1st leg)
Oct 6 vs Coventry City (h) 1-1
Att: 17,228 Ferguson

2nd Round (2nd leg)
Oct 27 vs Coventry City (a) 1-0
(aggregate 2-1)
Att: 13,770 Ferguson

3rd Round
Nov 11 vs Oxford United (h) 1-0
Att: 14,910 O'Keefe

4th Round
Dec 15 vs Ipswich Town (h) 2-3
Att: 15,759 McMahon 2

1982/83 SEASON

2nd Round (1st leg)
Oct 5 vs Newport County (a) 2-0
Att: 8,293 McMahon, King

2nd Round (2nd leg)
Oct 27 vs Newport County (h) 2-2
(aggregate 4-2)
Att: 8,941 King, Johnson

3rd Round
Nov 9 vs Arsenal (h) 1-1
Att: 13,089 Stevens

Replay
Nov 23 vs Arsenal (a) 0-3
Att: 19,547

1983/84 SEASON

2nd Round (1st leg)
Oct 4 vs Chesterfield (a) 1-0
Att: 10,713 Sharp

2nd Round (2nd leg)
Oct 26 vs Chesterfield (h) 2-2
(aggregate 3-2)
Att: 8,067 Heath, Steven

3rd Round
Nov 9 vs Coventry City (h) 2-1
Att: 9,080 Heath, Sharp

4th Round
Nov 30 vs West Ham United (a) 2-2
Att: 19,702 Reid, Sheedy

Replay
Dec 6 vs West Ham Utd. (h) 2-0 (aet.)
Att: 21,609 King, Sheedy

5th Round
Jan 18 vs Oxford United (a) 1-1
Att: 14,333 Heath

Replay
Jan 24 vs Oxford United (h) 4-1
Att: 31,011 Richardson, Sheedy, Heath, Sharp

Semi-Final (1st leg)
Feb 15 vs Aston Villa (h) 2-0
Att: 40,006 Sheedy, Richardson

Semi-Final (2nd leg)
Feb 22 vs Aston Villa (a) 0-1 (agg. 2-1)
Att: 42,426

FINAL (at Wembley)
Mar 25 vs Liverpool 0-0 (aet.)
Att: 100,000

Replay (at Maine Road)
Mar 28 vs Liverpool 0-1
Att: 52,089

1984/85 SEASON

2nd Round (1st leg)
Sep 26 vs Sheffield United (a) 2-2
Att: 16,345 Sharp, Mountfield

2nd Round (2nd leg)
Oct 10 vs Sheffield United (h) 4-0
(aggregate 6-2)
Att: 18,740 Mountfield, Bracewell, Sharp, Heath

3rd Round
Oct 30 vs Manchester United (a) 2-1
Att: 50,918 Sharp (pen), Gidman (og)

4th Round
Nov 20 vs Grimsby Town (h) 0-1
Att: 26,298

1985/86 SEASON

2nd Round (1st leg)
Sep 25 vs Bournemouth (h) 3-2
Att: 13,930 Lineker, Marshall, Hefferman

2nd Round (2nd leg)
Oct 8 vs Bournemouth (a) 2-0 (aggregate 5-2)
Att: 8,081 Lineker, Richardson

3rd Round
Oct 29 vs Shrewsbury Town (a) 4-1
Att: 10,246 Sharp, Hughes (og), Sheedy, Heath

4th Round
Nov 26 vs Chelsea (a) 2-2
Att: 27,544 Sheedy, Bracewell

Replay
Dec 10 vs Chelsea (h) 1-2
Att: 26,376 Lineker

1986/87 SEASON

2nd Round (1st leg)
Sep 24 vs Newport County (h) 4-0
Att: 11,957 Langley, Heath, Wilkinson 2

2nd Round (2nd leg)
Oct 7 vs Newport County (a) 5-1 (aggregate 9-1)
Att: 7,172 Wilkinson 3, Sharp, Mullen (og)

3rd Round
Oct 28 vs Sheffield Wednesday (h) 4-0
Att: 24,638 Wilkinson 2, Heath, Mountfield

4th Round
Nov 19 vs Norwich City (a) 4-1
Att: 17,988 Sheedy, Sharp, Steven (pen), Heath

5th Round
Jan 21 vs Liverpool (h) 0-1
Att: 53,323

1987/88 SEASON

2nd Round (1st leg)
Sep 22 vs Rotherham United (h) 3-2
Att: 15,369 Snodin, Wilson, Clarke (pen)

2nd Round (2nd leg)
Oct 6 vs Rotherham United (a) 0-0 (aggregate 3-2)
Att: 12,995

3rd Round
Oct 28 vs Liverpool (a) 1-0
Att: 44,071 Stevens

4th Round
Nov 17 vs Oldham Athletic (h) 2-1
Att: 23,315 Watson, Adams

5th Round
Jan 20 vs Manchester City (h) 2-0
Att: 40,014 Heath, Sharp

Semi-Final (1st leg)
Feb 7 vs Arsenal (h) 0-1
Att: 25,476

Semi-Final (2nd leg)
Feb 24 vs Arsenal (a) 1-3 (agg. 1-4)
Att: 51,148 Heath

1988/89 SEASON

2nd Round (1st leg)
Sep 27 vs Bury (h) 3-0
Att: 11,071 Sharp, McDonald (pen), McCall

2nd Round (2nd leg)
Oct 11 vs Bury (a) 2-2 (agg. 5-2)
Att: 4,592 Steven (pen), Sharp

3rd Round
Nov 8 vs Oldham Athletic (h) 1-1
Att: 17,230 Steven (pen)

Replay
Nov 29 vs Oldham Athletic (a) 2-0
Att: 14,573 Cottee 2

4th Round
Dec 14 vs Bradford City (a) 1-3
Att: 15,055 Watson

1989/90 SEASON

2nd Round (1st leg)
Sep 19 vs Leyton Orient (a) 2-0
Att: 8,214 Newell, Sheedy

2nd Round (2nd leg)
Oct 3 vs Leyton Orient (h) 2-2
(aggregate 4-2)
Att: 10,128 Whiteside, Sheedy

3rd Round
Oct 24 vs Luton Town (h) 3-0
Att: 18,428 Newell 2, Nevin

4th Round
Nov 22 vs Nottingham Forest (a) 0-1
Att: 21,324

1990/91 SEASON

2nd Round (1st leg)
Sep 25 vs Wrexham (a) 5-0
Att: 9,072 Cottee 3, McDonald, Nevin

2nd Round (2nd leg)
Oct 9 vs Wrexham (h) 6-0 (agg. 11-0)
Att: 7,415 Sharp 3, Cottee, Ebbrell, McDonald

3rd Round
Oct 30 vs Sheffield United (a) 1-2
Att: 15,045 Pemberton (og)

1991/92 SEASON

2nd Round (1st leg)
Sep 24 vs Watford (h) 1-0
Att: 8,264 Beardsley

2nd Round (2nd leg)
Oct 8 vs Watford (a) 2-1 (agg. 3-1)
Att: 11,561 Newell, Beardsley

3rd Round
Oct 30 vs Wolverhampton W. (h) 4-1
Att: 19,065 Beagrie 2, Cottee, Beardsley

4th Round
Dec 4 vs Leeds United (h) 1-4
Att: 25,467 Atteveld

1992/93 SEASON

2nd Round (1st leg)
Sep 23 vs Rotherham United (a) 0-1
Att: 7,736

2nd Round (2nd leg)
Oct 7 vs Rotherham United (h) 3-0
(aggregate 3-1)
Att: 10,302 Rideout 2, Cottee

3rd Round
Oct 28 vs Wimbledon (h) 0-0
Att: 9,541

Replay
Nov 10 vs Wimbledon (a) 1-0
Att: 3,686 Beardsley

4th Round
Dec 2 vs Chelsea (h) 2-2
Att: 14,457 Barlow, Beardsley

Replay
Dec 16 vs Chelsea (a) 0-1
Att: 19,496

1993/94 SEASON

2nd Round (1st leg)
Sep 21 vs Lincoln City (a) 4-3
Att: 9,153 Rideout 3, Cottee

2nd Round (2nd leg)
Oct 6 vs Lincoln City (h) 4-2
(aggregate 8-5)
Att: 8,375 Rideout, Snodin, Cottee 2

3rd Round
Oct 26 vs Crystal Palace (h) 2-2
Att: 11,547 Beagrie, Watson

Replay
Nov 10 vs Crystal Palace (a) 4-1
Att: 14,662 Watson 2, Ward (pen), Young (og)

4th Round
Nov 30 vs Manchester United (h) 0-2
Att: 34,052

1994/95 SEASON

2nd Round (1st leg)
Sep 20 vs Portsmouth (h) 2-3
Att: 14,043 Samways, Stuart (pen)

2nd Round (2nd leg)
Oct 5 vs Portsmouth (a) 1-1 (agg. 3-4)
Att: 13,605 Watson

1995/96 SEASON

2nd Round (1st leg)
Sep 20 vs Millwall (a) 0-0
Att: 12,053

2nd Round (2nd leg)
Oct 4 vs Millwall (h) 2-4 (agg. 2-4)
Att: 14,891 Hinchcliffe (pen), Stuart

1996/97 SEASON

2nd Round (1st leg)
Sep 18 vs York City (h) 1-1
Att: 11,527 Kanchelskis

2nd Round (2nd leg)
Sep 24 vs York City (a) 2-3 (agg. 3-4)
Att: 7,854 Rideout, Speed

1997/98 SEASON

2nd Round (1st leg)
Sep 16 vs Scunthorpe United (a) 1-0
Att: 7,145 Farrelly

2nd Round (2nd leg)
Oct 1 vs Scunthorpe United (h) 5-0
(aggregate 6-0)
Att: 11,562 Stuart, Oster 2, Barmby, Cadamarteri

3rd Round
Oct 15 vs Coventry City (a) 1-4
Att: 10,087 Barmby

1998/99 SEASON

2nd Round (1st leg)
Sep 15 vs Huddersfield Town (a) 1-1
Att: 15,395 Watson

2nd Round (2nd leg)
Sep 23 vs Huddersfield Town (h) 2-1
(aggregate 3-2)
Att: 18,718 Dacourt, Materazzi

3rd Round
Oct 28 vs Middlesbrough (a) 3-2 (aet)
Att: 20,748 Ferguson, Bakayoko, Hutchison

4th Round
Nov 11 vs Sunderland (h) 1-1 (aet.)
Att: 28,132 Collins
Sunderland won 5-4 on penalties

1999/2000 SEASON

2nd Round (1st leg)
Sep 14 vs Oxford United (a) 1-1
Att: 7,345 Cadamarteri

2nd Round (2nd leg)
Sep 22 vs Oxford United (h) 0-1
(aggregate 1-2)
Att: 10,006

2000/2001 SEASON

2nd Round (1st leg)
Sep 20 vs Bristol Rovers (h) 1-1
Att: 25,564 Campbell

2nd Round (2nd leg)
Sep 27 vs Bristol Rovers (a) 1-1 (aet.)
(aggregate 2-2)
Att: 11,045 Jeffers
Bristol Rovers won 4-2 on penalties

2001/2002 SEASON

2nd Round
Sep 12 vs Crystal Palace (h) 1-1 (aet.)
Att: 21,128 Ferguson (pen)
Crystal Palace won 5-4 on penalties

EUROPEAN CUP-WINNERS-CUP

1984/85 SEASON

1st Round (1st leg)
Sep 19 vs Univ. College Dublin (a) 0-0
Att: 9,750

1st Round (2nd leg)
Oct 2 vs Univ. College Dublin (h) 1-0 (aggregate 1-0)
Att: 16,277 Sharp

2nd Round (1st leg)
Oct 24 vs Inter Bratislava (a) 1-0
Att: 15,000 Bracewell

2nd Round (2nd leg)
Nov 7 vs Inter Bratislava (h) 3-0 (aggregate 4-0)
Att: 25,007 Heath, Sharp, Sheedy

Quarter-Final (1st leg)
Mar 6 vs Fortuna Sittard (h) 3-0
Att: 25,782 Gray 3

Quarter-Final (2nd leg)
Mar 20 vs Fortuna Sittard (a) 2-0 (aggregate 5-0)
Att: 20,000 Reid, Sharp

Semi-Final (1st leg)
Apr 10 vs Bayern Munich (a) 0-0
Att: 67,000

Semi-Final (2nd leg)
Apr 24 vs Bayern Munich (h) 3-1 (aggregate 3-1)
Att: 49,476 Sharp, Gray, Steven

FINAL (at Rotterdam)
May 15 vs Rapid Vienna 3-1
Att: 38,500 Gray, Steven, Sheedy

1995/96 SEASON

1st Round (1st leg)
Sep 14 vs KR Reykjavik (a) 3-2
Att: 6,000 Ebbrell, Unsworth (pen), Amokachi

1st Round (2nd leg)
Sep 28 vs KR Reykjavik (h) 3-1 (aggregate 6-3)
Att: 18,422 Stuart, Grant, Rideout

2nd Round (1st leg)
Oct 19 vs Feyenoord (h) 0-0
Att: 27,526

2nd Round (2nd leg)
Nov 2 vs Feyenoord (a) 0-1 (agg. 0-1)
Att: 40,000

UEFA CUP

1978/79 SEASON

1st Round (1st leg)
Sep 12 vs Finn Harps (a) 5-0
Att: 5,000 Thomas, King 2, Latchford, Walsh

1st Round (2nd leg)
Sep 26 vs Finn Harps (h) 5-0 (aggregate 10-0)
Att: 21,611 King, Latchford, Walsh, Ross, Dobson

2nd Round (1st leg)
Oct 18 vs Dukla Prague (h) 2-1
Att: 32,857 Latchford, King

2nd Round (2nd leg)
Nov 1 vs Dukla Prague (a) 0-1 (aggregate 2-2)
Att: 35,000
Dukla Prague won on Away Goals

1979/80 SEASON

1st Round (1st leg)
Sep 19 vs Feyenoord (a) 0-1
Att: 40,000

1st Round (2nd leg)
Oct 3 vs Feyenoord (h) 0-1 (agg. 0-2)
Att: 28,203

EVERTON 25 SEASONS 1977-78 TO 2001-02

THE 25 MEN WHO HAVE APPEARED MOST FREQUENTLY

LEAGUE APPEARANCES 1977-1978 TO 2001-2002

25 SEASONS TOTAL

1	Neville Southall	578
2	Dave Watson	423
3	Kevin Ratcliffe	359
4	Graeme Sharp	322
5	Kevin Sheedy	274
6	David Unsworth	245
7	Adrian Heath	226
8	John Ebbrell	217
9	Trevor Steven	214
10	Gary Stevens	208
11	Tony Cottee	184
12	Andy Hinchcliffe	182
13	Alan Harper	178
14	Mike Lyons	177
15	John Bailey	171
16	Billy Wright	166
17	Peter Reid	159
18	Andy King	155
19	Duncan Ferguson	150
20	Mark Higgins	149
21	Ian Snodin	148
22	Graham Stuart	136
23	Van Den Hawue	135
24	Trevor Ross	124
25	Barry Horne	123

EVER-PRESENTS (15)

7 campaigns: Neville Southall (1984-1985, 1988-1989, 1989-1990, 1990-1991, 1991-1992, 1993-1994 and 1995-1996)

2 campaigns: George Wood (1977-1978 and 1978-1979)

1 campaign: Mike Lyons (1977-1978), Andy King (1977-1978), John Bailey (1979-1980), Peter Eastoe* (1980-81), Kevin Ratcliffe (1986-1987), Peter Beardsley (1991-1992) and Thomas Myhre (1998-1999)

* includes one game as a substitute

THE 25 LEADING GOALSCORERS

LEAGUE GOALS 1977-1978 TO 2001-2002

25 SEASONS TOTAL

1	Graeme Sharp	111
2	Tony Cottee	72
3	Adrian Heath	71
4	Kevin Sheedy	67
5	Bob Latchford	53
6	Duncan Ferguson	49
7	Trevor Steven	48
8	Andy King	40
9	Kevin Campbell	34
10	Gary Lineker	30
11	Paul Rideout	29
12=	Peter Eastoe	26
12=	David Unsworth	26
14	Peter Beardsley	25
15	Dave Watson	23
16	Graham Stuart	22
17	Andrei Kanchelskis	20
18	Derek Mountfield	19
19=	Nicky Barmby	18

19=	Wayne Clarke	18
19=	Francis Jeffers	18
22=	Mike Lyons	16
22=	Pat Nevin	16
22=	Kevin Richardson	16
22=	Trevor Ross	16
22=	Gary Speed	16

SEASON-BY-SEASON: LEADING GOALSCORERS

1977-1978	30 – Bob Latchford
1978-1979	12 – Andy King
1979-1980	10 – Brian Kidd
1980-1981	15 – Peter Eastoe
1981-1982	15 – Graeme Sharp
1982-1983	15 – Graeme Sharp
1983-1984	12 – Adrian Heath
1984-1985	21 – Graeme Sharp
1985-1986	30 – Gary Lineker
1986-1987	14 – Trevor Steven
1987-1988	13 – Graeme Sharp
1988-1989	13 – Tony Cottee
1989-1990	13 – Tony Cottee
1990-1991	10 – Tony Cottee
1991-1992	15 – Peter Beardsley
1992-1993	12 – Tony Cottee
1993-1994	16 – Tony Cottee
1994-1995	14 – Paul Rideout
1995-1996	16 – Andrei Kanchelskis
1996-1997	10 – Duncan Ferguson
1997-1998	11 – Duncan Ferguson
1998-1999	9 – Kevin Campbell
1999-2000	12 – Kevin Campbell
2000-2001	9 – Kevin Campbell
2001-2002	6 – Duncan Ferguson and Tomasz Radzinski

LEADING SCORERS (15 DIFFERENT MEN)

5 campaigns: Tony Cottee

4 campaigns: Graham Sharp

3 campaigns: Kevin Campbell, Duncan Ferguson (joint top scorer in 2001-02)

1 campaign: Peter Beardsley, Peter Eastoe, Adrian Heath, Andrei Kanchelskis, Brian Kidd, Andy King, Bob Latchford, Gary Lineker, Tomasz Radzinski (joint top scorer in 2001-02), Paul Rideout and Trevor Steven

INDIVIDUAL MATCH SCORING FEATS

FOUR GOALS IN A MATCH (TWO IN TOTAL)

Two Everton strikers netted as many as four goals in a League game during the 25 seasons up to the summer of 2002. They were Bob Latchford and Graeme Sharp. Ironically these two fine feats were carried out on the opposition's own territory.

Bob Latchford
vs Queen's Park Rangers (A) 10th September 1977

Graeme Sharp
vs Southampton (A) 3rd October 1987

HAT-TRICKS (15 IN TOTAL)

Fifteen other hat-tricks were bagged by players wearing Everton colours in League football during those 25 seasons. Four were registered by Tony Cottee, while Latchford and Gary Lineker both hit three. Five other men – Andy King, Adrian Heath, Clarke, Andrei Kanchelskis and Kevin Campbell – were hat-trick heroes on one occasion. Only one (bagged by Kanchelskis in April 1996) of these 15 hat-tricks was registered outside Goodison Park.

Tony Cottee (4 hat-tricks)
vs Newcastle United (H) 27th August 1988
vs Tottenham Hotspur (H) 5th October 1991

vs Sheffield United (H) 21th August 1993
vs Swindon Town (H) 15th January 1994

Bob Latchford (3 hat-tricks)
vs Coventry City (H) 26th November 1977
vs Leeds United (H) 13th November 1979
vs Crystal Palace (H) 20th September 1980

Gary Lineker (3 hat-tricks)
vs Birmingham City (H) 31st August 1985
vs Manchester City (H) 11th February 1986
vs Southampton (H) 3rd May 1986

Andy King (1 hat-trick) vs Bristol City (H) 10th February 1979

Adrian Heath (1 hat-trick) vs Notts County (H) 4th February 1983

Wayne Clarke (1 hat-trick) vs Newcastle United (H) 20th April 1986

Andrei Kanchelskis (1 hat-trick) vs Sheffield Wednesday (A) 27th April 1996

Kevin Campbell (1 hat-trick) vs West Ham United (H) 8th May 1999

SEASON-BY-SEASON TOTAL GOALS AND AVERAGE SCORING RATES

		Scored		Conceded	
	Games	Goals	Average	Goals	Average
1977-1978	42	76	1.81	45	1.07
1978-1979	42	52	1.24	40	0.95
1979-1980	42	43	1.02	51	1.21
1980-1981	42	55	1.31	58	1.38
1981-1982	42	56	1.33	50	1.19
1982-1983	42	66	1.57	48	1.14
1983-1984	42	44	1.05	42	1.00

1984-1985	42	88	2.10	43	1.02
1985-1986	42	87	2.07	41	0.98
1986-1987	42	76	1.81	31	0.74
1987-1988	40	53	1.33	27	0.68
1988-1989	38	50	1.32	45	1.18
1989-1990	38	51	1.34	33	1.15
1990-1991	38	50	1.32	46	1.21
1991-1992	42	52	1.24	51	1.21
1992-1993	42	53	1.26	55	1.31
1993-1994	42	42	1.00	63	1.50
1994-1995	42	44	0.95	51	1.21
1995-1996	42	64	1.52	44	1.05
1996-1997	38	44	1.16	57	1.50
1997-1998	38	41	1.08	56	1.47
1998-1999	38	42	1.11	47	1.24
1999-2000	38	59	1.55	49	1.29
2000-2001	38	45	1.18	59	1.55
2001-2002	38	45	1.18	57	1.50

LEAGUE ATTENDANCES AT GOODISON PARK

The largest crowd for a League game at Goodison Park during the quarter of a century up to the summer of 2002 was the 53,131 who watched the 1978-79 local derby. Liverpool attracted the largest crowds in 21 of the 25 seasons. The lowest gate was registered in 1982-83, when only 12,972 saw Coventry City's visit.

The highest average Goodison gate, during the 25 seasons, was the 39,513 recorded in 1977-78. The lowest average was recorded as 19,343, in 1983-84.

Season	Average	Highest	Lowest
1977-1978	39,513	52,759 vs Liverpool	33,402 vs Ipswich Town
1978-1979	35,456	53,131 vs Liverpool	22,958 vs Birmingham City
1979-1980	28,711	53,013 vs Liverpool	20,356 vs WBA
1980-1981	26,105	52,565 vs Liverpool	15,352 vs Stoke City
1981-1982	24,673	51,847 vs Liverpool	15,460 vs Nottingham Forest

1982-1983	20,277	52,741 vs Liverpool	12,972 vs Coventry City
1983-1984	19,343	51,245 vs Liverpool	13,016 vs Notts County
1984-1985	32,725	51,045 vs Liverpool	20,013 vs Coventry City
1985-1986	32,226	51,509 vs Liverpool	23,347 vs Leicester City
1986-1987	32,935	48,247 vs Liverpool	25,553 vs Wimbledon
1987-1988	27,770	44,162 vs Liverpool	20,351 vs Wimbledon
1988-1989	27,765	45,994 vs Liverpool	16,316 vs Charlton Athletic
1989-1990	26,280	42,453 vs Liverpool	17,591 vs Nottingham Forest
1990-1991	25,028	39,847 vs Liverpool	14,590 vs Wimbledon
1991-1992	23,148	37,681 vs Liverpool	15,201 vs Southampton
1992-1993	20,445	35,826 vs Liverpool	14,051 vs Southampton
1993-1994	22,876	38,157 vs Liverpool	13,265 vs Southampton
1994-1995	31,291	40,011 vs Manchester U	23,295 vs Norwich City
1995-1996	35,435	40,127 vs Aston Villa	30,009 vs QPR
1996-1997	36,189	40,177 vs Liverpool	30,368 vs Leicester City
1997-1998	35,376	40,479 vs Manchester U	28,533 vs Wimbledon
1998-1999	36,202	40,185 vs Liverpool	30,357 vs Newcastle United
1999-2000	34,880	40,052 vs Liverpool	30,490 vs Leicester City
2000-2001	34,130	40,260 vs Liverpool	27,670 vs Aston Villa
2001-2002	34,003	39,948 vs Manchester U	29,503 vs Tottenham Hotspur

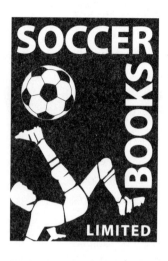